INTRODUCTION

to

INTELLECTUAL

PROPERTY LAW

INTRODUCTION
to
INTELLECTUAL PROPERTY LAW

Donald A. Gregory
Charles W. Saber
Jon D. Grossman

Dickstein, Shapiro & Morin

The Bureau of National Affairs, Inc., Washington, D.C.

Library of Congress Cataloging-in-Publication Data

Saber, Charles W.
Introduction to intellectual property law / Charles W. Saber, Donald A. Gregory, Jon D. Grossman.
p. cm.
Includes index.
ISBN 0-87179-823-9
1. Intellectual property--United States. I. Gregory, Donald A. II. Grossman, Jon D. III. Title.
KF2979.S22 1994
346.7304'8--dc20
[347.30648]
93-51096
CIP

Published by BNA Books
1250 23rd St. NW, Washington, DC 20037
International Standard Book Number: 0-87179-811-5
Printed in the United States of America

Foreword

by ***Ralph Oman***
Former Register of Copyrights of the U.S.A.
Of Counsel, Mudge Rose Guthrie Alexander & Ferdon

In my twenty years in the intellectual property field—first on the Senate Subcommittee on Patents, Copyrights, and Trademarks as a staff lawyer and ultimately as Chief Counsel, and then as the Register of Copyrights of the United States—I have lived through a dramatic transformation. Back in the 1970s, patents, copyrights, and trademarks cowered in the shadow of the antitrust laws. They were disfavored monopolies, and the courts, the Ford and Carter Administrations, and Congress took every opportunity to limit their scope and expand the ambit of unbridled competition.

Then it slowly dawned on Congress and other U.S. policymakers that the world was changing. As the United States shifted its focus away from the smokestack industries and an essentially domestic market, toward its high-tech future in a world economy, the importance of strong protection for patents, copyrights, trademarks, and trade secrets became clear. The United States insisted on a strong intellectual property component as an integral aspect of the General Agreement on Tariffs and Trade (GATT) negotiations. In the process, intellectual property law moved out of the legal backwaters and into the forefront of economic and cultural policymaking at home and abroad. The mounting U.S. trade deficit fueled this heightened interest, and as the industries that depend on intellectual property protection grew in importance, so too did the intellectual property legal portfolio grow in importance.

On the copyright side of the shop alone, the software, sound recording, motion picture, publishing, and music industries now account for six percent of our gross domestic product. They contribute $45 billion to our favorable balance of international trade. Add the patent-dependent industries and the value of our trademarks to this figure, and you are talking about a big chunk of U.S. productivity. That we see a burgeoning interest in intellectual property law can come as no surprise.

Today, as the practice of law grows more complex, practicing lawyers need to understand the fundamentals of intellectual property law. Mr. Gregory, Mr. Saber, and Mr. Grossman have given practitioners the tools they need to operate in this dynamic discipline.

Introduction to Intellectual Property Law gives legal generalists a solid introduction to the essentials of intellectual property law. The authors enumerate the rights and remedies on which authors and inventors rely, and they explain the underlying rationale for the statutory provisions. Especially useful, they describe in a very straightforward manner how a lawyer should advise clients in drafting a contract, registering a claim to copyright, transferring rights, applying for a patent, or registering a mark. They also go into great detail on the practical aspects of the enforcement of rights.

The volume gives legal generalists this basic information, but it's not just a primer for generalists. It also gives the intellectual property specialist a very valuable tool. The authors present a coherent view of the whole interwoven tapestry of the law, and that perspective is of growing importance as serious overlaps develop. For instance, both patents and copyrights afford protection for computer software, and for the patent lawyer with only a vague or rusty understanding of copyright principles, this book, with a separate chapter on the protection of computer software, ties it all together.

The book will help the specialist in other ways as well. It updates the specialist who has drifted off into a subspecialty and lost touch with the latest developments in the broader intellectual property field. Congress has changed the law with great frequency in recent years, especially in the copyright area, to accommodate the new technologies, and this volume provides up-to-the-minute analysis on the state of the law and the latest regulations of the Copyright Office and the Patent and Trademark Office.

Two hundred years ago, our founding fathers wove intellectual property protection into the fabric of the Constitution. We were the first country to do so. With the Constitution as our guide, we have grown from a small, agrarian nation into a powerhouse—the world's leading creator and exporter of scientific know-how and popular culture. To survive and prosper in such a world, American lawyers need a solid foundation in intellectual property law. Sooner or later, an inventor, a songwriter, a computer programmer, a film maker, a novelist, a painter, a photographer, a poet, or an executive from a multinational corporation that exploits inventions or creations, will knock on their door with a sticky legal problem. And when that time comes, *Introduction to Intellectual Property Law* will give them comfort.

15 March, 1994

About the Authors

Donald A. Gregory is a partner with Dickstein, Shapiro & Morin, a Washington, D.C. law firm having international expertise in the areas of patent law, copyrights, and trademarks. Mr. Gregory is a frequent writer and speaker on issues concerning intellectual property licensing and counseling in the United States and abroad. Mr. Gregory received his J.D. from the College of William and Mary and his undergraduate degree from the University of Virginia.

Charles W. Saber specializes in trademark law and intellectual property litigation and has written articles and lectured on these subjects in the United States and abroad. He is a partner with Dickstein, Shapiro & Morin. Mr. Saber is an honors graduate of the Georgetown University Law Center and is a graduate of the University of Massachusetts.

Jon D. Grossman is a principal with Dickstein, Shapiro & Morin. Mr. Grossman has experience on issues concerning the acquisition of computer technology protection. Mr. Grossman is also an Adjunct Professor at the Johns Hopkins University and teaches in areas concerning technology law. Mr. Grossman is a graduate of American University Law School, holds a master degree from the Johns Hopkins University and received his undergraduate degree from the University of Chicago.

Acknowledgments

This book was, in large part, a group collaborative effort. Many individuals made significant contributions without which this book would have never gotten off the ground. Our recognition, and especially our thanks, go out to the following individuals.

Brett N. Dorny
Alisa A. Harbin
Deborah H. Miller
Charles S. Murray
Gabrielle S. Roth
Kenneth N. Sheehan
Oscar A. Towler
James S. Trussell

Special thanks are also due to Gabrielle Roth for her able assistance in organizing and arranging this book.

Special thanks are also due to the extremely valuable assistance provided by Kathy Walvick and Barbara Bruce. Finally, our thanks are also extended to Anne M. Heath who, above and beyond her daily workload, typed a large part of this book.

The course on intellectual property sponsored by the Cambridge Institute and the course book we prepared for use in teaching that course served as a source and inspiration for this book.

Donald A. Gregory
Charles W. Saber
Jon D. Grossman

Contents

1 Introduction

1.1 What Is Intellectual Property?

Property law refers to a set of legal rules defining the rights of ownership of something having value, including the exclusive rights of the owner to use and dispose of the property. There are two types of property: tangible and intangible. Tangible property, whether real or personal, relates to a physical object. Intangible property, on the other hand, refers to a set of rights defined by the law that are not related to a physical object. Intellectual property is an intangible that is not easily described. The law creates the property by defining what will be protected from others. Intellectual property is created and protected based upon policy considerations as to what types of intellectual activities should be encouraged. As with all types of property, intellectual property may be sold, transferred, or otherwise disposed of.

A significant aspect of intellectual property that differs from tangible property is limits in the duration of the property. Tangible property is owned as long as the physical object exists. Intellectual property, on the other hand, is often limited to a certain period of time by the law that creates it. The purpose of intellectual property is to encourage the development of new ideas and creations. The creator is provided with the exclusive rights to the ideas in exchange for free use by all others after a given period of time.

Generally, intellectual property includes the rights provided by the laws of patents, copyrights, and trademarks. However, the laws recognize other protections for the results of intellectual creativity, including trade secret, trade dress, personality, false designation of origin, and other types of unfair competition. In addition, contracts between individual parties can create rights between the parties relating to intellectual property. The types of intellectual creativity or knowledge that can be protected are discussed in section 1.2, together with a brief description of the laws that create and protect each type of intellectual property.

Intellectual property is governed by federal and state statutory laws and by state common law. However, in the areas of patents and copyrights, the federal statutes explicitly preempt any state law rights that are covered by the federal statute. The authority for Congress to protect intellectual property is contained in article 1, section 8, clause 8 of the Constitution, which provides that Congress shall have the power "[t]o promote the Progress of Science and useful Arts, by securing for limited Times to Authors and Inventors the exclusive Right to their respective Writings and Discoveries." The policy nature of intellectual property rights is noted in the fact that this clause provides that these rights are for the purpose of promoting the arts and sciences. Congress also uses the power to regulate commerce among the states to protect certain types of intellectual property. Generally, state power to regulate intellectual property is provided by the police power of the state.

1.2 Types of Intellectual Property and Their Protection

(a) Ideas and Inventions

The broadest form of protection for intellectual property relates to protection of ideas. Ideas refer to general intellectual efforts such as ways of thinking. Ideas also relate to ways of doing things and to understandings of the way things operate. Certain types of ideas are protected under patent law and trade secret law.

Patent law provides protection for inventions. An invention refers to an innovation, or a new or improved product or process of making a product. Inventions also relate to new methods of doing things. However, patents are explicitly limited to "new and useful process, machine, manufacture, or composition of matter, or any new and useful improvement thereof."[1] Patent law does not protect abstract ideas, mathematical formulas or algorithms, or methods of doing business.

[1]35 U.S.C. §101.

Although these types of ideas are important and have value to the discoverer, the policies of patent law exclude them from protection.

A patent is obtained through an application describing the invention, which is provided to the U.S. Patent and Trademark Office (PTO). To obtain a patent, the invention must be "new." Therefore, patent law only protects ideas that have not existed before. If the PTO determines that the invention is of an appropriate type and is new, the inventor is given exclusive rights in the invention for a 17-year period. At the end of this time, anyone is free to use the invention that has been explicitly disclosed in the patent.

Trade secret law, which is embodied in state common law and/or state statutes such as the Uniform Trade Secrets Act,[2] also provides protection for ideas. Trade secret law, however, is not explicitly limited in the types of ideas that can be protected or in duration. Trade secret law can apply to any concept or idea not generally known or used by others and of value to the owner of the secret. The concept or idea is protected only if it can be maintained as a secret and only as long as it is maintained as a secret. Furthermore, it is protected only from those who wrongly appropriate the idea from the owner. Anyone who has the same idea or concept is free to use or disclose it in any manner whatsoever, which can destroy the value of the idea as a secret.

Significant value is derived from the knowledge and experience obtained by a person or organization with respect to a specific business or process. This knowledge can result in improved performance or capabilities. Generally, knowledge or experience is not a protected form of intellectual property. However, under trade secret law or unfair competition law, contracts and tort principles can be used to create and/or protect know-how and experience as a form of intellectual property. To the extent that a company is able to devise better methods of operating its business, although not protected by patent law, the company can prevent the use of this information by others to whom it is disclosed in a confidential manner, such as employees. This, however, does not prevent others from similarly gaining knowledge and experience which improve their performance in the same business.

(b) Expressions and Works of Authorship

In addition to protecting ideas, intellectual property law protects the manner in which the idea is presented or expressed. Federal copy-

---

[2] 14 U.L.A. 433 (1985).

right law protects all works of authorship, such as books, music, artistry, sculpture, movies, drama, architecture, and computer software. The copyright in a work of authorship exists for 50 years after the author dies. The copyright protects only the expression, not the ideas that are being expressed. For example, a copyright can be obtained on a book that discusses a new accounting system. The copyright prevents others from copying the book and the manner in which the accounting system is described. However, others are free to use the accounting system or to write another book that describes the same system.[3]

(c) Good Will and Designations of Origin

Competition is an important part of the American economy. Although free competition is an important principle in American society, some activities are considered anticompetitive and are, therefore, restricted. The restriction of anticompetitive activities and the prevention of consumer confusion create a significant amount of intangible intellectual property.

Trademark law, available at both the federal and state level, is intended to prevent consumer confusion about the source of a product and to protect the good will that an owner creates in the name or image of its product. Trademark law provides the first user of a word or design on certain products the exclusive right to use that word or design with respect to those products. The trademark rights exist as long as the trademark is being used by that person or company or any successors. In addition, trade dress law protects the overall appearance of the product and packaging. Furthermore, unfair competition law protects the general reputation of a company by preventing false or misleading statements about its business or products or about a competitor's business or products.

1.3 Federal Preemption—Limitations on Intellectual Property Protections

As noted previously, intellectual property is protected under both federal and state laws. However, both the patent and copyright acts

[3]Baker v. Selden, 101 U.S. (11 Otto) 99 (1879).

explicitly preempt conflicting state law rights that are similar to those covered by federal statutes. Federal preemption prevents states from expanding intellectual property rights in certain areas. Other than these specific areas, the states are free to create new intellectual property rights or to change the protection provided to this property.

Generally, "unfair competition" is the basis of state law expansions of intellectual property rights. However, the U.S. Supreme Court has held that the patent and copyright laws prevent creation of new protections from competition for ideas or expressions that could be covered by federal law.

In *Sears, Roebuck & Co. v. Stiffel Co.*,[4] the Supreme Court held that state unfair competition law could not prevent Sears from selling a pole lamp that was similar to a Stiffel pole lamp. The Stiffel lamp was the subject of an invalid patent and, therefore, could be copied. Although the state could prevent consumers from being misled as to the source of the product through labeling, it could not prohibit copying of an article that was neither patented nor copyrighted.

More recently, the Supreme Court has reiterated the significance of federal preemption. *Bonito Boats, Inc. v. Thunder Craft Boats*[5] involved a Florida statute that made duplication of a boat hull or component by direct molding unlawful. The state trial court found the statute to be invalid due to federal preemption and dismissed the complaint. The dismissal was upheld on appeal in the state courts and finally went to the Supreme Court. The Supreme Court held that any state law that substantially interferes with the enjoyment of an unpatented design or utilitarian conception which has been freely disclosed contravenes federal patent policy. Therefore, the states cannot prevent the copying of articles or ideas that have already been freely disclosed to the public.

In spite of the sweeping language of these cases relating to federal preemption of state unfair competition claims, other state law claims relating to protection of intellectual property have been upheld. Trade secret law, which is solely state created, has been upheld as conforming with federal patent and copyright laws. The federal statutes are intended to foster public disclosure of the intellectual property. If information is not publicly disclosed, then the state may protect the owner from disclosure or use by persons who received the information in confidence or by improper means. Unlike the unfair competition cases, protection

---

[4]376 U.S. 225, 140 USPQ 524 (1964).
[5]489 U.S. 141, 9 USPQ2d 1847 (1989).

of trade secrets does not remove material from the public domain. It only prevents public disclosure of information that has not yet entered the public domain.

In addition, contract law can be used to create and protect some intellectual property without being preempted by federal law. Agreements have been upheld in which one party agrees to pay royalties or refrain from using information in order to receive confidential knowledge or know-how. Although the information may later become publicly available, the contracting party is still bound by its contract.

1.4 Summary

Many types of intellectual property are created and protected by a variety of state and federal laws. This book reviews the principal laws defining intellectual property and how it is created. In addition, the procedures for protecting this property are set forth. Although the many intricacies of this field of law are beyond the scope of this book, the basic structures and elements provided herein will assist you, the reader, in understanding the nature, extent, and potential value of proper protection for the various forms of intellectual property.

2
Patents

2.1 Introduction

(a) Basis—Constitution

The U.S. patent system is one of long and illustrious history. In fact, the U.S. Constitution authorizes Congress to provide a patent system: "The Congress shall have power . . . to promote the Progress of Science and useful Arts, by securing for limited Times to Authors and Inventors the exclusive Right to their respective Writings and Discoveries."[1] Congress enacted the first patent act in 1790 and appointed Thomas Jefferson as the first "patent examiner," and the U.S. patent system was born.

(b) Purpose

The success of the U.S. patent system is founded upon a type of reciprocity between an inventor and the public. An inventor is encouraged to invent and publicly disclose the invention to the public, which then benefits from and perhaps even improves upon the original invention. In exchange for the public disclosure of the invention, the public,

[1]*See* U.S. Const. art. 1, §8, cl. 8.

acting through Congress and ultimately through the U.S. Patent and Trademark Office (PTO), gives the inventor or patent owner a statutory right, for a limited period of time, to exclude others from making, using, or selling the patented invention.

The right to exclude others is the incentive for the inventor to publicly disclose the invention. Otherwise, the inventor would have little incentive to invest in the development of an innovative product that any member of the public could freely copy and exploit. Public disclosure of the invention more than justifies the limited right to exclude granted to the inventor. For example, if the nature of the invention is such that it is easy to "reverse engineer," in the absence of an award of exclusive rights, the owner/inventor might prefer to keep the invention secret. As a result, the public would not benefit from the disclosure of the invention. Thus, the reciprocity between the inventor and the public serves the needs of and provides benefits for all concerned parties.

A subtle but important point is that the grant of a patent does not confer upon the owner a right to make, sell, or use the patented invention himself or herself but merely the right to exclude others from so doing. The patent owner's right to exclude others even extends to those individuals who are practicing the invention as a result of independent development of the invention.

(c) Structure of Patent Law

As mentioned above, the supreme patent law is that of the U.S. Constitution itself. Most of the issues related to obtaining and enforcing patents are governed by federal law. State law governs issues related to licenses and assignments of inventions and patents.

The patent law is codified at Title 35 of the U.S. Code, which provides the entire legal framework both for obtaining and enforcing patents. Should a state decide to enact a law that involves obtaining or enforcing patents as its subject matter, such a law is likely to be struck down or preempted by federal law.

In addition to federal statutes, the PTO has promulgated regulations having the force and effect of law. The patent regulations are located at 37 C.F.R. pt. 1 and set forth the rules of practice within the PTO.

The next level of authority that regulates obtaining and enforcing patents is the *Manual of Patent Examining Procedure* (MPEP). Each patent examiner employed by the PTO is trained in the use and application of the practice guidelines set forth in the MPEP. Additionally, to be licensed to practice before the PTO, each private patent lawyer must pass an examination to demonstrate proficiency in the substance of the patent law and the MPEP guidelines.

2.2 Types of Patents

There are several types of patents that may be obtained, including utility patents, design patents, and plant patents. Briefly, utility patents cover the way something functions or works. Design patents cover the merely ornamental features of an article of manufacture. And plant patents cover asexually reproduced plants. Reexamination and reissue patents are patents that have been issued and subsequently gone back through an examination process in the PTO under special reexamination or reissue procedures.[2] Reexamination patents and reissue patents are given their own series of numbers to distinguish them from originally issued utility patents.

Some other commonly used names for patents do not refer to distinctive types but identify subcategories of the types of patents described above. "Process patents" are utility patents that claim the steps for carrying out a method. "Paper patents" are patents that are issued on inventions that have not been actually practiced; there is no requirement that the invention be made or used before or after a patent is issued. "Improvement patents" are generally patents that claim inventions that are improvements on other patents and, if practiced, would infringe the underlying patents. "Pioneer patents" are patents that mark a great advance in technology.

(a) Utility Patents

Utility patents may be issued to protect any new, useful, and nonobvious process, machine, article of manufacture, or composition of matter, as well as any new and useful improvement thereof. In

---

[2]37 C.F.R. §§1.171–179, 1.501–570.

addition, certain plants can be the subject of a utility patent.[3] A utility application directed to a plant must contain the same formalities and is examined as any other utility application.

Once a utility patent is granted, it confers upon the patent owner, who is not necessarily the inventor, the right to exclude others for a limited time from making, using, or selling the invention as claimed in the patent.[4] As mentioned above, the granting of a patent does not confer any right to the patent owner to make, use, or sell the patented invention himself or herself. It is therefore possible that a patent owner may not be able to practice his or her own claimed invention. For example, Smith invents and obtains a patent for a bucket. Jones adds a handle onto the bucket of Smith and is granted a patent on the combination. Due to Smith's exclusionary rights, Jones cannot make, use, or sell a bucket with or without a handle without obtaining a license from Smith. Further, Smith cannot make, use, or sell a bucket with a handle without obtaining a license from Jones.

The exclusive rights conferred by a U.S. patent extend only throughout the United States, its territories, and its possessions.[5] The rights are granted for a term of 17 years for utility patent applications and are measured beginning from the date the patent issues. It is possible to extend the 17-year term of a patent only in certain extraordinary circumstances, such as to make up time awaiting government approval to market the invention.

To maintain a utility patent in the United States, three maintenance fees must be paid at specified times. The current times for payment of the maintenance fee are 3.5, 7.5, and 11.5 years after the issue date of the patent. The patent owner can lose the exclusive rights conferred by the patent by failing to pay the required maintenance fee. The patent will then become "abandoned" and will become part of the public domain. Then anyone is free to make, use, or sell the invention. The PTO does allow some abandoned patents to be "revived" upon a requisite showing and payment of a fee.

The exclusive rights conferred by a patent are not effective until the patent issues. Thus, marking a product with the words "patent pending" merely notifies the public that an application is pending in the PTO. The true purpose of marking an object "patent pending" is for notification; however, should the patent owner ever sue an infringer

---

[3]Ex parte Hibberd, 227 USPQ 443 (Bd. Pat. App. & Int. 1985).

[4]35 U.S.C. §154.

[5]35 U.S.C. §§100(c), 154.

on the patent, the issue of the infringer's notification of the infringed patent directly affects the amount of damages awarded to a patent owner. Failing to mark the products with the patent number once the patent issues could result in loss of entitlement to damages for infringements occurring prior to actual notice to the infringer.

Prior to the issue date, all U.S. patent applications are held in confidence and remain unpublished. This aspect of the U.S. system differs from the majority of other patent systems. For example, the European Patent Office publishes patent applications approximately 18 months after they are first filed and grants patents for a term of 20 years beginning from the date of filing the application.

(b) Design Patents

The patent statute also provides for obtaining patents for designs for any "new, original and ornamental design for an article of manufacture for a term of 14 years."[6] The requirements for a valid design patent are similar to those for a utility patent except that the design must be "ornamental" rather than having some practical usefulness as required for utility patents. Design patents are intended to encourage the decorative arts, contemplating appearance rather than utility.

The subject matter of an ornamental design may not be the result of purely functional requirements; however, there may be a mixture of functional and ornamental configurations. "If the patented design is primarily functional rather than ornamental, the patent is invalid."[7] Thus, when a configuration or structure of an object is the result of functional considerations only, the resulting design is not patentable as an ornamental design for the simple reason that it is not "ornamental," that is, was not created for the purpose of ornamenting.[8] In the past, courts have held that a device that is concealed in use may not be the subject of a design patent; however, the law has shifted somewhat to now allow patents granted even if design is concealed.

---

[6]35 U.S.C. §171.

[7]Power Controls Corp. v. Hybrinetics, Inc., 806 F.2d 234, 238, 231 USPQ 774, 777 (Fed. Cir. 1986).

[8]*Id.* (citing In re Carletti, 328 F.2d 1020, 1022, 140 USPQ 653, 654 (C.C.P.A. 1964)).

A design application contains the following parts: (1) a drawing of the ornamental design of the article, (2) a description that includes a title, (3) an identification of each figure of the drawing, (4) one single claim that describes the drawing, (5) an oath, and (6) the prescribed fee.

As with utility inventions, an ornamental design for an article of manufacture must be novel and unobvious.[9] Among other requirements, this means that the design must not have been described in a previous publication or patent (i.e., not part of the "prior art") and must not have been obvious to an ordinary designer in view of the current state of the art. A determination of what constitutes the prior art is made in accordance with 35 U.S.C. §102 and is discussed at section 2.4(c)(iv) below. A design patent is infringed when the patented ornamental design and the accused article are visually compared and found to be similar.

(c) Plant Patents

Original plants can be protected in at least three ways: (1) by plant patents, (2) through the Plant Variety Protection Act (PVPA),[10] and (3) by utility patents. A "plant patent" may only be used to protect asexually reproduced plants.[11] A plant patent is granted for a period of 17 years (which may not be extended) and excludes others from asexually reproducing the plant or selling or using a plant so produced.

Plant patent applications differ from utility patent applications in several ways. The specification must point out where and in what manner the new variety of plant was reproduced. Two copies of the specification must be submitted and the application may not contain more than one claim. The drawings must be artistically and competently executed and if in color, two copies must be submitted.

For plants reproduced sexually, a Certificate of Plant Variety Protection (which operates like a plant patent in many ways) can be obtained from the Department of Agriculture. This certificate grants the person who first reproduces the plant (the breeder) the right to exclude others from selling, offering for sale, reproducing, importing, or exporting the variety, or using the variety in producing a hybrid or

---

[9] *See* 35 U.S.C. §§102, 103, discussed at sections 2.4(c)(iv)–(v) in this chapter.
[10] 7 U.S.C. §2321 *et seq.*
[11] 35 U.S.C. §§161–164.

different variety therefrom. This form of protection extends for a period of 18 years.

2.3 Patent Applications

A utility application consists of the following parts: a specification having a title, a written description, claims, drawings, and an abstract of the disclosure; an oath by the inventor; and a prescribed fee.

(a) Specification

(i) Title

The title is short, yet should accurately describe the invention. The recent trend of computer database searching increases the need and importance of a concise and descriptive title.

(ii) Written Description

The written description is the portion of the patent application that "teaches" others how to practice the invention. The application may include drawings to illustrate specific embodiments of the invention as well as a description of those embodiments. The PTO prefers the written description to have the following elements in order: (a) field of the invention, (b) background of the invention, (c) summary of the invention, (d) brief description of the drawings, and (e) detailed description of the invention.

The patentee generally describes the state of the prior art (what is currently known in the field of the invention) in the background of the invention section. United States patent law requires the applicant to disclose any known prior art that is material to the examination of the application. This requirement is termed the "duty of disclosure."[12] The duty of disclosure is generally stricter in the United States than in foreign countries. Thus, if an applicant is filing a U.S-originated

[12] 37 C.F.R. §§1.56, 1.96, 1.98.

application abroad, the applicant can edit the background discussion of prior art to save on translation costs.

In the United States, practice is to summarize the invention as a whole in the summary of the invention. Additionally, the summary section may contain the objects of the invention, that is, what the invention is designed to accomplish. In Europe, the summary of invention section merely recites the first independent claim.

The detailed description is a substantial portion of the application: it is where the invention is taught. The detailed description sets out each example and embodiment, as well as the methods for making and using the invention. In addition, the detailed description may also contain tables and experimental data where applicable.

For patent applications directed to nucleotide and amino acid sequences, the PTO has promulgated rules relating to the specific format required for the presentation of the sequence information in an effort to maintain uniformity of these patent applications.[13] The rules require that all sequences over 10 nucleotides or 4 amino acids in length, whether disclosed in the specification or in the claims, must be presented in the format described therein. For example, each reference to a sequence must identify it by the following: SEQ NO:X. Each application must contain the sequence in a listing as described in the rules. The PTO has developed a software package called "PATENTIN," which generates a sequence listing having the required format. For an application to comply with the rules, it must contain a computer readable sequence listing and a verified statement that the paper and computer readable sequence listings are an actual part of the specification. This can be added to the application by amendment if it is not submitted initially with the application.

(iii) Claims

Following the detailed description are one or more "claims" that formally define the invention sought to be patented. Patent claims define the scope of the exclusive rights to which the inventor believes he or she is entitled. They appear as numbered one-sentence paragraphs at the end of the text of the patent specification. When a patentee asserts infringement, the accused device is compared to the patent claims, not to the patent specification. Thus, it is particularly important

[13] 37 C.F.R. §§1.821–825.

that the applicant, or his or her attorney, carefully draft the claims to accurately define the scope of the invention.

Patent law also requires that the claims of the patent particularly point out and distinctly claim the subject matter that the applicants regard as their invention. Compliance with this provision requires a determination whether those skilled in the relevant art would understand what is claimed. It is only required that the claims reasonably apprise those skilled in the art as to their scope, and that the claims be as precise as the subject matter permits.[14]

Structurally, there are two different types of patent claims. The first type is called an independent claim. An independent claim stands alone and does not refer to any other claim of the patent. On the other hand, the second type, a dependent claim, includes a reference to at least one other claim in the patent. A dependent claim incorporates all of the limitations or words of the claims to which the dependent claim refers.

(iv) Drawings and Abstract

The drawings and abstract of the disclosure are the remaining parts of the application. An applicant is not required to submit drawings for every patent application. Instead, drawings are required only when they are necessary to describe the invention. Almost all applications for mechanical and electrical inventions contain drawings. The PTO requires that drawings conform to certain rules.[15] Drawings that do not conform must be corrected.

Each patent application must contain an abstract. The abstract should be a one-paragraph overall description of the invention not exceeding 250 words in length. Although the abstract appears at the end of the patent application, it ultimately will be printed on the first page of the patent issued by the PTO and, thus, is an important searching tool. The abstract, therefore, should provide as much detail as possible about the scope of the invention.

---

[14]35 U.S.C. §112; *see* Amgen, Inc. v. Chugai Pharmaceutical Co., 927 F.2d 1200, 1217–18, 18 USPQ2d 1016, 1030 (Fed. Cir.), *cert. denied,* 112 S. Ct. 169, 60 USLW 3261 (1991); Hybritech Inc. v. Monoclonal Antibodies, 802 F.2d 1367, 1385, 231 USPQ 81, 94 (Fed. Cir. 1986), *cert. denied,* 480 U.S. 947 (1987).

[15]37 C.F.R. §§1.81–88.

(b) Oath

The Constitution allows only the inventors to apply for a patent in the United States. Thus, the application must be signed by the inventors in an oath or declaration.[16] This greatly contrasts with the majority of the rest of the world where an assignee can file for patents in its own name. In the case of joint inventors in the United States, each of the joint owners owns an individual share of the patent and, absent an agreement to the contrary, may independently exploit the patent rights.[17] Specific laws govern the ownership of inventions made under government contract.[18] On the other hand, employees in the private sector are not obligated to assign their inventions to their employer unless they have an express or implied obligation to do so.

(c) Preparation of the Application

A patent application is prepared by the inventors or by an attorney or agent acting on behalf of the inventors. The application filed with the PTO must include the specification, drawings if necessary, an accompanying application fee, and an oath by the inventors stating that the invention is theirs and that they believe the invention meets the standards of patentability.[19] The oath must also list all prior filed applications related to the newly filed application. Applicants almost always obtain the aid of a patent attorney or agent because of the complexity of the process of obtaining a patent.

The preparation of a patent application usually begins with the disclosure of the invention by the inventor to a patent attorney. The patent attorney may then conduct a patent search of the records of the PTO to locate any prior art that may be relevant to the patentability of the invention. There is no legal requirement to conduct this search. Next, the attorney reviews the results of the patent search and any other available relevant information to determine the scope of patent protection to which the invention is entitled. In addition, the patentability search results enable the inventor's attorney to focus the patent

[16] 35 U.S.C. §111.
[17] 35 U.S.C. §262.
[18] 35 U.S.C. chp. 38.
[19] 35 U.S.C. §111.

application on the likely patentable aspects of the invention. Generally, the attorney or agent then drafts the application and files it with the PTO and the examination process begins. The invention does not need to be physically constructed or tested before filing the patent application.

(d) Other Types of Applications

(i) Continuation Applications

Before an allowed patent issues, an applicant may file a "continuation" patent application based on a "parent" pending application. A parent pending application is one that has neither issued nor been abandoned and that forms the basis for the later filed application. A continuation application contains exactly the same disclosure as the pending application and is awarded the filing date of the original application. It cannot, however, contain any new matter (i.e., additional disclosure). Generally, the purpose of filing continuation applications is to seek additional and broader patent claims. A continuation application may also be filed to continue prosecution. United States law does not limit the number of continuation applications that may be filed. Thus, it is theoretically possible that a chain of applications may extend over the entire life of the first issued patent in the chain or, possibly, even longer. The PTO may require the applicant to disclaim a portion of the term of that patent that issues from a continuation application. Generally, if the term is disclaimed, it is shortened so that it does not extend past the date of expiration of the first issued patent.

(ii) Continuation-in-Part (CIP) Applications

An applicant may also file a continuation-in-part (CIP) application from a pending parent application. A CIP application is similar to a continuation application in that it is based on the pending application. One major difference is that unlike a continuation application, a CIP application may contain new matter, that is, additional disclosure. Because the CIP is a hybrid application it is awarded two filing dates: (1) the matter disclosed in both the CIP and the parent application is awarded the filing date of the parent application, and (2) the newly added matter is awarded the filing date of the CIP application.

(iii) Divisional Applications

A divisional application is another type of application filed from a pending parent application. Like a continuation application, a divisional application contains exactly the same disclosure as the parent application and is awarded the same filing date as the parent application. An applicant will generally file a divisional application when the parent application was subject to a restriction requirement (section 2.4(a) below) and the applicant decides to pursue protection on the inventions that were not elected in the parent application. When filing a divisional application, the applicant may simply present the claims withdrawn from prosecution in the parent case for prosecution in the divisional application.

(e) Other Considerations in Filing Patent Applications

(i) Invention Secrecy Act

Special provisions apply to patent rights and inventions that relate to national security, atomic energy, and aeronautics and space. First, the Invention Secrecy Act of 1951[20] authorizes the Commissioner of Patents and Trademarks to issue "secrecy orders" when public knowledge of the subject matter disclosed in a U.S. patent application is believed to be detrimental to the national security of the United States. The Invention Secrecy Act also prohibits anyone from filing an application in a foreign country based on an application originally filed in the United States until six months after filing the U.S. application without a foreign filing license from the Commissioner. A secrecy order is directed to all applicants, their successors, and any and all assignees and their legal representatives.

The applicant may seek review of the secrecy order by filing a Petition for Recision or Removal with the Commissioner. In addition, the applicant may file a Petition for a Permit or Modification of a secrecy order in order to disclose the invention or to file the application for a patent in a foreign country. If the patent application is otherwise eligible to issue as a patent, the PTO notifies the applicant and the agency responsible for the secrecy order. The PTO then places the

---

[20] 35 U.S.C. §§181–88.

application in a condition of suspension until the secrecy order is removed.

An applicant whose patent is withheld by a secrecy order is entitled to compensation. The applicant may request compensation during the time beginning on the date on which the applicant is notified that, except for such order, the application is otherwise in condition for allowance and ending six years after a patent is issued thereon. The owner of the right to the invention may recover damages caused by the secrecy order and the use of the invention by the government. The recoverable compensation is the damages caused by the secrecy order and/or the use of the invention by the government. This recovery can be either by administrative agreement or by suit in the U.S. District Court or Court of Claims.

If a secrecy order is violated, that is, the invention is published or disclosed without the consent of the Commissioner, the Commissioner can deem the application or patent abandoned. The abandonment is effective as of the time of violation and constitutes a forfeiture of all claims against the United States based on the invention. Even inadvertent disclosure can be cause for abandonment. Additionally, criminal penalties may be imposed upon persons who, with knowledge of a secrecy order and without due authorization, willfully publish or disclose or authorize or cause to be published or disclosed the invention, or material information with respect to the invention.

(ii) Atomic Energy Act

The Atomic Energy Act of 1954[21] includes a number of provisions relating to patent rights in inventions directed to atomic energy. For example, the Atomic Energy Act prohibits the patenting of any invention or discovery that is solely directed to the use of special nuclear material or atomic energy in an atomic weapon. For atomic energy inventions that are not useful in weapons, a patent shall not confer exclusive rights to the extent the invention or discovery is directed to the utilization of special nuclear material or atomic energy in atomic weapons. The Department of Energy (DOE) is authorized to provide for compulsory licensing of patented inventions of primary importance in the production or utilization of special nuclear material or atomic energy. The Commissioner of Patents and Trademarks is directed to

[21]42 U.S.C. §2011 *et seq.*

notify DOE of all applications that, in the opinion of the Commissioner, disclose inventions or discoveries that are useful in the production or utilization of special nuclear material or atomic energy and to grant to DOE access to all such applications.

In addition, the Atomic Energy Act contains special procedures for determining ownership of inventions made or conceived in the course of or under any contract, subcontract, or arrangement with DOE. The Atomic Energy Act allows DOE to assert title to a patent or invention that is (1) useful in the production or utilization of special nuclear material or atomic energy and (2) made or conceived in the course of or under any contract, subcontract, or arrangement entered into with or for the benefit of DOE.[22] When an application relates to atomic energy, the Commissioner of Patents and Trademarks must request, prior to issuing a patent, a statement under oath setting forth the full facts surrounding the making or conception of the invention, and whether the invention was made or conceived in the course of or under any contract, subcontract, or arrangement entered into with or for the benefit of DOE. That statement must be filed within 30 days of the request.

(iii) National Aeronautics and Space Act

The National Aeronautics and Space Act of 1958 establishes special procedures for determining ownership of inventions made in the performance of any work under contract of the National Aeronautics and Space Administration (NASA) that has significant utility in conducting aeronautical and space activities. Basically, the procedures are essentially the same as those under the Atomic Energy Act. Aeronautical and space activities are defined as (1) research into, and the solution of, problems relating to flight within and outside the earth's atmosphere; (2) the development, construction, testing, and operation for research purposes of aeronautical and space vehicles; and (3) such other activities as may be required for the exploration of space.[23]

---

[22]The Atomic Energy Act uses the term "Commission" in some places rather than "Department of Energy," but the restructuring of the federal entities having the mandate to regulate atomic energy has resulted in DOE having the pertinent responsibilities.

[23]42 U.S.C. §2452.

2.4 Examination of Applications

(a) Award of Filing Date

When an application arrives in the PTO, it receives a filing date that is treated prima facie as the date of the invention sought to be patented. As set forth above, for an application to receive a filing date, it must include the following: (1) the specification, (2) the identity of the inventors, (3) one or more claims, and (4) the drawings (if required for the invention). Everything else may be, and often is, submitted at a later date. Once the application receives a filing date, it is then assigned a serial number and it begins to work its way through the PTO. Usually within 12–24 months, a patent examiner will review the application in detail. Even though an inventor has no exclusive rights prior to the patent's issuance, the inventor may, upon learning that someone else is using the invention, request the PTO to expedite the processing of the application. A request for expedited processing can result in the patent issuing in a time period as short as six to nine months compared with the PTO's 18-month goal, which is not always achieved.

The effective date of invention for each claim is determined independently and is initially presumed to be the date on which the original application for a patent was filed in the PTO. An earlier date of invention can be proven by establishing (1) conception and reduction to practice, (2) priority based upon an earlier filed domestic application, or (3) foreign filing priority.

An inventor can establish an invention date earlier than the effective filing date of his or her patent application if the inventor proves that he or she conceived the invention before the filing date and thereafter diligently reduced it to practice. The inventor may prove an invention date only by reference to activities conducted within the United States. An inventor who made his or her invention in another country is entitled to a date of invention prior to filing the application in the United States only if the inventor proves that he or she subsequently practiced the invention in the United States prior to the filing date.

Patent law entitles a U.S. application to the filing date of (1) a copending previously filed U.S. application, that is, a continuation application discussed in section 2.3(d)(i) above, or (2) a foreign counterpart application if it is filed within one year of the foreign filing. An applicant may antedate prior art by relying on the benefit of a previously filed application to establish an earlier effective date. Under patent law, the claims set forth in a U.S. patent application are entitled to the earlier priority date only if the earlier application supports those claims.[24]

Before an examiner begins to "examine" the application "on the merits," the examiner will determine whether the claims are directed to more than one invention. If they are, then the examiner will issue a restriction requirement which requires the applicant to select one group of claims for prosecution (continuing attempt to obtain a patent). In applications that contain several variations (species) of a broader invention (genus), the applicant may be required to elect a species for prosecution. The applicant is required to elect a single invention or species he or she wishes to prosecute regardless of whether the applicant disagrees with the examiner's restriction requirement.

Patent Cooperation Treaty (PCT) applications, discussed at section 2.6(c) below, may also be subjected to restriction, for example, limiting of invention. However, if a PCT application remains unrestricted throughout the preliminary stages in the International Examining Bureau, the national offices may not require the applicant to restrict the former PCT application.

(b) Examination

Next, the examiner examines the application "on the merits." To do this, the examiner will conduct a search for "prior art" documents that may render the application unpatentable. This prior art search by the examiner resembles the patentability search performed by the patent attorney.

After the examiner reviews the patent application in view of the prior art, the examiner issues an "office action." Frequently, the office action rejects some or all of the pending patent application claims.[25] The office action reflects the examiner's view of the application and considers the criteria set forth below.

---

[24]35 U.S.C. §119; *see* In re Gosteli, 872 F.2d 1008, 1010, 10 USPQ2d 1614, 1616 (Fed. Cir. 1989).

[25]35 U.S.C. §132.

(c) Criteria for Examination

(i) Statutory Subject Matter

The first criterion is that the type of subject matter sought to be patented is "statutory" subject matter.[26] In other words, it must be a type of subject matter that is protectable by a patent as defined by the patent statute and interpreted by the courts. The types of statutory subject matter are as follows: any new and useful process, machine, article of manufacture, or composition of matter, as well as any new and useful improvement thereof.

Life forms are now considered statutory subject matter. An applicant may obtain a patent directed to a living animal.[27] In *Allen,* the applicant claimed "polyploid" oysters resulting from a process that included exposing the fertilized oyster eggs to very high pressure shortly after fertilization. The patent examiner, noting a long-established trend in the PTO that animals are not patentable subject matter, rejected the claims. The Board of Appeals reversed the examiner and declared that the test for patentability is whether the claimed subject matter is a nonnaturally occurring product of human intervention. If it is, then the claimed subject matter is patentable if it meets all other conditions for patentability. Because the oysters were produced by human intervention, they were proper subject matter for a patent. *Allen* opened the possibility for patents on higher life forms. In keeping with the holding of *Allen,* if the life form is naturally occurring, then it is improper subject matter for a patent; however, if it is the result of human intervention, it is proper subject matter for a patent.

There has been a popular misconception that patents may not be obtained for software under 35 U.S.C. §101 as it constitutes unpatentable "mental steps." It is unclear how this viewpoint came about. One source may have been the initial unwillingness on the part of the Supreme Court to allow patents for software. That initial unwillingness was expressed in a 1972 Supreme Court decision declaring that an algorithm used in a digital computer for converting the form of a number was not proper subject matter for a patent.[28] Subsequent decisions by that Court and lower courts have indicated that the inclusion of an algorithm does not by itself prohibit patent coverage for an invention,

---

[26]35 U.S.C. §101.

[27]Ex parte Allen, 2 USPQ2d 1425 (Bd. Pat. App. & Int. 1987).

[28]Gottschalk v. Benson, 409 U.S. 63 (1972).

software often being regarded as an algorithm. Instead, the crucial consideration is whether the invention is directed to an algorithm that merely constitutes a method of calculation not drawn to a structure or process that patent law was designed to protect or, as the Supreme Court termed it, an algorithm having no postsolution activity.

The PTO position closely follows the recent court decisions. As articulated in the *Manual of Patent Examining Procedure* §2106, "statutory" software (eligible for patent) under 35 U.S.C. §101 must fulfill the following test:

1. The patent claim must first be considered as a whole to see if it directly or indirectly recites a *mathematical* algorithm. If the claim does not directly recite a mathematical algorithm, reference must be made to the specification to see if the claim indirectly recites the formula. If no mathematical formula is directly or indirectly recited, then the claim is statutory.
2. However, if the claim directly or indirectly involves a mathematical formula, then the second step determines whether that formula is applied in a structure or process that as a whole performs a postsolution function that patent law was designed to protect.

Under this test, for example, the fact that software is used in a manufacturing process does not forbid a claim to a manufacturing process including that software or the computer program steps.

Note that the mathematical algorithm limitation cannot be circumvented by simply limiting the use of the formula to a particular technological environment. Insignificant postsolution activity (with regard to the formula) thus will not transform an unpatentable principle into a patentable process. An example of this is claims for formulas for updating an alarm limit inside a computer or for gathering data. As the postsolution activities in both claims are simply *numbers,* or the acquisition of numbers, the claims are nonstatutory.

In conclusion, claims directed to a computer program are nonstatutory only in those instances when they are restricted to mathematical algorithms having no application that affects a known process or structure.

(ii) Sufficiency of the Patent Disclosure

Patent law requires that the specification of a patent enable a person skilled in the relevant art to make and use the claimed invention.[29] The

---

[29]35 U.S.C. §112.

requirement is satisfied if one skilled in the art could make the invention without undue experimentation. That some experimentation is required is not fatal. This enablement requirement is met if the description in the patent specification enables any mode of making and using the claimed invention.[30]

In addition, the application must set forth the "best mode" of practicing the invention.[31] This is satisfied by the inventor disclosing the best mode of which he or she is aware at the time of filing the application. It is a subjective test; the inventor need not disclose the absolute best mode that may exist if the inventor has not yet contemplated it.

For a deposit of biological material constituting the invention into a depository where the specimen will be publicly available, the inventor is required to supplement the disclosure in an application relating to biological material that cannot be adequately described by words alone within the sufficiency of disclosure requirements of 35 U.S.C. §112.[32] Every patent is required to describe the invention in a manner that is adequate to instruct a person of ordinary skill in the art to make and use the invention. In the case of biological inventions, a written description alone may not provide an adequate disclosure. The biological material referred to in the rules is "material that is capable of self-replication either directly or indirectly."[33] Such material includes plasmids, bacteria, viruses, fungi, yeast, algae, protozoa, eucaryotic cells, cell lines, plant tissue cells, and seeds. In addition, viruses and other nonliving material existing in and reproducible from a living cell can be deposited by depositing a host cell. Biological material need not be deposited if it is known and readily available to the public or can be made or isolated without undue experimentation. The deposit must be maintained throughout the term of the patent.

(iii) Usefulness

An invention must be useful under 35 U.S.C. §101. The utility requirement is usually not an issue because most inventions are able to accomplish their purported functions. Efficiency of the invention is

---

[30]In re Vaeck, 947 F.2d 488, 495, 20 USPQ2d 1438, 1444 (Fed. Cir. 1991); Engel Indus. v. Lockformer Co., 946 F.2d 1528, 1533, 20 USPQ2d 1300, 1304 (Fed. Cir. 1991).

[31]35 U.S.C. §112.

[32]37 C.F.R. §§1.802, 1.807, 1.809.

[33]37 C.F.R. §1.801.

not required, as long as it works. Certain types of inventions, such as perpetual motion machines and cures for baldness, are presumed to be unpatentable for lack of utility.

(iv) Novelty of the Invention

Another requirement for a valid patent is that the invention defined in the claims must be new or novel.[34] Anything that destroys its novelty is called an anticipation. There are several categories of events, all defined by statute, that can anticipate and invalidate a claim of a patent. They are:

1. The invention was publicly known in the United States before the patentee invented it.
2. The invention was publicly used in the United States either (a) before the patentee invented it, or (b) more than one year before the patentee filed the patent application.
3. The invention was described in a printed publication anywhere in the world either (a) before the patentee invented it, or (b) more than one year before the patentee filed the patent application.
4. The invention was patented in another patent anywhere in the world either (a) before the patentee invented it, or (b) more than one year before the patentee filed the patent application.
5. The invention was on sale in the United States more than one year before the patentee filed the patent application.
6. The invention was invented by another person in the United States before the patentee invented it, and such other person did not abandon, suppress, or conceal the invention.
7. The invention was described in a patent granted on a patent application filed in the United States before the patentee made the invention.[35]

There is no anticipation unless every one of the elements of the claim is found in a single prior publication, prior public use, prior invention, prior patent, prior knowledge, or prior sale. It is not permitted to combine two or more items of prior art to make out an anticipation.[36]

---

[34] 35 U.S.C. §102.

[35] *Id.*

[36] Shatterproof Glass Corp. v. Libbey-Owens Ford Co., 758 F.2d 613, 619, 225 USPQ 634, 637 (Fed. Cir.), *cert. dismissed,* 474 U.S. 976 (1985); Lindemann Maschinenfabrik GmbH v. American Hoist & Derrick Co., 730 F.2d 1452, 1458–59, 221 USPQ 481, 485 (Fed. Cir. 1984).

An accidental achievement of a product or process does not constitute an anticipation. A true accident gives no assurance that the same result can be reached by others at a later time. On the other hand, anticipation is not avoided where the prior achievement was deliberate or a necessary consequence of what was intended, even though the achiever did not fully appreciate or recognize the uses, purposes, or properties of the product or process. In addition, the prior publication, prior public use, prior invention, etc., must be enabling, thus placing the allegedly disclosed matter in the possession of the public.[37]

An invention is anticipated if it was known by others in the United States before it was invented by the patentee. "Known" in this context means known to the public. Private knowledge, secret knowledge, or knowledge confined to a small, limited group is not necessarily an invalidating anticipation. Things that were known to the public only outside the United States do not invalidate the patent.[38]

An invention is anticipated if it was used by others before it was invented by the patentee, or more than one year before the patentee filed a patent application. "Use" in this context means a public use. Public use is any use of the invention by a person other than the inventor who is under no limitation, restriction, or obligation of secrecy by the inventor. An invention is publicly used when it is accessible to any member of the public, even a single person, whether or not the public could reasonably learn the invention by analyzing or inspecting the thing used. Secret use by a third party is not an invalidating public use. Thus, if the particular device, composition, or process is used by a third party, under circumstances of secrecy, that does not invalidate the patent.[39]

An invention is anticipated if it was described in a printed publication before it was invented by the patentee or more than one year prior

---

[37]Verdegaal Bros. v. Union Oil Co. of Cal., 814 F.2d 628, 2 USPQ2d 1051 (Fed. Cir.), *cert. denied,* 481 U.S. 827 (1987); Akzo N.V. v. United States Int'l Trade Comm'n, 808 F.2d 1471, 1479, 1 USPQ2d 1241, 1245 (Fed. Cir. 1986), *cert. denied,* 482 U.S. 909 (1987); Reading & Bates Constr. Co. v. Baker Energy Resources Corp., 748 F.2d 645, 651, 223 USPQ 1168, 1173 (Fed. Cir. 1984).

[38]Continental Can Co. USA v. Monsanto Co., 948 F.2d 1264, 1267–69, 20 USPQ2d 1746, 1748–50 (Fed. Cir. 1991); Filterite Corp. v. Tate Eng'g, 318 F. Supp. 584, 590, 167 USPQ 450, 453–54 (D. Md. 1970), *aff'd per curiam,* 447 F.2d 62, 170 USPQ 190 (4th Cir. 1971).

[39]Carella v. Starlight Archery & Pro Line Co., 804 F.2d 135, 138–39, 231 USPQ 644, 646–47 (Fed. Cir. 1986); W.L. Gore & Assocs. v. Garlock, Inc., 721 F.2d 1540, 1548–50, 220 USPQ 303, 309–11 (Fed. Cir. 1983), *cert. denied,* 469 U.S. 851 (1984).

to the filing date of his or her patent application. The essence of a printed publication is accessibility to the public. It must be reasonably accessible to at least some segment of the public. So long as the required accessibility or dissemination is shown, the manner in which the information is recorded is unimportant. It is only required that the information be maintained in some permanent form, such as magnetic tape, microfilm, photographs, photocopies, etc. It is not necessary that the printed publication be available to every member of the public, but it must be available, without restriction, to that segment of the public most likely to avail itself of the publication's contents. For a publication to constitute an anticipation of an invention, it must be capable, when taken in conjunction with the knowledge of people of ordinary skill in the art, of placing the invention in the possession of the reader. The disclosure must be enabling and meaningful.[40]

An invention is anticipated if it was patented in the United States or a foreign country, either before it was invented by the patentee or more than one year before he or she filed a patent application. The effective date for this type of anticipation is the date on which two things co-existed: (1) the owner of the reference patent had the right to enforce the patent, and (2) the reference patent was available to the public.[41]

An invention is anticipated if it was placed on sale by the inventor in the United States more than one year prior to the application filing date. The law requires that the invention was "on sale," not that a sale was actually consummated. An offer of sale, solicitation of orders, promotional activities, or advertisements can constitute being "on sale," even though no actual sale takes place. In order to be on sale, the invention must have been developed to the point of demonstrating that it will work for its intended purpose.[42]

---

[40]Scripps Clinic & Research Found. v. Genentech, Inc., 927 F.2d 1565, 18 USPQ2d 1001 (Fed. Cir. 1991); Constant v. Advanced Micro-Devices, 848 F.2d 1560, 1568–69, 7 USPQ2d 1057, 1062–63 (Fed. Cir.), *cert. denied,* 488 U.S. 892 (1988).

[41]Minnesota Mining & Mfg. Co. v. Johnson & Johnson Orthopaedics, 976 F.2d 1559, 1572, 24 USPQ2d 1321, 1332 (Fed. Cir. 1992); Continental Can Co. USA v. Monsanto Co., *supra* note 38.

[42]Buildex Inc. v. Kason Indus., 849 F.2d 1461, 1462, 7 USPQ2d 1325, 1326 (Fed. Cir. 1988); King Instrument Corp. v. Otari Corp., 767 F.2d 853, 860, 226 USPQ 402, 407 (Fed. Cir. 1985), *cert. denied,* 475 U.S. 1016 (1986); Barmag Barmer Maschinenfabrik AG v. Murata Mach., 731 F.2d 831, 836–40, 221 USPQ 561, 565–68 (Fed. Cir. 1984).

An invention is anticipated if it was invented by another person, in the United States, before it was invented by the patentee, and that other person did not abandon, suppress, or conceal the invention. To be a prior invention, the patented composition and process must have actually been made and carried out and sufficiently tested to demonstrate that it would work for its intended purpose, and its effective date as an anticipation is the date those acts were completed. A prior invention, even if put in physical form and shown to produce the desired result, is not an invalidating anticipation unless some steps were taken to make it public.[43]

An invention is anticipated if it has been described in a U.S. patent issued on a patent application filed by another person before the invention was made by the inventor named in the patent application. The effective date of a prior application for purposes of this issue is the date on which it was filed in the United States. Foreign-filed patent applications do not apply. If the patent application claims the benefit of more than one U.S. application, its effective date as an anticipation is the filing date of the first U.S. application that sufficiently discloses the invention.[44]

(v) Obviousness of the Invention

To grant a patent, an examiner must determine that an invention is not obvious. The criterion of non-obviousness is by far the most difficult to apply. An invention may be determined to be novel, but still may be found to be obvious and therefore unpatentable. United States patent law requires that the invention would not have been obvious to one ordinarily skilled in the relevant art at the time the invention was made.[45] This requirement means that if the invention is not shown by a single prior art reference and is therefore novel, it is nonetheless unpatentable if it would have been obvious at the time the invention was made for one of ordinary skill in the relevant art to have

[43]Kimberly-Clark Corp. v. Johnson & Johnson, 745 F.2d 1437, 1444–47, 223 USPQ 603, 607–10 (Fed. Cir. 1984); General Motors Corp. v. Toyota Motor Co., 467 F. Supp. 1142, 1164, 205 USPQ 158, 180–81 (S.D. Ohio 1979), *aff'd in part and rev'd in part,* 667 F.2d 504, 221 USPQ 659 (6th Cir. 1981), *cert. denied,* 456 U.S. 937 (1982).

[44]In re Wertheim, 646 F.2d 527, 532–34, 209 USPQ 554, 559–62 (C.C.P.A. 1981); In re Hilmer, 359 F.2d 859, 877, 149 USPQ 480, 495 (C.C.P.A. 1966).

[45]35 U.S.C. §103.

combined the teachings of two or more of the prior art references to arrive at the invention. Notably, when determining obviousness, the scope of the prior art (i.e., the prior art to which the examiner looks) can extend beyond the defined field of technology to analogous fields. In addition, the examiner must consider the level of skill of one ordinarily skilled in the art, as well as the differences between the invention and the prior art, before rendering a final decision.

The test for determining obviousness of a claim was set forth by the Supreme Court.[46]

1. Compare the scope and content of the prior art relied upon;
2. Identify the difference or differences between each claim of the patent and the prior art;
3. Determine the level of ordinary skill in the pertinent art at the time the invention of the patent in suit was made; and
4. Consider objective indicia of nonobviousness such as commercial success as a result of the invention, long-felt but unsolved need filled by the invention, failure of others to solve the problem solved by the invention, and acquiescence in the validity of the patent by others.

The first factor, the scope and content of the prior art, includes the same items that are considered prior art under the novelty requirement.[47]

The next factor is the difference or differences between the prior art and the claimed invention. Although it is proper to note any such differences between the claimed invention and the prior art, those differences are not "the invention." The test is whether the claimed invention as a whole would have been obvious to one of ordinary skill, in light of all of the prior art. Each claim must be considered in its entirety and separately from the other claims.[48]

The next factor is the level of ordinary skill in the art. The test is not whether the subject matter of the patent was obvious or nonobvi-

---

[46]Graham v. John Deere Co., 383 U.S. 1, 17, 148 USPQ 459, 467 (1966); *see also* Ryko Mfg. Co. v. Nu-Star, Inc., 950 F.2d 714, 716, 21 USPQ2d 1053, 1055 (Fed. Cir. 1991); Standard Oil Co. v. American Cyanamid Co., 774 F.2d 448, 453–54, 227 USPQ2d 293, 297 (Fed. Cir. 1985); Structural Rubber Prods. Co. v. Park Rubber Co., 749 F.2d 707, 721, 223 USPQ 1264, 1274 (Fed. Cir. 1984).

[47]Lindemann Maschinenfabrik GmbH v. American Hoist & Derrick Co., *supra* note 36 at 1460, 221 USPQ at 488; Stratoflex, Inc. v. Aeroquip Corp., 713 F.2d 1530, 1535–36, 218 USPQ 871, 876–77 (Fed. Cir. 1983).

[48]Medtronic, Inc. v. Cardiac Pacemakers, 721 F.2d 1563, 1572–74, 220 USPQ 97, 103–05 (Fed. Cir. 1983); Stratoflex, Inc. v. Aeroquip Corp., *supra* note 47, at 1536–38, 218 USPQ at 877–79.

ous to the actual inventors. The level of skill of the person of "ordinary skill" is that of one who has been working in the field at the time that the invention was developed. The person of ordinary skill in the art is one who thinks along the wisdom of the art. The issue is not whether the claimed invention would be obvious to a layman, to a judge, or to a genius in the art, but whether it would have been obvious to one of ordinary skill in the art at the time it was made. Factors to be considered in determining the level of ordinary skill in the pertinent art include:

1. The educational level of the inventor;
2. The types of problems encountered in the art;
3. The prior art patents and publications;
4. The activities of others;
5. Prior art solutions to the problem encountered by the inventors;
6. The sophistication of the technology; and
7. The education of others working in the field.[49]

The last factor is objective indicia of nonobviousness. These include:

1. Commercial success of products covered by the patents due to the merits of the invention and not other factors such as advertising;
2. A long-felt need in the art that was satisfied by the invention;
3. The failure of others to make the invention;
4. Copying of the invention by others in the field;
5. Unexpected results achieved by the invention;
6. Praise of the invention by persons in the field;
7. Expressions of disbelief by experts and those skilled in the art; and
8. The patentee proceeded contrary to accepted wisdom of prior art.

There must be a causal connection between the evidence showing the existence of one or more of the listed factors and the claimed invention. For example, if commercial success is due solely to advertis-

---

[49]Standard Oil Co. v. American Cyanamid Co., *supra* note 46, at 454, 227 USPQ at 297; Environmental Designs v. Union Oil Co. of Cal., 713 F.2d 693, 696–97, 218 USPQ 865, 868 (Fed. Cir. 1983), *cert. denied,* 464 U.S. 1043, 224 USPQ 520 (1984); Orthopedic Equip. Co. v. United States, 702 F.2d 1005, 1011–12, 217 USPQ 193, 198 (Fed. Cir. 1983) (*per curiam*).

ing, promotion, salesmanship, or the like, or is due to features of the product other than those claimed in the patent in suit, then it is not established that commercial success has a relation to the invention itself.[50]

The question of nonobviousness is simple to ask but difficult to answer. A person of ordinary skill in the art is presumed to have knowledge of the relevant prior art at the time of the invention. The question is whether it would then have been obvious to a person of ordinary skill in the art to combine or coordinate the elements in the prior art in the same manner as the claims in the application. The difficulty that attaches to all honest attempts to answer this question can be attributed to the strong temptation to rely on hindsight while undertaking this evaluation. It is wrong to use the application as a guide through the maze of prior art references, combining the right references in the right way so as to achieve the result of the application.[51] There must be a teaching or motivation in the prior art to combine the prior art elements in the same manner as the claims in the application. The prior art must also suggest to one of ordinary skill in the art a reasonable likelihood of success in carrying out the combination of references.[52]

The prior art might indicate that what the inventors did was obvious to try. If so, this does not necessarily indicate the patent is invalid for obviousness. "Obvious-to-try" is not the standard.[53] The standard is whether the invention as a whole would have been obvious to one of ordinary skill in the field to which the invention pertains at the time the invention was made.

It is also necessary to consider whether the prior art would lead one of ordinary skill in the art away from the claimed invention. Rather than suggesting the claimed combination, the closest prior art may discourage one of ordinary skill in the art from attempting what the applicant did.[54]

---

[50]Gillette Co. v. S.C. Johnson & Son, 919 F.2d 720, 725, 16 USPQ2d 1923, 1928 (Fed. Cir. 1990); Perkin-Elmer Corp. v. Computervision Corp., 732 F.2d 888, 895–96, 221 USPQ 669, 675 (Fed. Cir.), *cert. denied,* 469 U.S. 857 (1984); W.L. Gore & Assocs. v. Garlock, Inc., *supra* note 39 at 1555–56, 220 USPQ at 315.

[51]In re Vaeck, *supra* note 30 at 493, 20 USPQ2d at 1442; Orthopedic Equip. Co. v. United States, *supra* note 49 at 1012, 217 USPQ at 199.

[52]In re Dow Chem. Co., 837 F.2d 469, 473, 5 USPQ2d 1529, 1531 (Fed. Cir. 1988).

[53]Gillette Co. v. S.C. Johnson & Son, *supra* note 50, at 725–26, 16 USPQ2d at 1928–29.

[54]*Id.* at 725, 16 USPQ2d at 1928.

If an invention is novel, useful, and unobvious, and the application disclosure is enabling, then the application meets all statutory requirements and the PTO will grant a patent for the invention.

(vi) Double Patenting

United States patent law forbids an applicant from receiving more than one patent for the same invention, that is, "double patenting." Generally, there are two forms of double patenting: (1) statutory, and (2) the judicially created category of "obviousness-type" double patenting. Statutory double patenting simply provides that the same claim cannot appear in more than one patent. Obviousness-type double patenting provides that a claim that is an obvious modification of an already patented claim cannot appear in a second patent having the same inventors and assignee. When presented with an obviousness-type double patenting rejection, the usual strategy to overcome the rejection is simply to file a terminal disclaimer. The terminal disclaimer disclaims that portion of the term of the second patent that extends beyond the term of the first, already granted patent.

(d) Applicant's Response to an Office Action

After receiving the office action (section 2.4(b)), the patent attorney and inventor review and examine it along with the prior art references cited therein to make their own determination as to whether the examiner correctly analyzed the application and the references. An initial consideration is whether the pending claims should be amended to distinguish the claimed subject matter from the newly cited prior art documents. If an amendment to the application is necessary, the attorney prepares a document that makes changes to the specification and the claims. The document includes arguments that attempt to persuade the examiner as to the patentability of the amended claims.

Sometimes an amendment is accompanied by evidence relating to the issue of patentability. This evidence may, for example, be directed to the date of invention if it is necessary for the applicant to "swear behind" the effective date of a cited reference.[55] In addition, the evidence may be directed to addressing other concerns regarding

---

[55] *See* 37 C.F.R. §1.131 for the procedure for filing a Rule 131 affidavit.

the sufficiency of the disclosure of the specification, the meaning or inoperability of a cited prior art reference, and the advantages of the invention.[56] The accompanying evidence may also relate to various "secondary considerations" such as the commercial success of products embodying the invention, whether the invention filled a long-felt but unsolved need, the failure of others to make the invention, copying of the invention by others in the field, unexpected results obtained by the invention, praise of the invention by others in the field, that it became the industry standard, or that it revolutionized the industry.[57]

After the inventor, patent agent, or attorney replies to the examiner's action by submitting an amendment, the examiner again reviews the claims and may search for further references. If the examiner determines that the claims in the application are now patentable, he or she will issue a "notice of allowance."[58] The applicant will then have three months to submit formal drawings and pay the issue fee for the allowed patent before it will issue to the inventor or the assignee.[59] Alternatively, if the patent examiner either maintains the previous rejection or proffers a new rejection, the patent will not issue. In such event, the applicant can either attempt another amendment or can appeal to the Board of Patent Appeals and Interferences.[60] If the applicant is unsuccessful before the Board, the applicant can appeal directly to the Court of Appeals for the Federal Circuit or first to the District Court for the District of Columbia and then to the Federal Circuit.[61] Finally, on rare occasions, the Supreme Court will grant certiorari for appeals from the Federal Circuit.

(e) Reexamination of Patents

Reexamination occurs when any person, not just the patent owner, submits prior art documents to the PTO and requests reexamination of an existing patent.[62] Only printed publications and prior patents are

[56]*See* 37 C.F.R. §1.132 for the procedure for filing a Rule 132 affidavit.

[57]Graham v. John Deere Co., *supra* note 46; Perkin-Elmer Corp. v. Computervision Corp., *supra* note 50; Stratoflex, Inc. v. Aeroquip Corp., *supra* note 47.

[58]35 U.S.C. §151.

[59]35 U.S.C. §§131, 152.

[60]35 U.S.C. §§7, 134.

[61]35 U.S.C. §§141, 145.

[62]35 U.S.C. §§301–302.

considered by the PTO. Within three months, this submission will be reviewed by a patent examiner and an initial determination will be made of whether the reexamination request, including the prior art documents, raises substantial new issues of patentability. If no new issues are raised, the examiner denies the request and the proceeding terminates. If new issues are raised, the examiner grants the reexamination. If the reexamination request is filed by a third party, a copy of the request is forwarded to the patent owner; however, the patent owner may not respond until the reexamination is granted. Once the request is granted only the patent owner participates in the reexamination proceedings regardless of who requested reexamination. Thus, the requester has only initial involvement in the proceedings unless the requester is also the patent owner. No proposed amendment or new claim enlarging the scope of a claim of the patent is permitted in reexamination proceedings. A patent issued after reexamination keeps the same expiration date as the original patent.

Reexamination is generally considered in the context of actual or prospective litigation. Reexamination is useful because an alleged infringer or prospective licensee can settle questions of alleged patent invalidity via reexamination proceedings without immediately risking a possible damage award in an infringement suit. The nonpatent owner-requester also benefits from this procedure because reexamination is less expensive than litigation and places the issue of validity based on patentability before a patent examiner rather than a jury or judge. In fact, many courts will grant a stay of a litigation proceeding already underway once reexamination proceedings begin. The negative side to reexamination from the standpoint of the nonpatent owner-requester is that once a proceeding is initiated, it is "ex parte." This means that it is between the patent owner and the PTO; the requester, who is not the patent owner, is not entitled to participate. In addition, the nonpatent owner-requester has no right to appeal a ruling favorable to the patent owner and may eventually face a strengthened patent in a subsequent infringement suit in future court litigation. Thus, requesting reexamination, while having some advantages, can also present a major risk for an alleged infringer.

An advantage of reexamination for the patent owner is that, unlike an infringement suit, the patent owner avoids the adversarial arguments of the alleged infringer against the patentability of the invention. The patent owner needs only to convince the patent examiner of the patentability of the claims over the newly cited prior art. Thus, a patent owner may be able to strengthen his or her validity argument in subsequent litigation by requesting that prior art, which may be cited by a potential defendant, be examined. If the patent owner prevails during the reexamination, the alleged infringer is in a more difficult position because the PTO has considered the prior art references and issued the reexamined patent. Thus, the patent's presumption of validity is stronger and much more difficult to rebut.

A particular point of interest is that once a reexamination proceeding has begun, it cannot be stopped. Even the patent owner is powerless to stop reexamination proceedings regardless of whether the dispute with the alleged infringer is resolved. Thus, an adverse reexamination result could affect settlement terms and market leverage.

(f) Reissue of Patents

Reissue is another procedure generally considered if litigation is contemplated. If a patent is deemed wholly or partly inoperative or invalid because it contains claims that are too broad or too narrow, the patent can be reissued.[63] Consequently, if a patent owner learns of prior art not considered during the original patent examination, he or she can raise the prior art in a reissue application.

When a patent issues with claims narrower than are warranted by the invention, the patent owner may seek broader protection for the invention through a reissue patent. The patent owner must apply for the reissue within two years from the date of issuance of the original patent if seeking broader protection, but may do so any time during the life of the patent if seeking narrower protection. In addition, the inventor must execute the reissue application seeking broader protection; otherwise, the assignee may execute the application.

Unlike reexamination proceedings, reissue proceedings can be commenced only by the patent owner and not by other members of the public. Also unlike reexamination proceedings, reissue proceedings are not ex parte. Therefore, interested persons may participate in the reissue proceedings, whereupon the proceedings become adversarial with the parties having discovery rights. Furthermore, reissue proceedings can consider any issue of patentability, not just printed publications and prior patents. Another major difference between reissue and reexamination is that the patent owner may dismiss the reissue proceeding

---

[63] 35 U.S.C. §251.

once it is begun. If the patent owner dismisses the proceeding, the patent is left as it was originally issued.

2.5 Other Methods of Protection

(a) SIR—The Statutory Invention Registration

In 1984, Congress authorized the Commissioner of Patents and Trademarks to publish a Statutory Invention Registration (SIR).[64] The Commissioner publishes the SIR without examination if the application meets the requirements of §112 (discussed in section 2.4(c)(ii) above), appropriate fees are paid, and the applicant waives the right to receive a patent on the invention within such period as may be prescribed by the Commissioner. By statute, a SIR has all the attributes of a patent under the patent law except those that entitle the patent holder to the right to obtain an injunction or receive damages for infringement. Consequently, the SIR is only defensive. Its real practical effect is to create prior art and thereby prevent subsequent inventors of the same material from obtaining a patent.

(b) The Document Disclosure Program

The PTO has developed a program whereby it accepts a disclosure document as evidence of the date of conception of an invention. This document is kept in confidence for two years. After two years, the disclosure document is destroyed unless a separate document references it in a related patent application. If a patent issues that refers to a disclosure document within this two-year period, the disclosure document is then made available to the public.

The disclosure document is not a patent application. The date of receipt by the PTO will not become the effective filing date of any patent application subsequently filed. Instead, it is intended to provide a more credible form of evidence of the dates of conception than some other practices that exist.

[64]37 U.S.C. §157.

The two-year retention period should not be considered a "grace period" that allows the inventor to wait to file the patent application without possible loss of benefits. Thus, if the invention were ever in a priority contest, the disclosure document could be used to establish the date of conception. The applicant must then establish diligence in completing the invention (actual reduction to practice) or in filing the patent application (constructive reduction to practice) in order to be awarded the disclosure document's date as the date of conception. It is important to note that the existence of a disclosure document will not preclude an application from being unpatentable due to any public use or sale of the invention more than one year before the filing date of the patent application.

2.6 Foreign Filing of Applications

The exclusive rights provided by a U.S. patent are not extraterritorial, that is, they do not extend beyond the geographic area of the United States, including its territories and possessions. Similarly, patents issued by a foreign country are effective only within that country's boundaries. Therefore, an owner of an invention must apply for an individual patent in each country where protection is desired.

Prior to the 1980s, an applicant could file foreign applications only by depositing a formal patent application in each country's patent office. Formal foreign patent applications required the preparation of foreign language translations of the patent specifications, as well as the compliance with other formal requirements of each individual country. In addition, each country required payment of filing fees. Fortunately, applicants now have additional options available whereby a single filing can initiate patent protection in a number of countries.

(a) Claiming Foreign Priority

Each country's patent laws are unique; however, one feature of the patent law of most foreign countries is the "absolute novelty" provision. Absolute novelty requires that any public disclosure of the invention at any time prior to the filing of a patent application will bar the issuance of a valid patent. The absolute novelty provisions of other countries contrast with U.S. law, which provides for a one-year grace period. The grace period runs from the initial disclosure of an invention to the filing date of the patent application. Most of the developed countries, with the notable exception of Taiwan, are members of the Paris Convention, which allows a patent owner to file initially in his or her home country and then delay filing in member foreign countries up to one year after the original filing date. Consequently, an applicant may file a patent application in his or her resident country and have one year to ascertain the economic significance of the invention in various countries prior to undertaking the expensive and time-consuming task of filing the patent application abroad.

One difference between design applications and utility applications is the application of 35 U.S.C. §119 relating to foreign filing dates. An applicant for a design patent has only six months from the time that he or she filed in a foreign country to claim a foreign priority date for the U.S. application as compared with the one year for utility applications.

(b) European Patent Office Filing

The member countries of the European Patent Convention (EPC) established a European Patent that is examined and issued at a central patent examining office, the European Patent Office (EPO) located in Munich. The European patent application for the European Patent designates those member countries in which the European Patent is to be effective. As a general rule, applicants save money by seeking a European Patent if protection is desired in three or more member countries. In deciding whether to file a patent application in the EPO, applicants should consider the high standard of examination in the EPO as compared with other countries that may have lower standards of examination such as France and Italy. However, too much emphasis should not be placed on the varying standards of examination because all the members of the EPC have conformed their laws regarding obtaining patent protection. Nevertheless, because the standard of examination differed in countries prior to the formation of the EPO, it is still possible for an applicant to obtain a patent in some countries while the EPO may refuse to grant a patent for that same invention. If the EPO grants the application, it is lodged in each designated country and has substantially the same effect as a national patent of that country.

(c) International Applications and the Patent Cooperation Treaty

Another option available to applicants is the "international" patent application available under the Patent Cooperation Treaty (PCT).[65] Filing a PCT application effects filing in many more countries than the EPC application, such as countries in South America and Africa. An EPC application may also be filed through the PCT application. The PCT application differs from the European application because no "international" patent ever issues. Instead, the PCT application must be lodged in each designated national or regional patent office for subsequent examination and issuance of a patent. The primary advantage of filing a PCT application is that the substantial expense of preparing translations and formal application papers may be delayed 20 months from the date the original priority patent application was filed. In addition, an applicant can obtain an additional 10 months by requesting delay of preliminary examination in the PCT Office. Thus, an applicant may be able to delay foreign filing of the application for 30 months from the date of filing the PCT application. PCT applications may be filed based upon a U.S. application if the PCT application is filed one year from the filing date of the original U.S. application, and vice versa.

(d) Foreign Filing Licenses

The filing of foreign patent applications by U.S. inventors is subject to technology export restrictions. Therefore a U.S. applicant seeking to file a foreign patent application must first obtain a foreign filing license. When a U.S. applicant files a U.S. patent application or an international application under the PCT in the U.S. PTO, the filing is construed as an application for a license to export the information contained in the patent application. The licensing and review section of the PTO reviews each application filed in the United States and notifies the applicant if the foreign filing license is granted. Usually this notification is provided on the filing receipt issued by the PTO. In addition, an applicant may file the application abroad six months

---

[65] 3 World Intellectual Property Organization, *Manual of Industrial Property Conventions* (1971), *reprinted in* 6 D. S. CHISUM, PATENTS, Appendix 4 (1992).

after filing in the United States if the applicant has not received any information to the contrary. If an applicant files foreign applications without an export license, the U.S. patent may be rendered unenforceable unless the applicant successfully petitions the PTO for a retroactive foreign filing license.

Such licenses are implicitly granted six months after the filing date of the U.S. application. Thus, unless the applicant requests an expedited foreign filing license, the applicant must wait until the close of the six-month deadline before filing the application abroad.

2.7 Establishing a Strong Patent Position in the Development of New Products

During the 1980s, the U.S. patent gained increased strength and importance. A greater number of patents are being issued, enforced, and upheld by the courts. In 1982, a single federal appeals court, the Court of Appeals for the Federal Circuit, was established in Washington, D.C., to hear all appeals from the PTO and all patent infringement suits from all federal trial courts throughout the United States. Prior to the establishment of the Court of Appeals for the Federal Circuit, PTO appeals were taken to the Court of Customs and Patent Appeals, and patent infringement appeals were heard in the 10 separate circuits of the federal courts throughout the United States. The Court of Customs and Patent Appeals, and each of the 10 circuit appellate courts, established its own body of law. Although all appeals ultimately went to the Supreme Court, the Supreme Court can decline to hear the appeal and, as it happened, seldom agreed to hear appeals in patent cases. As a result, a wide disparity of patent law developed among the circuits. In some of the circuits, patents were usually not upheld by the courts. Because of this, the value and economic importance of patents suffered.

In the years following the establishment of the Court of Appeals for the Federal Circuit, it has considered and decided many of the points of law on which the other circuits had taken diverse paths. Therefore, the patent law followed in the PTO and followed in the trial courts throughout the United States has been made more uniform and consistent. Now, the patent owner and patent attorney have a clearer path to follow to secure a patent that will meet the legal requirements applied by the Court of Appeals for the Federal Circuit. As a result, approximately 70 percent of patents litigated are being upheld by the courts. Patents in the United States are enjoying a renewed strength and importance. Damages awarded in the United States in some patent infringement cases have reached record amounts, for example, in the hundreds of millions of dollars.

Faced with the increased strength of the U.S. patent, manufacturers and importers of goods made, sold, or used in the United States can take steps to strengthen their patent position and minimize the risk of patent infringement associated with participating in the U.S. market. These steps include finding out what patent protection others have, and designing around it or taking a license, getting a legal opinion that the product does not infringe, and maintaining a strong patent portfolio for offensive and defensive posture.

(a) Avoiding Infringement

(i) State of the Art Study

At the early stages of product development, the manufacturer or designer should perform a "state of the art" study to determine the scope of similar products developed by others. Such a search is conducted by reviewing the issued U.S. patents and foreign patent documents and literature contained in the files of the PTO. The public records of the PTO are organized into hundreds of classes that contain many thousands of subclasses. A search properly focused on the pertinent subclasses can quickly reveal a large amount of background material.

Two major benefits may be obtained from conducting state of the art studies. Those benefits are (1) guidance for research, and (2) an indication early in the design process of patents that may need to be avoided.

State of the art studies can provide a wealth of information concerning an area of technology for research and development purposes. For example, while most scientists are familiar with literature studies in an area of technology in which they are interested, a study of the patents issued in that same technological area can provide much more detailed information concerning developments in that area of technology, and at modest cost.

Because state of the art studies can be as focused or as broad as desired, they can function as a researcher's tool at a small cost to the company. A properly performed state of the art study will provide details of the problems encountered in a particular area of technology and the solutions developed to solve those problems.

By conducting a state of the art study in the early stages of the design of a product, potentially troublesome unexpired patents can be identified at a time when the product design decisions are at an early stage. For example, if a certain approach is to be followed with the design of a product, a state of the art study may uncover a patent that potentially would be infringed by that design.

By uncovering potentially troublesome patents early during the design process, the product may be designed to avoid any difficulties with existing patents, while at the same time achieving the design goals for that product. Also, since any potentially troublesome patents have been uncovered long before the product design is finalized, it is far more efficient to modify the design before tooling, production, advertising, marketing, and other sales expenses have been incurred.

(ii) Designing Around a Patent

To "design around" a patent claim owned by another means to design or manufacture a product so that it is not covered by the patent claim. In the United States a patent claim gives an exclusive right, not an inclusive right. Therefore, the patent gives the patent owner the right to exclude others from making, using, or selling what is claimed. But the patent does not give the patent owner the right to do himself or herself what is claimed. For example, Smith invents a pencil having a graphite rod encased in wood, and obtains a patent. Call the graphite rod Element "A," and the wood casing Element "B." Smith has the right to exclude all others from making, using, or selling such a pencil, if it includes both A and B. Now, Jones improves Smith's pencil construction by adding an eraser to the end. Jones's pencil with an eraser is different from Smith's, and Jones obtains an improvement patent claiming a pencil having a graphite rod encased in wood (A and B, like Smith's) and also having an eraser affixed to one end. Call the eraser Element "C." Jones now has the right to exclude others from making, using, or selling such a pencil if it includes all of A, B, and C. But Jones does not have the right himself to make, use, or sell such a pencil. This is because Smith has the dominant patent, the patent on A and B. Jones is practicing Smith's claimed invention (A plus B), when Jones makes, uses, or sells a pencil with A, B, and C.

To design or manufacture around the patent claim, Jones must eliminate from his product one of the elements of the claim. For example, a pencil that included only a graphite rod (Element A) and an attached eraser (Element C) and did not include a wood casing (Element B), would not infringe Smith's patent claim on A plus B, because B has been eliminated.

(iii) Infringement Study

It is often prudent to conduct an infringement study prior to introducing a product into the marketplace, even after a state of the art study has been conducted, because patents may have been issued in the period between the time of the state of the art study and the time of introduction of the product to the market. The results of the state of the art study will nevertheless provide valuable assistance to the patent attorney performing the infringement study.

To determine whether there is a potential risk of infringement, one must conduct a proper infringement study. A "proper infringement study" is one on which a prudent or reasonable business person would rely. It is important that a proper infringement study be conducted, because if it is not, and then the accused infringer loses in a patent infringement litigation, the damages could be tripled for willful infringement. (See section 2.7(b) and Chapter 3, section 3.6(c), for a discussion of willful infringement.)

Moreover, if the infringer has actual notice of a patent right, he or she has an affirmative duty to use due care to determine whether there is, or is not, an infringement. Conducting a proper infringement study includes a search conducted in the relevant classifications of the PTO to uncover any patents whose claims could be infringed. Any patents whose claims are potentially infringed are reviewed by first resorting to the plain words of the claims. The determination of infringement, however, requires more than consideration of the phraseology of the claims and must include an analysis of the patent and its claims and an understanding of the inventive concept.

Once an initial determination is made that the product may fall within the claims of a patent, a copy of the application file history of that patent is obtained from the PTO in order to determine the full meaning of the words of the claims. During the prosecution of the patent application, the patent applicant and the examiner may make amendments and remarks in writing that explain and interpret the meaning of the claim language. The prosecution history is, in essence, the patent, and the meaning and scope of the patent claims cannot be conclusively determined without taking into account the prosecution history.

After determining the meaning and scope of a claim, a factual determination is made as to whether the product falls within the scope of the claim. If it does, then the claim is considered to be infringed, but if it does not, then the product is not considered to infringe the claim.

A patented method may be infringed by importing into the United States a product that was produced outside the United States using the patented method. Therefore, if manufacturing will be carried out overseas, not only the construction of the product but also the method of manufacture of the product should be considered for patent infringement.

(iv) Validity Study

At times, none of the elements of a patent claim can be eliminated from the product without resulting in an inferior or economically uncompetitive product. In this case, the next step is to examine the patent claim for validity and enforceability. Many patents that are issued are not valid. Although, as noted previously, more patents are being upheld in the courts, an invalid patent is less likely to be litigated. Relatively few patent infringement claims are not resolved by the parties and thus result in a lawsuit. A patent could be invalid because the patent examiner did not correctly apply the prior art that was before him or her, or more commonly, all of the prior art was not before and considered by the examiner. This can be determined by conducting a search for additional art in the PTO and in other searching offices such as the EPO. A patent could be invalid because the invention was not adequately disclosed to the PTO or because the best mode of practicing the invention was not disclosed to the PTO.

A patent could be unenforceable because inequitable conduct occurred during the procurement of the patent, for example, the failure of the patent application to disclose material prior art to the examiner, or the misrepresentation of the prior art to the examiner can form the basis of inequitable conduct if the omission or misrepresentation was accompanied by the requisite intent to deceive the PTO on the part of the applicant or the applicant's attorney. (See Chapter 3, section 3.3(c) for a more complete discussion of inequitable conduct.)

Generally, the discovery of previously unconsidered and pertinent prior art is the most common basis for a conclusion of invalidity where the parties are not in litigation. However, during litigation, discovery information from the patent owner's files and from depositions may support the other grounds of invalidity.

If it is not practical to design around the patent claim and there are no grounds to conclude that the patent claim is invalid, then it may be desirable to approach the patent owner to take a license under the patent. Whether this is a practical business solution depends upon the willingness of the patent owner to grant a license, because he or she is generally not compelled to do so, and to what extent the negotiated royalties affect the economics of marketing the product.

(b) Legal Opinions

To minimize and avoid the risk of litigation, it is important to obtain an infringement opinion prior to introducing the product into the market. It is even more important that the scope and content of the infringement opinion meet the tests set forth by the Court of Appeals for the Federal Circuit with respect to willful infringement.

If a court finds that an infringement has been "willful," then the court can increase the patentee's damages to up to three times the amount found[66] and also award attorneys' fees to the patentee.[67]

Prior to the decisions of the Federal Circuit on the issue of willful infringement, courts had generally held that a patentee was entitled to increased damages and attorneys' fees based upon a finding of willful infringement. These findings were generally based on the infringer's failing to obtain an opinion of counsel after being charged with infringement, copying the patentee's product, misappropriating trade secrets in connection with the patent infringement, or putting forth untenable defenses.

The Federal Circuit has increasingly upheld awards based on a willful infringement finding in which a legal opinion was indeed obtained, but the scope and content of the opinion by patent counsel were determined to be inadequate and the prudent businessman should have known not to rely on the opinion.

The Federal Circuit has set forth the requirements for the scope and content of a proper infringement opinion. The court has said that advice of counsel does not shield the company from a finding of willful infringement when it commenced infringement activity with knowledge of a patent and had not first obtained an adequate opinion. The court

---

[66]35 U.S.C. §284.
[67]35 U.S.C. §285.

found that an award of multiple damages is proper when (1) the company embarked on the activity prior to consulting counsel, or (2) counsel did not do a full study including obtaining and reviewing the file history.

The court has also found that advice of counsel did not shield the company from a finding of willful infringement when it recruited a key employee of the patentee and commenced infringement with knowledge of the patent and had not obtained an adequate opinion. The court upheld an award of multiple damages as proper when (1) counsel's advice of probable invalidity of the patent was based solely on prior art in the file history, and (2) the company took no steps for two years to verify that its operations fell within the parameters specified in counsel's advice of noninfringement.

A proper infringement opinion has the following features: (1) it should be rendered in writing by competent patent counsel; (2) it should be requested before the subject device is manufactured, used, imported into, or placed on sale in the United States; (3) to assess the validity of the patent under consideration, counsel should obtain and review a patent search before any potentially infringing activities occur; (4) it should include a review of the prosecution file history of the patent alleged to have been infringed; and (5) it should set forth a comparison of the subject device and the claims of the patent under consideration together with reasons why the subject device does not fall within the scope of those claims. Counsel should review any design changes after an opinion of noninfringement has been rendered and issue a supplemental opinion.

If a competent infringement opinion based upon a proper infringement study is obtained and that opinion indicates that no valid claim of the patent is believed to be infringed by the subject device, then the manufacturer, user, seller, or importer of that device in the United States may reasonably rely upon that infringement opinion in asserting a defense of nonwillful infringement in litigation brought by the patentee.

In the patent counsel's infringement opinion, the focus is on the meaning of the patent claims. As stated previously, the language of the claim or claims of a patent is the measure of the exclusive rights conferred by that patent. In construing a claim, the courts consider not only the literal meaning of its terms, but also the prior art and the prosecution history of the patent in the PTO.

Claims are interpreted by the courts during patent infringement litigation. In determining infringement, the courts apply two traditional doctrines. Those two doctrines are the doctrine of equivalents and the doctrine of "file wrapper" or "prosecution" estoppel.

Under the doctrine of equivalents, an accused product or process will infringe a claim, though outside the literal terms of that claim, if it does the same work in substantially the same way to accomplish substantially the same result as the patented product or process.

Under the doctrine of "file wrapper estoppel" or "prosecution history estoppel," a patent owner may not expand the claim through the doctrine of equivalents, so as to recapture subject matter deliberately surrendered during the course of the proceedings in the PTO to obtain the patent.

As early as about 1890, the Supreme Court recognized that proper construction of the language of claims required consideration of both the content of the prior art and the prosecution of the application for the patent in the PTO.[68]

If the patent applicant narrows claims by amendment or cancellation to meet the objections of the patent office examiner as to the patentability of the original claims in light of the prior art, the applicant and his or her assigns cannot later "recapture" by construction the full scope of the claims that were previously surrendered.[69]

(c) Maintaining a Strong Patent Portfolio

While owning a patent does not automatically mean that the owner can practice the invention for which that patent is granted in the United States since it may infringe other patents, it does enable the owner of the patent to prevent others from making, using, or selling the protected invention. Obtaining maximum patent protection for inventions enables the patent owner to legally prevent his or her competitors from making, using, or selling the inventions protected by the patent. Thus, a strong patent portfolio is important to legally limit the patent owner's competitors. Moreover, filing a patent application establishes priority to an invention and precludes others who invented and filed later from obtaining the right to exclude the prior inventor's use of his or her invention. Also, a strong patent portfolio is useful for cross-licensing when seeking to settle infringement disputes with competitors.

In seeking meaningful patents, claims should be drafted with a view toward protecting the business of that patent owner. For example,

---

[68]Hoff v. Iron Clad Mfg. Co., 139 U.S. 326 (1891); Crawford v. Heysinger, 123 U.S. 589 (1887).

[69]Keystone Driller Co. v. Northwest Eng'g Corp., 294 U.S. 42 (1935).

the claims should recite the invention in such a manner that the competitors of the patent owner would necessarily have to use all of the claimed elements in order to effectively compete with the patent owner.

Consider as an example, that first 3.5-inch computer hard disk drive. While such a device may contain many separately patentable features, it is important also to consider protecting this device as a whole, as well as the subsequent market for this small hard disk drive.

Claims can be written to protect certain features of the hard disk drive that will in all likelihood be used by others when developing such drives. For example, the achievement of a certain storage capacity using a certain size disk may of necessity be utilized by the patent owner's competitors, simply because it otherwise would be impossible to achieve an equivalent or better storage capacity in order to compete effectively with the patent owner.

In addition, by using such a market driven claim drafting approach, a patent owner will obtain more valuable patent protection than if the claims of the patent are directed to a few of the subfeatures that may ultimately be designed around.

A strong patent portfolio can provide a company with an additional source of revenue. That is accomplished by permitting others, for the payment of a royalty, to practice its patented inventions in a predetermined, prescribed manner.

By obtaining a significant patent portfolio in the United States, a company can cross-license that patent portfolio to other companies with large patent portfolios or potentially valuable patent rights, thus obtaining rights to use such other companies' patented inventions.

In addition, when threatened with infringement of a particular patent or group of patents, potential infringement litigation can be avoided by the alleged infringer's agreeing to cross-license its patents in return for a license of the allegedly infringed patent and, frequently, additional patents owned by the other company. In addition to obtaining a license of another company's patents in return for a cross-license, other intangible property rights such as know-how, trade secrets, technical data, and technical assistance may also be obtained.

3

Enforcing Patents

3.1 Introduction

Patent litigation refers to any action that finds as its basis an issued U.S. patent. Most commonly this would take the form of an action by a patent owner to enforce the rights conferred by the patent grant. In this situation, the patent owner would ordinarily file suit in an appropriate federal district court seeking damages for the infringement by the alleged infringer and for an injunction to prevent further infringement.

Alternatively, a declaratory judgment action may be brought against a patent owner in an appropriate federal district court to have an issued patent declared invalid or noninfringed. Whether such a declaratory judgment action is proper will depend upon the existence of actions on the part of a patent owner giving rise to a reasonable apprehension by a party that it will be sued for infringement.

Suits for patent infringement are brought exclusively in the federal courts. As a result, the rules of procedure common to all federal litigation would apply in patent cases. There are additional procedural considerations and substantive law specific to patents that arise only in the context of patent litigation. It is this latter set of considerations and law that will be addressed in this chapter.

3.2 Infringement Actions

(a) General

Patents are not self-enforcing. The only recourse available to a patent owner against one who is infringing an issued patent, without a right to do so, is to enforce the patent by means of a suit for infringement. In preparing to initiate such a suit, there are certain preliminary considerations that should be addressed. These considerations can be broadly categorized as follows: (i) Is there a proper basis for an infringement suit? (ii) Who is an appropriate defendant in such a suit? (iii) What is the appropriate forum for the suit? and (iv) What remedy will be sought? Each of these categories will be treated separately below.

(i) Proper Basis for Lawsuit—The Infringement Analysis

A determination as to the propriety of an infringement action must start with an analysis of the activities of the potential defendant to see if they are proscribed by patent law. A patent owner considering a lawsuit should, to the extent reasonably possible, investigate the potential defendant's product to determine if infringement exists. This is typically done by examining the defendant's product, discerning technical information as to how the product is made, and obtaining the appropriate legal analysis from patent counsel.

The most frequently encountered activities that constitute infringement of a patent are set forth in 35 U.S.C. §271(a).[1] Under this section, the making, using, or selling of a process or device that is covered by one or more claims of an issued patent infringes that patent. The language "makes, uses or sells" is sufficiently broad that little difficulty should be encountered in categorizing accused activity as being one or more of these. Reference should be made to the case law, which is replete with examples of the types of activities falling in each category. Infringement by any one of these activities is termed "direct" infringement.

---

[1]This section provides that: "(a) Except as otherwise provided in this title, whoever without authority makes, uses or sells any patented invention, within the United States during the term of the patent therefor, infringes the patent."

The next step in the process is to determine if the accused activity infringes the claims of the patent. In utility patents, the patent claims appear in numbered paragraphs at the end of the patent. Each claim, which represents what was actually invented, contains a number of specific "limitations." In order to infringe a patent claim, each and every limitation of that claim must be present in the accused process or device. A patent is infringed if any one claim is infringed.

A design patent has only one claim—the design of the product. A design patent is infringed if the design of the accused product is so similar to the patented design that the "ordinary observer" would be deceived. A more detailed discussion on how to prove infringement of both utility and design patents can be found in section 3.3(a) below.

The plaintiff does not have to prove intent on the part of the defendant to succeed on a claim of direct infringement. The defendant need not even have knowledge of the patent or patented device or process. This would be true even if the device or process that forms the basis for the infringement claim were independently developed by the defendant. If, however, the defendant did intend to infringe the patent willfully, this can form the basis of a claim for treble damages.

As stated above, direct infringement includes making, using, or selling the patented product or process. There are, however, additional activities that constitute infringement of a patent. The most common of these grounds are "inducing infringement" and "contributory infringement."

"Inducing infringement"[2] covers situations where a party does not "directly" infringe a patent but "induces" another to infringe. The variety of activities falling within this section is quite diverse. One frequently arising situation in which infringement by inducement has been found is where a party is selling a noninfringing product with instructions for using that product in an infringing manner. While the seller technically does not infringe the patent, he or she "induces" infringement by telling someone else how to infringe.

"Contributory infringement"[3] covers the situation where a party sells a component that is specially made or adapted for use with a patented invention. "Staple" items (goods that are ordinarily sold in trade for many purposes) as well as "specialty" items that are capable of substantial noninfringing use are excluded from the scope of the contributory infringement section.

---

[2]35 U.S.C. §271(b).
[3]35 U.S.C. §271(c).

Unlike direct infringement, an underlying element of any claim for inducing infringement or contributory infringement is that there be knowledge on the part of the contributory or inducing[4] party before infringement will be found. Thus, if a patent owner believes there is an inducement or contributory infringement, it is important to put that party on notice about the existence of the patent and that the party's activity is a violation of patent law. Such notice will eliminate possible problems with proving "knowledge" if an infringement action is later commenced.

Further, there must be direct infringement of a patent before there can be contributory infringement or inducement. The direct infringement, however, need not occur in the United States. Section 271(f) provides a remedy to a patent owner where the contributory activity occurs inside the United States, but the direct infringement occurs outside the United States and thus outside the territorial scope of the patent law of this country.[5]

The most recent addition to §271, codified in 35 U.S.C. §271(g), makes actionable the importation, sale, or use of a product made by a patented process. This section is particularly beneficial in situations where the product itself is old, but where a patent is obtained on a new process for making that product. Prior to the enactment of §271(g), one could capitalize on the advantages of such a process without obtaining a license simply by manufacturing the product outside the United States and then importing it into this country. Such activities are now subject to a charge of infringement of the patent covering the new process for making the product.

In order to succeed on a claim for infringement of a patent claim, the patent owner would have to prove, by a preponderance of the evidence, infringement under one of the provisions of §271 discussed above. Since each claim of a patent has a varying scope, infringement would have to be proved individually as to each claim that is believed to be infringed.

In some circumstances, it may also be prudent to conduct an analysis of the validity of the patent before filing suit against an in-

---

[4]Although not specifically codified in §271(b), courts have interpreted that section as requiring knowledge on the part of the inducer before infringement will attach.

[5]Section 271(f) was enacted in 1984 in response to the Supreme Court decision in Deepsouth Packing Co. v. Laitram Corp., 406 U.S. 518, 173 USPQ 769 (1972), where the Court held that the use of a machine outside the United States did not directly infringe a combination patent and thus there could be no contributory infringement resulting from the sale of the component parts in the United States.

fringer. Patents are presumed to be valid, but if there is additional information available that was not known at the time the patent was obtained, this information should be considered to ensure that there is a proper basis for the lawsuit.

(ii) Who May Be Liable

As pointed out in the previous section, direct infringement under 35 U.S.C. §271(a) can result from any one of the three listed activities, that is, making, using, or selling the patented product or process. It is frequently the situation that a single product will result in direct infringement by a number of different entities. One such situation occurs where company "A" manufactures and distributes an infringing product to a retailer, company "B," which in turn sells the product for use by consumers. In this situation, each entity, including each consumer who used the infringing product, would be liable as an infringer. It is noted, however, that it is rare that a patent owner would sue an ordinary consumer for patent infringement. This situation might be different where the "user" is a large commercial entity that uses the patented product or process in large volume.

In addition to direct infringers, there may also be infringers under one of the alternate provisions of §271 discussed in the previous section. In particular, §271(b) has been given a broad scope by the Court of Appeals for the Federal Circuit in terms of who can be held liable for inducing infringement. In the corporate arena, the scope of infringement under §271(b) has been found sufficiently broad to encompass corporate officials who actively aid and abet their corporations' infringement of a patent.[6]

Each of these infringers is liable to the full extent of the damages resulting from their infringement with the limitation that the patent owner may recover its damages only once. Identifying all potential defendants and their relative assets can be critical to ensuring full recovery since it may be impractical or impossible to obtain a judgment against one or more of these infringers (e.g., an infringer is insolvent or no longer exists).

Where an action is brought against a party who bought an infringing product manufactured and sold by another, that purchaser may have a remedy against the manufacturer. This remedy arises under

---

[6]Power Lift, Inc. v. Lang Tools, 774 F.2d 478, 227 USPQ 435 (Fed. Cir. 1985).

Uniform Commercial Code §2-312, which contains an express warranty against infringement. This warranty extends to purchasers of goods from one who regularly deals in such goods and holds that such goods will be free from infringement.

The breach of this warranty would entitle the purchaser to recover any damages the purchaser suffers as a result of the purchaser's infringement. The warranty against infringement may be disclaimed, however, if done expressly and in writing, and clauses disclaiming such warranties are frequently contained in sales agreements. Further, the warranty does not apply where the purchaser provides the manufacturer with specifications for making the infringing goods.

(iii) Appropriate Forum for Infringement Suit

As with any lawsuit, the selection of an appropriate forum for a patent infringement action requires that both jurisdiction and venue be addressed. Patent infringement lawsuits must be brought in a federal district court. Subject matter jurisdiction for patent infringement, which is governed by 35 U.S.C. §271, is exclusively federal and a patent infringement lawsuit cannot be brought in a state court.

The second issue that must be addressed is in which of the federal district courts an infringement action may be brought. The plaintiff must establish personal jurisdiction and venue against each defendant. Personal jurisdiction is determined in patent cases in the same way as it would be in any case in federal court. Venue in patent infringement cases is governed by 28 U.S.C. §1400(b), which provides that these actions "may be brought in the judicial district where the defendant resides, or where the defendant has committed acts of infringement and has a regular and established place of business." In addition, the general venue statute, 28 U.S.C. §1391, as amended in 1988,[7] acts to extend the patent venue statute by broadly defining corporate residence.

---

[7]Prior to the 1988 amendment to this section, it was uniformly held that the venue in patent cases was decided solely under 28 U.S.C. §1400(b) and that the general venue statute did not modify that section. The inclusion of the wording "[f]or purposes of venue under this chapter" in the 1988 amendment created uncertainty as to whether Congress then intended the general venue statute to apply in patent cases. This uncertainty was settled by the Federal Circuit in 1990, with the court's holding that Congress did in fact intend the general venue statute to apply in patent cases. VE Holding Corp. v. Johnson Gas Appliance Co., 917 F.2d 1574, 16 USPQ2d 1614 (Fed. Cir. 1990), *cert. denied,* 111 S. Ct. 1315, 59 USLW 3636 (1991).

When infringing goods are being imported into the United States, the patent owner may also institute a proceeding before the International Trade Commission (ITC) to obtain a ruling prohibiting such importation.[8] While damages may not be recovered in a proceeding before the ITC, the preclusive nature of the ruling has made this a potent weapon, which has been used successfully by patent owners, to extract licenses from foreign manufacturers. In addition, the ITC is required to issue a ruling no later than 12 months from the institution of the proceeding by the ITC.[9] Thus, this type of proceeding can be substantially shorter than an infringement action brought in federal district court.[10]

Appeals from patent cases are also vested solely in the federal courts. Before 1982, appeals from patent cases were brought in the court of appeals in the same judicial circuit as the district court deciding the case below. In 1982, Congress created the Court of Appeals for the Federal Circuit and granted exclusive jurisdiction in that court to hear all patent appeals.[11] The Court of Appeals for the Federal Circuit also hears all appeals from decisions of the ITC.

(iv) Remedy Sought

This section addresses only the prelitigation considerations relating to remedies. For a more detailed discussion of remedies in patent infringement actions, see section 3.6 in this chapter.

The remedies available to a patent owner for infringement of its patent normally take the form of damages and/or injunction. Where it can be shown that the infringer's actions were willful, the patent owner may also be entitled to receive increased damages.

Damages are available to compensate the patent owner for any loss it experienced as a result of the infringement. Where the patent holder and the alleged infringer are competitors, the patent holder's actual losses, usually in the form of lost profits, are sometimes recoverable.[12] Even where the patent holder and the alleged infringer are not

---

[8] 19 U.S.C. §1337.

[9] This time period can be extended to 18 months if the ITC designates a case "more complicated." 19 C.F.R. §210.59.

[10] For a more complete discussion of ITC proceedings, see Chapter 5, section 5.5(d).

[11] 28 U.S.C. §1295.

[12] The factors that a patent holder must establish to obtain an award of lost profits are discussed in the section on remedies (section 3.6(b)).

competitors, the patent holder is still entitled to damages in the form of reasonable royalties because the patent statute specifically states that, at a minimum, a patent holder is entitled to recovery of a reasonable royalty for infringement of the patent.[13] Damages may be claimed for the six years preceding the filing of the complaint.[14]

Where the infringing activity is ongoing, the patent holder is typically entitled to an injunction against further infringement of the patent. Injunctive relief may also be had prior to any act of infringement actually occurring. Such relief must be sought by means of a declaratory judgment action wherein it must be shown that the defendant is engaged in activities directed toward infringement or making meaningful preparation for such activity and the defendant has indicated a refusal to change the course of its actions.[15]

3.3 Defenses

The defenses that may be affirmatively raised in an action for infringement of a patent include the statutory defenses[16] of noninfringement, invalidity, and unenforceability and the common law defenses of laches and estoppel. Each of these defenses will be described in the sections that follow.

(a) Noninfringement

When the noninfringement defense is raised, the plaintiff is put to its proof on the issue of infringement. The plaintiff bears the burden of proving infringement by a preponderance of the evidence. As stated above, infringement of a utility patent exists when it is shown that

---

[13]35 U.S.C. §284 provides in pertinent part as follows: "Upon finding for the claimant the court shall award the claimant damages adequate to compensate for the infringement, but in no event less than a reasonable royalty for the use made of the invention by the infringer. . . ."

[14]Any recovery for infringement occurring more than six years prior to the filing of the complaint is barred by statute. 35 U.S.C. §286.

[15]Lang v. Pacific Marine & Supply Co., 895 F.2d 761, 13 USPQ2d 1820 (Fed. Cir. 1990).

[16]35 U.S.C. §282.

each and every limitation in at least one of the numbered "claims" of the patent is present in an accused process or device. (See section 3.2(a)(i) for a definition of patent "claims.")

In order to determine if the claims of a patent are infringed, the claims must first be properly construed. Proper claim construction requires the application of the so-called "canons of construction." Some of the more commonly encountered canons of construction are discussed below.

The canons of construction require that each claim be considered in light of the specification and prosecution history so that it can be understood what the invention is that is being claimed. The scope of the claim should not extend unreasonably beyond the invention disclosed in the patent. As to the wording of a claim, the canons of construction require that words be given their ordinary and accustomed meaning unless it is clear that the inventor intended some other meaning. Here, the patentee is permitted to be his or her own "lexicographer," within reason, in assigning meaning to words.

The prior art must also be considered in construing patent claims. This is necessary because patent claims are construed to uphold their validity, if possible. Thus, the prior art is considered to make sure that the claims are not construed to mean the same thing as something previously invented.

The accused process or device is then compared to the properly interpreted claims. If found to contain all of the limitations of a claim, the claim is said to "read on" that accused process or device. By way of example, a fictitious claim directed to a utensil will be examined. This supposedly new, useful, and nonobvious utensil has a handle and three tines. A claim directed to this utensil might read as follows:

> A utensil comprising (1) a handle, (2) a first tine connected at one end to said handle, (3) a second tine connected at one end to said handle, and (4) a third tine connected at one end to said handle, (5) each of said tines being parallel to said other tines.

In order to find infringement of this claim, each of the limitations (which are numbered in this claim for convenience) must be found in the accused device. Thus, a fork having two parallel tines and a handle would not infringe this claim since one element, a third parallel tine, is not present in the accused device. On the other hand, this claim would "read on" a fork that has a handle and three parallel tines since each element of the claim can be found in the accused device.

Unless the wording of the claim specifically excludes adding further elements, the existence of elements in addition to those found in the claim is not material to the determination of infringement. Thus, one cannot avoid infringement by adding elements to a patented invention. Using our example, a fork having four parallel tines and a handle would still infringe the utensil claim above since there is a handle and at least three parallel tines as disclosed in the claim. The fourth tine in this fork is superfluous for purposes of determining infringement.

This one-to-one correspondence of the claim elements to the accused process or device can be satisfied in one of two ways. The first of these, called "literal infringement," exists where each and every limitation of a claim is actually or "literally" found in the accused process or device. In our example, the fork with a handle and three or four tines parallel to each other "literally" infringes the claim because it "literally" has every limitation of the claim.

A process or device that does not literally infringe may still be an infringement under the "doctrine of equivalents." Under this doctrine, infringement will be found if a process or device uses (a) substantially the same means (b) in substantially the same way (c) to achieve substantially the same result as that of the claimed invention.[17] All aspects of the *Graver Tank* test must be met before the accused device will be considered equivalent to an element in the patent claim. In other words, an accused device that accomplishes substantially the same result and uses substantially the same means, but does *not* perform in substantially the same way as one element in the patent, will not be considered an equivalent of an element in a patent claim. The doctrine of equivalents does not mean that claim limitations can be ignored. Each claim limitation or its substantial equivalent must be found in the accused process or device in order to find infringement. Further, the Federal Circuit has indicated that the doctrine of equivalents should be applied as the exception, not the rule.[18]

The breadth of the doctrine of equivalents is measured in large part by the importance assigned an invention by those in the art. For inventions that provide great advances over the prior art, called "pioneer" inventions, a larger scope of equivalents would be allowed as opposed to an invention claiming a small advance in an already crowded field. True pioneer inventions are relatively rare. Most patents represent relatively small advances.

---

[17]Graver Tank & Mfg. Co. v. Linde Air Prods. Co., 339 U.S. 605, 85 USPQ 328 (1950).

[18]London v. Carson Pirie Scott & Co., 946 F.2d 1534, 20 USPQ2d 1456 (Fed. Cir. 1991).

In applying the doctrine of equivalents, one must also be aware of the limitation imposed by the doctrine of prosecution history estoppel.[19] The doctrine of prosecution history estoppel prohibits a patentee from recapturing during litigation anything surrendered in order to obtain the patent. In other words, a patentee is estopped from arguing a position that is inconsistent with or broader than that taken during the prosecution of the patent.

Thus, if an applicant enters amendments to the claims of a patent application or enters arguments during the prosecution of that application to distinguish the claimed invention from the prior art, these amendments or arguments will operate as a limit on the scope of equivalents afforded the patent. It is important to note that courts do not review whether such limiting amendments or remarks were necessary to obtain the patent, but only that they were made and the extent of the estoppel that results from them.

If a plaintiff establishes a prima facie case of infringement, a defendant is entitled to rebut this showing by presenting evidence that its device or process does not have one or more limitations of the patent claims. A defendant may also show noninfringement under the "reverse doctrine of equivalents." If this doctrine applies, an accused device or process will be found not to infringe a patent claim even if it literally "reads on" that claim, that is, even if all of the limitations of the claim are present in the accused device or process.

The underlying premise for the reverse doctrine of equivalents is that the scope of a patent claim should be reasonably construed in light of the invention disclosed in the specification. Thus, there will be no infringement by a device that is far removed from the patented invention, either in the way it achieves a particular result or in the purpose it serves, even if a literal one-to-one correspondence of patented claim elements can be found.

For example, if the owner of the patent on the three-tined utensil discussed above asserted the patent against a manufacturer of three-tined pitchforks, the pitchfork manufacturer may be able to raise the reverse doctrine of equivalents where the patent disclosure makes clear that the invention really concerns forks used for eating purposes. In

---

[19]This doctrine was formerly referred to as file wrapper estoppel, referring to the PTO folders ("file wrappers") in which all prosecution papers are kept. The Federal Circuit coined the new phrase "prosecution history" estoppel to make it clear that the doctrine of equivalents is limited by the whole prosecution history, not solely by what is contained in the PTO file.

this situation, although the patent claim may "read on" a "pitchfork" with three parallel tines, there may still be no infringement because a pitchfork serves a purpose that is completely different from a fork used for eating.

The test for infringement of a design patent is somewhat different from the test of infringement of a utility patent. Unlike a utility patent, a design patent has only one claim—a picture (generally with various views) that shows the design of the product. In essence, a product infringes a design patent if it is so similar to the patented design that the "ordinary observer" would be deceived. This infringement test was articulated by the Supreme Court in *Gorham Co. v. White*[20] as follows:

> [I]f, in the eye of an ordinary observer, giving such attention as a purchaser usually gives, two designs are substantially the same, if the resemblance is such as to deceive such an observer, inducing him to purchase one supposing it to be the other, the first one patented is infringed by the other.[21]

Under this test, infringement is not tested through the eyes of an expert, but instead through the eyes of an ordinary observer.

The ordinary observer test is subject to several refinements or qualifications. First, the similarity is to be determined as though the ordinary observer has seen the patented design for the first time.[22] Second, the similarity is not necessarily to be determined by a side-by-side comparison.[23] What is being compared is the overall impression resulting from the patented design and the accused design, not whether individual elements of the patented design appear in the accused design.

A third qualification is that the similarity must be attributable to the novel elements of the patented design.[24] This limitation exists because there is no protection for designs that existed before the invention was made. Likewise, since a design patent covers only the "ornamental" features of a design—not the "functional" aspects of the design—a device that copies the utilitarian or functional features of a patented design is not an infringement unless the ornamental aspects are also copied so that the overall resemblance is such as to deceive.

---

[20]81 U.S. (14 Wall.) 511 (1872).

[21]*Id.* at 528.

[22]Sanson Hosiery Mills v. Warren Knitting Mills, 202 F.2d 395, 96 USPQ 247 (3d Cir. 1953).

[23]Ashley v. Weeks-Numan Co., 220 F. 899 (2d Cir. 1915).

[24]Litton Sys. v. Whirlpool Corp., 728 F.2d 1423, 1444, 221 USPQ 97, 109–10 (Fed. Cir. 1984).

For example, consider a design patent for a doorknob that combines several features to give it a new and ornamental appearance. If "old" parts of the design are copied, these features may not be considered in making the comparison of the accused device and patent claim. The fact that doorknobs have a round appearance is well known. Thus, even if the design patent and the doorknob both are round, this similarity may not be considered when deciding infringement.

Further, in our doorknob example, functional features must not be considered in making the comparison of the accused doorknob and patent claim. The existence of a keyhole in the door would be a functional feature and therefore would not be considered. Note, however, that the particular shape or placement of the keyhole may be ornamental and, therefore, any such similarities between the design patent and the accused doorknob should be considered in determining infringement. As explained in Chapter 2, section 2.2(b), a design patent is invalid if the design is primarily functional, rather than ornamental.

(b) Invalidity

An alleged infringer can also raise a defense that the patent claims at issue are invalid and the patent should not have issued. Before examining this affirmative defense, it is instructive first to address the presumption of validity that is vested in every issued U.S. patent. 35 U.S.C. §282 provides that a patent is presumed valid and each claim of that patent is presumed to be valid independent of the validity of the other claims of the patent.

As a result of this presumption, Congress has provided that the party asserting the invalidity of a patent claim bears the burden of proof on that issue. This burden can be satisfied only through a showing, by clear and convincing evidence, of the invalidity of the patent claim.

The most common grounds for asserting that a patent is invalid are "anticipation," "obviousness," and the failure to comply with the requirements for the patent specification found in 35 U.S.C. §112 (such as "enablement" and disclosure of the "best mode" of the invention). These grounds are discussed below.

A patent claim is invalid if it is anticipated by a single "prior art" reference. In order to have anticipation of a patent claim, every limitation of the patent claim must be found in that single piece of prior art. If the prior art is missing just one limitation of the patent claim, there is no anticipation.

Prior art for anticipation is specifically defined in 35 U.S.C. §102(a)–(g). Most notably, prior art includes other patents and printed publications from anywhere in the world or inventions publicly known by others in the United States that predate the time that the patent applicant invented the claims of the patent-in-suit. Prior art also includes any prior patent or printed publication anywhere in the world that predates the filing of the U.S. patent application for the patent-in-suit by more than one year. Finally, prior art includes public uses or offers for sale of the invention in the United States more than one year before the filing of the patent application. This prior public use or offer for sale can be by the patent holder itself or anyone else.[25]

As in the infringement analysis, it is first necessary to interpret the correct meaning of the patent claim before it is compared to the prior art. It is important to note, however, that the claim interpretation must be the same one used in determining infringement. In other words, a patent holder cannot argue that the patent claim means one thing for purposes of determining infringement and then argue that the claim means something else to avoid invalidity.

Invalidity based on obviousness is similar to that based on anticipation except that the invention need not be found in a single piece of prior art. A patent is invalid for obviousness if the differences between the patent and the prior art are such that the invention in the challenged patent "would have been obvious at the time the invention was made to a person having ordinary skill in the art."[26] In *Graham v. John Deere Co.*,[27] the Supreme Court set forth the following four primary factual inquiries that must be considered in determining obviousness:

1. The scope and content of the prior art;
2. Differences between the prior art and the claims at issue;
3. The level of ordinary skill in the pertinent art; and
4. Secondary considerations that would tend to show that the invention is nonobvious.

The first inquiry identified in *Graham,* determining the scope of the prior art, requires an identification of the relevant areas of technology that are considered close to the invention. Only prior art in such areas will be considered. There may also have to be a determination whether a prior publication or prior invention is early enough to be

[25]*See* Chapter 2, section 2.4(c)(iv), for more discussion of prior use.
[26]35 U.S.C. §103.
[27]383 U.S. 1, 17, 148 USPQ 459, 467 (1966).

considered prior art. For example, a prior patent issued before the date of the application of the patent involved in litigation may or may not be prior art. If the prior patent is dated before the invention of the patent-in-suit, it will be considered prior art. If, however, the existing patent was issued after the invention of the patent-in-suit, it will not be considered prior art.

The second *Graham* inquiry requires that each piece of prior art that is believed to teach or suggest an element of the claim be reviewed for differences from the claimed invention. This needs to be done because the ultimate question on obviousness is whether these differences would have been "obvious" to a person of ordinary skill in the art at the time of the invention.

The third *Graham* inquiry is to determine the level of ordinary skill in the art. Some factors that have been found to be relevant to this determination are the level of education and training that the ordinary practitioner in that field has and what others in that field were doing at the time of the invention. It is important to note that it is the level of ordinary skill in the art at the time of the invention that is important, not at some later time.

The Supreme Court in *Graham* also identified certain secondary considerations that would tend to show that an invention is nonobvious.[28] These secondary considerations[29] include a showing that the invention has enjoyed commercial success, that it has satisfied a long-felt but unsolved need, failure of others, and any other evidence that would tend to show that this invention was not in fact obvious. The Federal Circuit has mandated that these secondary considerations, if present, must be considered in making the obviousness determination.

Once these factual inquiries have been made, the relevant prior art must be considered as it would have been by one of ordinary skill in the art to determine if the invention would have been obvious at the time of the invention. The mere existence of all of the elements in the various prior art references is not sufficient to prove obviousness if one of ordinary skill would not have thought to combine these references. Similarly, the absence of an element in the prior art does not defeat obviousness if adding that element would have been obvious

---

[28]*Id.* at 17–18, 148 USPQ at 467.

[29]While the Supreme Court described these as "secondary" considerations, the Federal Circuit has held that in certain factual situations these considerations can in fact outweigh a prima facie showing of obviousness. Simmons Fastener Corp. v. Illinois Tool Works, 739 F.2d 1573, 222 USPQ 744 (Fed. Cir. 1984), *cert. denied,* 471 U.S. 1065 (1985).

to one of ordinary skill in the art. Typically, this comparison is done at trial by a patent expert.[30]

As explained in Chapter 2, the U.S. Patent and Trademark Office (PTO) will perform a search of the prior art when examining a patent application. Likewise, the applicant is required to submit relevant prior art of which it is aware. While these prior art references may be used during an infringement trial to show invalidity, prior art references that were not considered during prosecution may also be used. In fact, where possible, it is preferable to raise prior art references at trial that were not considered by the examiner during prosecution. The Federal Circuit has held that, in some circumstances, the patent's presumption of validity can be more easily overcome by prior art that was not considered during prosecution of the patent application.

Invalidity may also be alleged for failure to satisfy a requirement of 35 U.S.C. §112. This section sets forth the requirements of a patent application and most importantly sets forth the "enablement" and "best mode" requirements.[31] Pursuant to the enablement requirement, a patent must provide sufficient detail to enable a person of ordinary skill in the art to practice the invention without undue testing or experimentation. The enablement requirement is part of the quid pro quo given by the inventor in exchange for the right to exclude others from making, using, or selling the invention. Since the inventor is receiving a 17-year right to exclude others, the inventor must contribute his or her knowledge to the public domain so that other inventors can use that information to create still further advancements.

The "best mode" requirement requires that the patent specification disclose the best way known by the inventor of practicing the invention on the day that the patent application is filed. In order to satisfy the best mode requirement, the inventor need not disclose what is actually the best way of practicing the invention; indeed, the inventor may not even know this. The inventor need only disclose what he or she believes to be the best mode. In addition, there is no requirement that the inventor supplement the application if he or she discovers after filing the patent application that there is a better way of practicing the invention.

---

[30]*See* Chapter 2, section 2.4(c)(v), for a discussion of obviousness considerations when a patent application is examined by the PTO.

[31]35 U.S.C. §112 states in pertinent part that the description of the invention must be set forth "in such full, clear, concise, and exact terms as to enable any person skilled in the art . . . to make and use the same, and shall set forth the best mode contemplated by the inventor of carrying out his invention."

(c) Unenforceability

Pursuant to the rules governing practice in the PTO, "[e]ach individual associated with the filing and prosecution of a patent application has a duty of candor and good faith" in dealings with the PTO.[32] A violation of this duty of candor and good faith, under certain circumstances, may be raised as the affirmative defense of inequitable conduct in a patent infringement case.

This defense is ordinarily grounded on a failure of the applicant, or its attorney, to reveal information to the PTO that is material to the patentability of the invention. Most often, this would arise as a failure to inform the PTO, during prosecution, of material prior art that the applicant or its attorney had in its possession. Other forms of misrepresentations or omissions can also form the basis of a claim of inequitable conduct.

The Court of Appeals for the Federal Circuit has indicated that a finding of inequitable conduct requires a showing and balancing of two elements. First, there must be a showing of materiality of the withheld or omitted information, and second, it must be shown that there was an intent to mislead the PTO. There are various levels of materiality and intent. Inequitable conduct, however, will not be found unless a defendant establishes a threshold existence of both materiality and intent. Assuming that the thresholds on both elements are met, materiality and intent are then balanced to determine if inequitable conduct exists. Thus, if there is a high degree of materiality (e.g., "but for" the withheld or omitted information the patent would not have issued), a lower degree of intent to deceive the PTO will suffice to support a finding of inequitable conduct. Likewise, if there is a conscious scheme to deceive (a high degree of intent), a lesser showing of materiality may suffice.

The defendant has the burden of proving inequitable conduct by clear and convincing evidence. If this is found, the patent becomes permanently unenforceable.

Patents may be found to be unenforceable for reasons arising after the issuance of the patent. Most notably, a patent may be found to be unenforceable based on a misuse of the patent. Misuse most frequently arises in licensing agreements where the patent owner is attempting to expand the scope of the patent beyond the legal monopoly granted by

---

[32] 37 C.F.R. §1.56(a).

that patent. Some examples would be extending royalty payments beyond the life of the patent, requiring licensees to take licenses on unrelated patents in addition to a desired patent, and requiring royalty payments for unpatented goods in addition to patented goods.

Even in these situations, misuse may not be found automatically. The market power of the patent holder must also be considered. Unlike a patent deemed unenforceable because of inequitable conduct, a patent held unenforceable on the basis of misuse may be remedied. If the misuse conduct and its effects end, the misuse is "purged" and the patent becomes enforceable once again.

Two additional forms of unenforceability arise under the doctrine of laches and estoppel. Whereas the previously discussed grounds for unenforceablity render a patent unenforceable against anyone, laches and estoppel render a patent unenforceable only as to the party raising this defense.

Laches and estoppel both arise out of a failure by the patent owner to take action within a reasonable time after discovering infringement. The defense of laches generally precludes a patent owner from recovering damages for the time period before a suit for infringement is brought. An injunction, however, remains an available remedy. The defense of estoppel precludes any recovery, including injunctive relief, for past or future infringement.

The defense of laches requires the infringer to prove that there was an unreasonable and inexcusable delay in bringing suit and that, as a result, the infringer was materially prejudiced. There is a common law presumption that the delay was unreasonable and inexcusable that arises after a six-year delay from the time the patentee learned of the infringement. After such a six-year delay, the burden of proof would then be upon the patent owner to show that the delay was neither unreasonable nor inexcusable. Thus, if the infringer proves that the patent owner knew about the alleged infringement but then waited several years to sue, during which time the defendant invested a large amount of capital into a business, the defendant may be able to avoid a damages award based on the laches defense.[33]

The defense of equitable estoppel in general requires that the party asserting the defense show that there was some action by the other party on which the party asserting the defense relied to its detriment. This typically translates into a showing by the infringer that the patent owner

---

[33]If the patent owner can show a good reason that its delay should be excused, then a laches defense will fail.

took some affirmative action that led the infringer to believe that no action for infringement would be brought and that the infringer would now be harmed if the patent owner were allowed to bring such an action.

3.4 Declaratory Judgment Actions

The declaratory judgment action provided in 28 U.S.C. §2201 primarily provides a means for potential infringers to obtain a determination as to the validity and infringement of a patent. In the patent context, the declaratory judgment action is ordinarily seen as a means of preventing the inequity that would result from a patent owner's informal charges of infringement on patents of questionable scope or validity. In the absence of a declaratory judgment suit, a patent owner could succeed in driving competition from a particular market without ever having to risk a challenge to the asserted patents.

Under the declaratory judgment statute, a party may sue for a declaration of invalidity or noninfringement of a patent. In order to satisfy Article III of the Constitution, which prohibits federal courts from issuing advisory opinions, there must be an actual controversy. This actual controversy requirement is satisfied in patent cases where there is a charge of infringement giving rise to a reasonable apprehension that a suit for infringement will be brought and where there is an ability and an intent to engage in the activity asserted to be infringing.

The first of these requirements (i.e., a charge of infringement) is broadly interpreted by the courts and can include any statements made by a patent owner, whether or not these are directed at a specific individual. A patent owner should be careful in making any public statements concerning its patent to ensure that it is not making infringement threats that could lead to expensive and time-consuming patent litigation.

The requirement that the party bringing the declaratory judgment action have an ability and intent to engage in the accused activity can be satisfied where the party is currently engaged in that activity or has the immediate ability and intent to engage in that activity.

3.5 Jury Trials

Until relatively recently, jury trials were uncommon in patent cases. This was likely the result of the perception of patent attorneys that jurors would be unable to comprehend, given the relatively short duration of a trial, all of the complex legal and technical issues that ordinarily arise in patent cases. Today, however, the demand for a jury trial is nearly reflexive, particularly on the part of plaintiffs. While one would hope this change in attitude toward juries has resulted from a rise in the level of sophistication of jurors, it is more likely the result of a recognition of the preexisting prejudices held by jurors. A more commonly encountered jury prejudice is sympathy toward patent owners, particularly small companies and independent inventors, over large corporations. Many also believe a jury is more likely to afford the actions of the PTO and the presumption of validity arising out of the issuance of the patent more weight than would a judge at a bench trial. Finally, juries have been more willing to grant substantial damage awards than judges in nonjury trials.

The allocation of the burden of proof on the different issues to be proven in patent cases also creates a distinct advantage to patent owners in jury trials. On the issue of infringement, the patent owner bears the burden of proof, but only by a preponderance of the evidence. The accused infringer, however, bears the burden of proof on the issue of invalidity and many of the unenforceability issues by clear and convincing evidence. To compound the difficulty this higher level of proof creates, the accused infringer must often rely on the combination of teachings from prior patents and articles to prove its case. These combinations, unless carefully presented, may be extremely hard for the jury to comprehend, and make it difficult for the jury to find a clear and convincing showing of patent invalidity.

The accused infringer and the patent owner are best served by educating the jury to at least a minimum level of understanding regarding the involved technology. This may be a daunting task given the low probability of finding even one juror having some prior understanding of the technology and the high level of sophistication required to understand some technologies. While it is easier to find at least one juror who has the requisite experience or education to understand a simple mechanical device, the chances of finding any jurors who have the capacity to understand involved chemical or electrical inventions are quite low.

In a jury trial, certain difficulties may arise in the allocation of responsibilities between the judge and jury. For example, a determination of whether the patent claim is invalid for obviousness is a legal issue for the judge. Nonetheless, it is the province of the jury to decide the underlying factual issues, such as the scope of the prior art, differences between the patent and the prior art, and the level of ordinary skill of people in the field of the invention. Likewise, in determining inequitable conduct, the jury will decide materiality and intent, but the judge will weigh the two factors and make the final determination on inequitable conduct.

Where the patent holder is a large company and the infringer is a small local company, the plaintiff patent holder may wish to avoid a jury trial. This can be accomplished by seeking only injunctive relief and voluntarily relinquishing a right to damages. The Seventh Amendment protects the right to a jury trial only for cases at common law. Since an action for an injunction is a purely equitable case, no party can demand a jury trial. Thus, in this situation, the patent holder effectively prevents the small local defendant from seeking a jury trial.

3.6 Remedies

The remedies available to the patent owner in an infringement action include injunctions, damages, increased damages, and the recovery of attorneys' fees and costs. Each of these remedies, and the situations in which they would be appropriate, are addressed below.

(a) Injunctions

Injunctive relief from the infringement of a patent is provided for in 35 U.S.C. §283,[34] which permits the grant of permanent injunctions and preliminary injunctions. The different requirements for the grant of each of these forms of injunctive relief are discussed below.

(i) Permanent Injunctions

The prerequisites to obtaining permanent injunctive relief from the infringement of a patent are relatively straightforward. General rules of equity require the party seeking such relief to show that no

---

[34] 35 U.S.C. §283 provides that: "The several courts having jurisdiction of cases under this title may grant injunctions in accordance with the principles of equity to prevent the violation of any right secured by patent, on such terms as the court deems reasonable."

adequate remedy at law exists before injunctive relief will be granted. It is presumed, however, that a remedy at law will not compensate a patent owner for the continued infringement of its patent and generally the patent owner need only prevail on the merits in the infringement action before a permanent injunction will issue. It is extremely difficult for an infringer to overcome this presumption and convince a court that a permanent injunction should not be issued.

One exception to this general rule is that a permanent injunction will not issue in the face of a strong public interest for the continued infringement. However, the showing of a public interest sufficient to an injunction is truly a formidable task, as is evident from cases such as *Polaroid Corp. v. Eastman Kodak Co.*[35] In the *Polaroid* case, Kodak was found to be infringing patents directed to instant camera film that were owned by Polaroid. The court in that case issued a permanent injunction against Kodak notwithstanding Kodak's assertion that it had a $200 million investment in the instant camera business, 4,500 employees of Kodak would lose their jobs, and 16 million Kodak camera owners would be unable to purchase instant film if this injunction issued.

The duration of a permanent injunction is ordinarily the term of the patent and thus injunctive relief will ordinarily not be available where suit is brought on an expired patent. An exception may exist where products are manufactured during the pendency of the patent. Here, the patent owner may be able to obtain an injunction preventing the sale of those products even after the patent expires.

(ii) Preliminary Injunctions

To obtain an injunction during the pendency of a lawsuit charging infringement of a patent, the patent owner must demonstrate a probability of success on the merits, that irreparable harm will be suffered if preliminary injunctive relief is not granted, that the balance of hardships favors the patent owner, and that the public interest would not preclude this relief. The court must then balance these elements to determine if preliminary injunctive relief is warranted.

Historically, courts were hesitant to issue preliminary relief in patent cases based on the judicially created requirement that the patent

---

[35]641 F. Supp. 828, 228 USPQ 305 (D. Mass. 1985), *aff'd,* 789 F.2d 1556, 229 USPQ 561 (Fed. Cir.), *cert. denied,* 479 U.S. 850 (1986).

owner make a strong showing[36] of validity of the patent. Typically, this required proof that the patent's validity had been upheld in prior litigation or that there had been industry acquiescence, usually evidenced by license agreements. The Federal Circuit has since done away with this extra showing and has held that the requirements for a preliminary injunction in a patent case are essentially the same as in any other type of case.[37]

To establish probability of success, however, the patent owner must still present a "clear showing" of patent validity. Mere reliance on the presumption of validity is insufficient for purposes of obtaining preliminary injunctive relief if validity is challenged. The second element required to establish probability of success is a showing of infringement. The proof submitted to establish infringement is similar to what will be presented at trial and typically requires application of the rules of claim construction in comparing the accused product to the patent claims.

Irreparable harm will be presumed if there is a clear showing of validity and infringement. A defendant, however, can present evidence showing that the patent holder will not suffer irreparable harm in the absence of a preliminary injunction.

The requisite showing regarding the balance of hardships requires that the patent owner demonstrate that the injury to the patent owner, in light of the relative strength of the showing of likelihood of success on the merits, outweighs the potential harm to the infringer if the injunctive relief is granted in error. The final element to be weighed by the court, the public interest, is rarely sufficient to counterbalance a showing by the patent owner that it is entitled to a preliminary injunction and thus is rarely the basis for denying this relief.

(b) Damages

Monetary recovery for the infringement of a patent is available in patent infringement actions pursuant to 35 U.S.C. §284. As provided by this section, damages are to be "adequate to compensate for the infringement, but in no event less than a reasonable royalty." The

---

[36]Many courts had required the patent owner to prove "beyond question" that a patent was valid before preliminary relief would issue.

[37]Atlas Powder Co. v. Ireco Chems., 773 F.2d 1230, 227 USPQ 289 (Fed. Cir. 1985).

purpose of this section is to place the patent owner financially in the same position it would have occupied had there not been infringement.

A patent owner who actively makes, uses, or sells products covered by the patent may seek a recovery of its actual damages, usually in the form of lost profits. To establish entitlement to lost profits, however, the patent owner must show that "but for" the infringement, the patent owner would have achieved the increased profits sought in the litigation. This causation is most easily understood in the context of a loss of sales due to competition by the infringer, but may also result from price erosion in the face of competition or increased costs, that is, marketing and advertising expenses, resulting from the infringer's activities. Where the infringer is not a competitor of the patent owner, however, actual damages will generally not be available because the patent owner will not be able to satisfy the "but for" test.

In order to recover lost profits from diverted sales, the patent owner would have to show a demand for the product, an absence of acceptable noninfringing substitutes, and a manufacturing and marketing ability on the part of the patent owner to exploit the demand.[38]

Patent owners who are not actively exploiting the patent or who cannot make the requisite showing entitling them to actual damages are entitled to recover a reasonable royalty instead. The statute sets a reasonable royalty as being the minimum to which a patent owner is entitled for infringement of its patent. The calculation of this reasonable royalty requires that both the royalty base and royalty rate be considered. The royalty base involves a determination of the products to which the royalty rate should be applied. The royalty rate is the amount of royalty per product. This royalty rate is typically measured as a percentage of gross sales or as a specific amount per unit. Sometimes, these issues are avoided and the reasonable royalty is set as a lump-sum payment, which is the equivalent of a "paid-up-license."

Where a patent claim is directed to an entire product or process, the royalty base will ordinarily include the entire infringing product or use of the infringing process. When the asserted claim is directed only to one portion of an entire product, however, issues arise as to whether apportionment of the value of the product between the patented and unpatented portions is proper and, if so, how that apportionment should be made.

---

[38]Central Soya Co. v. Geo. A. Hormel & Co., 723 F.2d 1573, 1578, 220 USPQ 490, 494 (Fed. Cir. 1983) (citing Panduit Corp. v. Stahlin Bros. Fibre Works, 575 F.2d 1152, 1156, 197 USPQ 726, 729–30 (6th Cir. 1978)).

On the issue of apportionment, the "entire market value rule" holds that the damages for infringement of a patented device will be based on the value of the entire device even if only one of several features of the device is patented.[39] To benefit from the entire market value rule, the patent owner must show a financial or marketing dependence on the patented feature, that is, the patented feature caused the demand for the device.

The royalty base can also be increased to include sales of collateral goods in addition to the patented device. These collateral goods can be included in the royalty base if " 'the patentee (or its licensee) can anticipate sale of such unpatented components as well as of the patented' " components.[40] This rule is frequently employed to cover supplies that are sold in conjunction with the sale of a patented machine that utilizes these supplies.

The determination of the appropriate royalty rate depends on a balancing of a number of factors.[41] In essence, the royalty rate is

---

[39]Paper Converting Mach. Co. v. Magna-Graphics Corp., 745 F.2d 11, 22 (Fed. Cir. 1984).

[40]*Id.* at 23 (citation omitted).

[41]A number of these factors are identified in Georgia-Pacific Corp. v. United States Plywood Corp., 318 F. Supp. 1116, 1120, 166 USPQ 235, 238 (S.D.N.Y. 1970), *modified,* 446 F.2d 295, 170 USPQ 369 (2d Cir.), *cert. denied,* 404 U.S. 870, 171 USPQ 322 (1971). The factors identified in *Georgia-Pacific* are:

1. The royalties received by the patentee for the licensing of the patent in suit, proving or tending to prove an established royalty.
2. The rates paid by the licensee for the use of other patents comparable to the patent in suit.
3. The nature and scope of the license, as exclusive or nonexclusive; or as restricted or nonrestricted in terms of territory or with respect to whom the manufactured product may be sold.
4. The licensor's established policy and marketing program to maintain his patent monopoly by not licensing others to use the invention or by granting licenses under special conditions designed to preserve that monopoly.
5. The commercial relationship between the licensor and licensee, such as, whether they are competitors in the same territory in the same line of business; or whether they are inventor and promotor.
6. The effect of selling the patented specialty in promoting sales of other products of the licensee; the existing value of the invention to the licensor as a generator of sales of his nonpatented items; and the extent of such derivative or convoyed sales.
7. The duration of the patent and the term of the license.
8. The established profitability of the product made under the patent; its commercial success; and its current popularity.
9. The utility and advantages of the patent property over the old modes

intended to be that to which a willing licensor and licensee would have agreed in an arm's-length transaction, although this rate can be adjusted due to the existence of other *Georgia-Pacific* factors.

A patent holder is not entitled to obtain an accounting of the defendant's profits for an infringement of a utility patent. Where a design patent is involved, however, a patent holder is entitled to a recovery of the infringer's profits.[42] The patent holder can combine this remedy with other monetary relief as long as it does not result in a double recovery.

Where an award of damages is made, the court is required under 28 U.S.C. §1961 to award postjudgment interest at the rate that is allowed by state law. An award of prejudgment interest is not required, but may be awarded from a date prior to the judgment[43] if necessary to make the patent owner whole. Prejudgment interest may be denied in certain circumstances, such as when the patent owner unreasonably delays in bringing suit.

---

or devices, if any, that had been used for working out similar results.

10. The nature of the patented invention; the character of the commercial embodiment of it as owned and produced by the licensor; and the benefits to those who have used the invention.
11. The extent to which the infringer has made use of the invention; and any evidence probative of the value of that use.
12. The portion of the profit or of the selling price that may be customary in the particular business or in comparable businesses to allow for the use of the invention or analogous inventions.
13. The portion of the realizable profit that should be credited to the invention as distinguished from nonpatented elements, the manufacturing process, business risks, or significant features or improvements added by the infringer.
14. The opinion testimony of qualified experts.
15. The amount that a licensor (such as the patentee) and a licensee (such as the infringer) would have agreed upon (at the time the infringement began) if both had been reasonably and voluntarily trying to reach an agreement; that is, the amount that a prudent licensee—who desired, as a business proposition, to obtain a license to manufacture and sell a particular article embodying the patented invention—would have been willing to pay as a royalty and yet be able to make a reasonable profit and which amount would have been acceptable by a prudent patentee who was willing to grant a license.

Id.

[42]35 U.S.C. §289.

[43]*See* 35 U.S.C. §284.

(c) Increased Damages

The section of the code that permits the recovery of damages for infringement of a patent also provides for the increase of these damages, up to three times, in certain cases.[44] This trebling of damages, which is available only in "exceptional" cases, typically requires a finding that the infringement was willful.

To prove that infringement was willful, the patent owner must establish that the infringer had knowledge of the patent and acted in disregard of that patent.[45] An infringer may therefore avoid a finding of willfulness by proving either that it had no knowledge of the patent or that it had a reasonable basis for believing that patent was invalid or was not infringed.

Lack of knowledge of relevant patents does not typically last long after potentially infringing activity begins, particularly in the case of large manufacturers, and thus this is not a generally available defense to a charge of willfulness. Ordinarily, the patent owner will contact a perceived infringer, once the infringing activity begins, through a letter that simply identifies certain patents as being owned by the patent owner and as possibly having relevance to the party to whom the letter is addressed. Any such letter must be carefully drafted so as not to give rise to a reasonable apprehension of suit on the part of the recipient of such letter, or the patent owner may find itself dragged prematurely into court on a declaratory judgment action.[46]

The party receiving such a letter should obtain an opinion from patent counsel regarding the validity of the identified patents and/or whether infringement exists. This opinion from counsel, if it provides a reasonable basis for believing the identified patents to be invalid or that the asserted activity does not infringe the patents, is important evidence in defense of a charge of willfulness.[47] The opinion, however, must set forth the analysis supporting its conclusion, which is best conducted by an attorney specially trained in patent law.

---

[44]*Id.* ("[t]he court may increase the damages up to three times the amount found or assessed").

[45]Stickle v. Heublein, Inc., 716 F.2d 1550, 1565, 219 USPQ 377, 388 (Fed. Cir. 1983).

[46]For a more detailed discussion of declaratory judgment actions, see section 3.4.

[47]Numerous courts have drawn a distinction between the opinion of outside counsel and that of in-house counsel. Courts generally afford the opinions of in-house counsel less weight in making willfulness determinations.

While advice of counsel is a defense to a charge of willful infringement, risks must be assessed before relying upon this defense in a patent infringement case. If the defense is raised, the attorney-client privilege will be waived, and it will be necessary to turn over the opinions to the patent holder in discovery. The scope of this waiver may be quite broad. It will usually require production of all opinions, including negative opinions, and may also require production of other materials related to the opinions. In addition, supplying the opinions to the patent holder may give the plaintiff a road map to the alleged infringer's defense. Thus, while it is always advisable to obtain opinions of counsel when a charge of infringement is made, careful thought should be given before raising an advice of counsel defense in litigation.

A party may also become aware of a patent through a search performed at its own behest prior to initiating any activity on a new project. This may be the most prudent way of operating for a number of reasons. The most important of these is that the party may be able to take steps to avoid infringement, prior to taking any actions that may be impossible or economically unfeasible to take later. Many research and development departments routinely obtain patentability and infringement studies prior to initiating or finalizing new projects. As explained in Chapter 2, section 2.7(b), obtaining a competent noninfringement opinion should avoid a finding of willful infringement if litigation later ensues.

(d) Attorneys' Fees and Costs

Reasonable attorneys' fees are available pursuant to 35 U.S.C. §285 in much the same situation as increased damages. In fact, §285 specifically states that attorneys' fees are available in "exceptional cases." While willfulness is generally necessary for an exceptional case finding, the court has the discretion whether to award attorneys' fees, and such fees are sometimes denied even if there is willful infringement.

A prevailing defendant is likewise entitled to attorneys' fees in an exceptional case. Generally, an exceptional case requires a finding that the patent holder engaged in inequitable conduct. Here again, however, the court has the discretion to deny an award of fees.

Court costs are governed by Rule 54(d) of the Federal Rules of Civil Procedure. As in other cases, court costs are routinely awarded to the prevailing party unless the court directs otherwise.

3.7 Appeals

In enacting 28 U.S.C. §1295(a),[48] Congress created the Court of Appeals for the Federal Circuit and granted to that court exclusive jurisdiction to hear all appeals from final decisions of the federal district courts in patent cases and all decisions from the ITC. In creating this court, it was in part the intention of Congress to "alleviate the serious problems of forums shopping among the regional courts of appeals on patent claims."[49] To this end, the Federal Circuit has acknowledged that it is "charged with the duty of increasing doctrinal stability in the field of patent law."[50] In its effort to achieve this consistency in patent law, the Federal Circuit has freely ignored or overruled pre–1982 appellate decisions from the various circuits when it disagrees. Thus, pre–1982 decisions of the various circuits on issues of substantive patent law should be viewed with caution.

The appellate process will end once a panel of the Federal Circuit renders its decision. A party may request, however, that the Federal Circuit rehear an appeal or rehear it en banc. The likelihood of the Federal Circuit accepting such a request and reversing itself is very low.

The final appellate avenue open to a party in a patent case is to petition the Supreme Court for a writ of certiorari to have a decision of the Federal Circuit reviewed. The Supreme Court, however, has very rarely granted certiorari to hear a patent case where issues of substantive patent law are concerned.

3.8 Judicial Attitude Toward Patents

With the advent of the Court of Appeals for the Federal Circuit in 1982, there has been a marked change in the treatment of patents

---

[48]Pub. L. No. 97-164, 96 Stat. 25 (Federal Courts Improvement Act of 1982).

[49]S. Rep. No. 275, 97th Cong., 2d Sess. 19–20 (1982), *reprinted in* 1982 U.S.C.C.A.N. 11, 29–30.

[50]Chemical Eng'g Corp. v. Marlo, Inc., 754 F.2d 331, 333, 222 USPQ 738, 740 (Fed. Cir. 1984).

in the courts. As stated in section 3.7, the Federal Circuit was created to alleviate the serious problem of forum shopping, which resulted primarily from the widely varying attitudes different courts held toward patents.

The open adversity exhibited toward patents in certain circuits prior to 1982 was in large part a carry-over of the general deep-rooted hostility in these courts toward monopolies. The patent grant, which essentially provides a limited 17-year exclusivity to the patent owner, was viewed with a jaundiced eye by many of the federal appeals courts.

The decisions of the Federal Circuit make it clear that that court has no predisposition against enforcement of patents. The court has eliminated many of the stumbling blocks that patent owners traditionally had to overcome in order to obtain relief in court. An example of this was the elimination of the required showing of validity "beyond question" before a preliminary injunction would issue (see section 3.6(a)(ii)). Another example was the elevation of the *Graham*[51] secondary considerations to the status of primary considerations such that evidence of secondary considerations may now overcome even a prima facie showing of obviousness.[52]

---

[51]Graham v. John Deere Co., *supra* note 27.

[52]Simmons Fastener Corp. v. Illinois Tool Works, *supra* note 29 at 1575–76, 222 USPQ at 747.

4
Trademarks, Trade Dress, and Dilution

4.1 Trademarks and Service Marks

(a) Definitions

A "trademark" is "any word, name, symbol, or device, or any combination thereof" adopted and used by a manufacturer or merchant to identify his or her goods and distinguish them from those manufactured or sold by others.[1] For example, Excedrin® is a trademark used to distinguish a particular painkilling medication of the Bristol-Meyers Squibb Co. from those of its competitors.

Although a trademark is typically a word or short phrase used to distinguish a product, the term "trademark" also includes symbols, numbers, slogans, nicknames of products, the appearance of the product's container, and perhaps even the configuration of the product itself. For example, the Pink Bunny with a Drum is a trademark for a particular type of battery, Formula 409® is a combination of a word and number and is a trademark for a particular type of household cleaner, the slogan "It takes a licking and keeps on ticking"® is a trademark for a specific type of watch, the nickname "Chevy"® is protectable as a trademark for Chevrolet® automobiles, and the shape

[1]15 U.S.C. §1127.

of a Coca-Cola® bottle is a trademark for a particular type of soft drink.

When a trademark is selected by a trademark owner, the owner must determine what products he or she intends the mark to cover. This is due to the fact that while trademark owners are entitled to protection of their respective trademarks in connection with specified goods, they are not entitled to protection of those marks in connection with every conceivable product that may exist. For example, the owner of the Apple® mark for computers is entitled to exclusive use of the Apple® trademark in connection with computers and computer-type products. In other words, the owner has a right to the exclusive use of the Apple® mark in connection with goods and services typically associated with this mark. The Apple® trademark owner is not, however, entitled to exclusive use of its mark for goods that are not of a type typically associated with the Apple® mark for computers, such as phonograph records. Thus, it is possible for different trademark owners to use the same or a similar trademark in connection with very different products.

A "service mark" is a "word, name, symbol, or device, or any combination thereof . . . to identify and distinguish the services of one person . . . from the services of others."[2] Macy's® is a well-known service mark identifying a distinctive department store service. Like trademarks, service marks are not limited to words. Symbols, slogans, numbers, and shapes may function as a service mark if they can be used to distinguish services of one person from those of another. For example, "7-Eleven" is a service mark that identifies the services offered by a particular convenience store and the well-known "Golden Arches" symbol is a service mark identifying a distinctive restaurant service.

"Collective marks" are trademarks and service marks "used by the *members* of a cooperative, an association, or other collective group or organization . . . and includes marks [known as collective membership marks] indicating membership in a union, an association, or other organization."[3] There are two types of collective marks. The first, called a collective trademark or service mark, is used "collectively" by members of a group and entitles each member to use the mark to identify and distinguish his or her own goods or services from those of nonmembers. For example, the "NFL" mark is a collective trademark

---

[2] *Id.*
[3] *Id.*

and service mark used by members of the National Football League in connection with the sale of their goods and services.

The second type of collective mark is called a collective membership mark. This type of collective mark is not used to identify and distinguish goods or services, but rather operates to indicate that the person displaying the mark is a member of the organized collective group. The "American Society of Hospital Pharmacists"® is a collective membership mark when used by its members to indicate they are members of that union.

A "certification mark" is a mark used on or in connection with the products or services of one or more persons other than the owner of the mark "to certify regional or other origin, material, mode of manufacture, quality, accuracy, or other characteristics of such person's goods or services or that the work or labor on the goods or services was performed by members of a union or other organization."[4] Although certification marks are used in connection with goods or services, unlike trademarks and service marks, they do not indicate the origin of the goods or services. Rather, a certification mark is used by persons, other than the owner of the mark, in connection with goods or services to certify quality, regional origin, or other origin.

One example of a certification mark is Underwriters Laboratories, Inc.'s "UL" mark often found on electrical appliances. Underwriters Laboratories does not sell the goods it certifies. In addition, the UL mark does not perform the function of identifying and distinguishing any particular seller and thus would not be considered a trademark. Rather, the mark simply certifies that the goods bearing the UL label meet certain standards or conditions upon which the consuming public can rely.

The symbol ® is commonly used by registrants to give notice to others that a particular trademark is registered in the U.S. Patent and Trademark Office (PTO). Once a registration has been obtained for a mark, it is beneficial to use the ® symbol next to the mark because failure to do so may result in the loss of certain statutory enforcement rights. In addition to the ® symbol (which can be used only after a federal registration issues), many trademark owners use the ™ symbol in connection with their unregistered marks or the ℠ symbol in connection with their unregistered services. Although the ™ or ℠ symbol does not provide a trademark owner with any statutory legal rights, it serves the practical purpose of notifying the public that the trademark

---

[4] *Id.*

owner is using the mark to indicate the source of the product and often helps to designate exactly which symbols or words the owner considers to be a trademark. In addition, use of either the ™ or ℠ symbol often discourages others from adopting a similar mark for similar goods. For these reasons, use of the ™ or ℠ symbol in connection with unregistered marks is often beneficial to the owner of the trademark or service mark, and its use is recommended.

The term "trade name" characterizes the names used by companies, firms, persons, and similar enterprises to describe their organization, as distinguished from the goods and/or services sold by that organization.[5] A trade name symbolizes the reputation of a business as a whole. For example, Sears, Roebuck & Co. is the trade name of the corporation that sells products pursuant to a variety of trademarks, such as Craftsman® tools.

In many cases, a trade name also functions as a trademark or service mark because it is used to describe the goods or services of the producing company. For example, products of the Sony Corporation are typically called Sony® products and the word "Sony" is therefore both a trade name and a trademark. However, some trade names are used solely as trade names and are not used at all in promoting goods and services. These trade names are therefore neither trademarks nor service marks. For example, many franchised fast food outlets are owned by corporations or individuals whose trade names are rarely used in the offering of goods and services.

Trademarks and trade names are treated separately under the law. Typically, trade name protection is obtained only by adopting a particular name for a business and obtaining permission from a state secretary of state to use that name. Obtaining such permission, however, may not provide any rights to actually use that trade name as a trademark or service mark. Similarly, obtaining permission to use a trade name may provide no basis for challenging the use by others of that same name as a trademark or a service mark.

(b) Purpose of Trademarks

When the Senate Committee reported out the bill that was to become the Federal Trademark Act of 1946 (the Lanham Act),[6] it noted that trademark law had two purposes:

---

[5] *Id.*

[6] 15 U.S.C. §1051 *et seq.*

> One is to protect the public so it may be confident that, in purchasing a product bearing a particular trade-mark which it favorably knows, it will get the product which it asks for and wants to get. Secondly, where the owner of a trade-mark has spent energy, time, and money in presenting to the public the product, he is protected in his investment from its misappropriation by pirates and cheats. This is the well-established rule of law protecting both the public and the trade-mark owner.[7]

As noted previously, a trademark or service mark (hereafter referred to collectively as "trademarks") is a symbol used by purchasers to identify goods and services with a certain price and quality. Consequently, trademarks serve the function of encouraging the production of quality products and lowering consumers' costs of shopping. Ultimately, in making purchasing decisions, consumers come to rely upon a trademark as indicating a certain level of quality. For example, a consumer has certain expectations with regard to quality and cost when purchasing a Honda® automobile. Thus, trademark law protects the public's expectations by minimizing the possibility of confusion by the public with respect to a certain product. For example, a new automobile company would not be permitted to sell automobiles or automobile parts under the name "Honda" or any similar name because the public would likely be confused as to the product it was actually purchasing.

Similarly, trademark law protects the good will that a trademark owner has developed in its products through the investment of time and money. Honda has spent many years and a great deal of money in both developing its automobile and automobile parts and advertising its name to the public so that consumers will associate the Honda trademark with a certain quality and reputation. Trademark law precludes a second company from trying to trade upon the good will of the trademark owner.

(c) Basis of Protection

Federal law, state law, and mere common law use of a trademark all provide a certain degree of protection to trademark owners. The advantages of and procedures for obtaining federal and state registra-

---

[7] S. Rep. No. 1333, 79th Cong., 2d Sess. (1946), *reprinted in* 1946 U.S.C.C.A.N. 1274.

tions are discussed more fully in sections 4.1(h) and 4.1(i) of this chapter.

Typically, federal law provides a trademark owner with the greatest degree of protection because once the owner establishes proper trademark usage and acquires a federal trademark registration, that owner is entitled to the exclusive nationwide use of his or her mark and can prevent the unauthorized use (anywhere in the United States) of the trademark by others if such use would likely lead to confusion by the consuming public.[8] The test for determining likelihood of confusion is discussed in detail in Chapter 5.

State law also provides a certain degree of protection to trademark owners. Most states have developed a system of registration that entitles trademark owners, in appropriate circumstances, to acquire state registrations for trademarks. Such state registrations often provide very limited rights to the trademark owner, and a state registration provides no rights outside of the state that issued the registration. Moreover, if state trademark law conflicts with federal trademark law, the federal law preempts the state law.

Finally, mere common law use of a trademark in connection with a particular product may provide a trademark owner some protection even if the owner has not obtained a federal or state registration for the mark. An owner who uses a mark without obtaining a registration develops certain common law rights in the mark. These rights entitle owners to use their marks and even gives them the right to prevent others from using the same or similar mark in connection with similar goods and/or services, provided they were the first to use the mark at issue. This common law use of a mark, however, merely entitles an owner to exclusive use of the mark in a strictly defined geographic area. Thus, while mere use of a mark provides a trademark owner with some protection, it certainly does not provide the owner with the broad degree of protection afforded by federal trademark law.

(d) Inherently Distinctive Marks

Some trademarks are entitled to protection as exclusive marks and federal registrations on the Principal Register (see section 4.1(h)) immediately upon use of the mark by the trademark owner. These

[8] 15 U.S.C. §1114(1).

marks are called "inherently distinctive" trademarks. On the other hand, however, when a mark is not inherently distinctive, a trademark owner is required to establish "secondary meaning" or "acquired distinctiveness" of the mark in order for the trademark owner to be entitled to exclusive use of that mark. Secondary meaning is a mental association in buyers' minds between the mark and a single source of the product. The requirements to establish secondary meaning are discussed in section 4.1(g) of this chapter.

There are three types of inherently distinctive marks: fanciful marks, arbitrary marks, and suggestive marks. Fanciful and arbitrary marks are considered the most distinctive trademarks and are generally afforded the most immediate protection. Fanciful marks are often made-up words that have no meaning except as trademarks. For example, Xerox® and Exxon® are fanciful marks that are considered distinctive immediately upon use.

Arbitrary marks consist of arbitrary words from the English language which, when used in connection with the goods or services at issue, have no apparent meaning. For example, the word "Dial"® has a specific meaning within the English language, but means nothing with respect to soap. Thus, when the word "Dial"® is arbitrarily used in connection with soap, it becomes an arbitrary trademark.

The final type of inherently distinctive marks is suggestive marks which, as the term indicates, suggest some quality or ingredient of the product without describing the product. A suggestive mark has been defined as one that requires imagination, thought, or perception on the part of the consumer to reach a conclusion as to the nature of the goods.[9] The mark Heartwise® is an example of a suggestive mark for low-fat, low-cholesterol foods because it requires both imagination and a multistage reasoning process for the consumer to conclude that such food is wise for the heart. Thus, the owner of the Heartwise® mark was able to obtain protection for the mark without proving secondary meaning.

(e) Noninherently Distinctive Marks

In contrast to the types of marks indicated in section 4.1(d), which are inherently distinctive, there also exist marks that are not inherently

[9] Stix Prods. v. United Merchants & Mfrs., 295 F. Supp. 479, 488, 160 USPQ 777, 785 (S.D.N.Y. 1968).

distinctive. When this is the case, a specific word or symbol can be registered or protected as a mark entitled to exclusive protection only if it can be proved that the word or symbol has acquired distinctiveness. In other words, the trademark owner must establish that the mark has acquired secondary meaning. The most common type of marks requiring this proof are referred to as "merely descriptive" marks.

Descriptive marks are those that describe or identify an ingredient, quality, characteristic, function, feature, purpose, or use of the goods or services to which the mark is applied. For example, the term "Little Tavern" for use in connection with restaurant and bar goods and services was deemed merely descriptive because the term describes characteristics of the products and services to which the term was used. Accordingly, to receive exclusive trademark protection for the term "Little Tavern," the trademark owner was required to prove that the mark had achieved secondary meaning in the marketplace.

Descriptive marks are not given exclusive protection without secondary meaning for two basic reasons. First, a descriptive term that merely informs the purchaser of a particular quality of the product does not automatically function to identify and distinguish any specific seller's product. Because a trademark serves to perform this very function, a descriptive mark is not capable of exclusive trademark protection without a showing of acquired distinctiveness (or secondary meaning).

Second, descriptive terms should be available to all sellers to describe their respective products. The Court of Customs and Patent Appeals stated that trademark law does not protect descriptive marks because it is necessary "to maintain freedom of the public to use the language involved."[10]

Other types of noninherently distinctive marks include those that are geographically descriptive and those that consist of personal surnames. A geographically descriptive term is one that indicates geographical location and is viewed by buyers as the place of origin of the goods and services. If, however, the geographic meaning of the mark is minor, obscure, remote, or unconnected with the goods or services, the mark should be afforded exclusive trademark protection. For example, the mark Jever® for beer coming from Jever, Germany, was not considered geographically descriptive because Jever was too remote a location. Similarly, use of the term Salem® for cigarettes was not geographically descriptive because the term "Salem" did not

[10]In re Abcor Dev. Corp., 588 F.2d 811, 813, 200 USPQ 215, 217 (C.C.P.A. 1978).

indicate the place of origin for the cigarettes. On the other hand, however, the term "Yellowstone Outfitters" was held a geographically descriptive term for outfitting services near Yellowstone Park and thus was not entitled to exclusive trademark protection absent acquired distinctiveness.

Personal names as trademarks may also be deemed descriptive and not inherently distinctive. Trademark law prohibits registration of marks that are primarily merely surnames for the policy reason that all persons having a certain surname should be equally entitled to use that name as a distinguishing mark. When a particular term has an ordinary meaning in the English language as well as its meaning as a surname, then it becomes necessary to determine the primary significance of the term. For example, the term "Bird" for radios was held not primarily merely a surname, even though Bird was the name of the president of the company selling the radios.

When a term that is primarily merely a surname or is geographically descriptive acquires secondary meaning, it becomes entitled to exclusive trademark protection. McDonald's® is such a mark. Although McDonald is a common surname, the fast-food restaurant chain, McDonald's® , has acquired distinctiveness and is a trademark entitled to exclusive protection. Accordingly, the owner of the McDonald's® mark can prevent someone with the surname McDonald from using the name in connection with those goods or services associated with McDonald's® restaurants.

(f) Marks That Are Incapable of Trademark Protection

Finally, there are some types of marks that are simply incapable of trademark significance and are thus not protected by trademark law. Even a claim of distinctiveness will not change the fact that such marks are not capable of trademark law protection.

Marks that consist of "generic" terms are the most common type of mark incapable of denoting origin or any specific source of the product. A generic term is the actual term given to a particular product or service. In other words, a generic term does not identify the source of a product, but rather is the accepted term for the product itself. For example, the term "car" or "automobile" is the actual name of a particular type of product and cannot be used as one's trademark.

Marks that begin as protected acceptable trademarks sometimes lose their trademark significance over time because the public comes to use the mark as the generic name for a particular type of product, rather than a brand name indicating the source of the product. Some well-known examples of words that were once protected trademarks include: "Thermos" for a vacuum-insulated bottle, "Aspirin" for acetyl salicylic acid, "Escalator" for a moving staircase, and "Cellophane" for transparent plastic wrap.

Some companies have gone to great lengths in an attempt to ensure that the public uses their trademarks properly and not in a generic sense. Xerox Corporation, for example, has placed advertisements in newspapers and magazines to inform the public that its Xerox® trademark should be used only in connection with Xerox Corporation's products. If consumers begin to refer to all copy machines as "Xerox," Xerox Corporation could become dangerously close to losing the protection afforded its Xerox® trademark. Thus, trademark owners must ensure that the public recognizes that their marks describe the product of a particular source and not the product itself.

In addition to generic marks, trademark law will not protect marks that are regarded as immoral or scandalous;[11] consist of matter that may disparage or falsely suggest a connection with persons living or dead, institutions, beliefs, or national symbols, or bring them into contempt or disrepute;[12] or consist of the flag, coat of arms, or other insignia of the United States, a state, a municipality, or a foreign nation.[13] Two examples of marks that were held not protectable pursuant to the above provisions include: (1) "Madonna" for wines because the use of a religious name may be regarded as immoral or scandalous, and (2) a mark consisting of a hammer and sickle with a cross through it because this was held to disparage a national symbol of the Soviet Union. On the other hand, the mark Old Glory Condom Corp®, accompanied by a design of a condom decorated with stars and stripes in a manner and color similar to the American flag, was found not to be scandalous and thus was registrable for condoms.

(g) Secondary Meaning

As indicated previously, to receive exclusive protection under trademark law for a mark that is not inherently distinctive, the trademark

[11] 15 U.S.C. §1052(a).
[12] *Id.*
[13] 15 U.S.C. §1052(b).

owner must prove that the mark has become distinctive in the marketplace. This acquisition of distinctiveness is often referred to as secondary meaning. To establish secondary meaning, a trademark owner must establish that a mental association has developed in consumers' minds between the mark and the source or origin of the goods or services bearing the mark. Generally, the less distinctive the mark, the greater the evidentiary burden to prove secondary meaning. As indicated in section 4.1(e), McDonald is a common surname and, hence, is not an inherently distinctive trademark. Nevertheless, the name of the fast-food restaurant chain McDonald's® is a trademark that has acquired secondary meaning and, thus, is entitled to exclusive protection.

Determining whether secondary meaning exists is a question of fact. The kinds of evidence generally presented to prove secondary meaning include extensive use of the mark in connection with particular goods and/or services, large expenditures for advertising and promoting the mark throughout various groups of purchasers, a high degree of consumer recognition of the company/seller's name, high sales volume, direct testimony of random consumers or consumer surveys indicating that they associate the mark with the source of the product bearing the mark, and evidence that actual confusion exists between marks. This final category of evidence is premised on the notion that Company B would not begin using a mark that is so similar to Company A's mark so as to cause actual confusion in the marketplace unless Company B were hoping to benefit from the secondary meaning developed by Company A between the mark and Company A's products.

Often, a trademark owner of a noninherently distinctive mark may only be able to prove the existence of secondary meaning in specific and limited geographic areas. When this is the case, the owner may only be able to have exclusive trademark rights in its mark within the geographic areas where secondary meaning is established. Thus, while the owner may not be able to prevent use by another of a similar mark in connection with similar goods or services in all areas, the owner will likely be able to prevent such use in the geographic areas where it can establish secondary meaning.

(h) Federal Registration

Federal registration can be sought on either the Principal Register or the Supplemental Register. The Principal Register is for marks that are inherently distinctive or noninherently distinctive marks that have achieved secondary meaning.[14] The Principal Register, which carries with it prima facie proof of the exclusive right to use the mark, is the preferable registration if it can be obtained. Registration on the Supplemental Register, which does not provide prima facie proof of exclusivity, is available for noninherently distinctive marks that do not have secondary meaning. Generic terms (and the other marks discussed in section 4.1(f)), cannot be registered.

Prior to November 16, 1989, a trademark applicant in the United States, with rare exceptions, could not even seek a federal registration for a mark unless the applicant had actually begun to use the mark in the sale of goods or services in interstate or foreign commerce. The Trademark Law Revision Act of 1988[15] changed this, however, and brought the United States' accepted bases for applying for registration into conformity with those of most foreign nations. Since November 16, 1989, several bases exist for submitting an application for trademark registration.

(i) Types of Trademark Applications

Use-Based Application.[16] Any applicant that has actually begun using a mark on or in connection with the sale of particular goods or services is entitled to apply for a federal trademark registration based on the dates of first use.

Intent to Use Use-Based Application.[17] Any applicant that has a bona fide intention to use a mark on particular goods and/or services can file an application for trademark registration based on that intention to use the mark. Ultimately, however, the federal registration cannot be issued to the applicant until the applicant actually begins using the mark and so notifies the PTO with a verified statement of the dates of first use of the mark.

---

[14]If the PTO initially determines that a mark is not inherently distinctive, the applicant can still obtain a registration on the Principal Register by submitting evidence that the mark has obtained secondary meaning. The applicant can submit the types of evidence discussed in section 4.1(g) of this chapter, or can submit a verified statement of substantially exclusive and continuous use of the mark by the applicant in the United States for the five years preceding the date of filing of the trademark application. *See* 15 U.S.C. §1052(f).

[15]Pub. L. No. 100-667, 102 Stat. 3935 (1988) (amending certain sections of 15 U.S.C. §§1051–1128).

[16]15 U.S.C. §1051(a).

[17]15 U.S.C. §1051(b).

It is important to note that no applicant is permitted to file a single trademark application based on actual use of the mark for some goods and an intent to use the mark in connection with other goods. When a trademark applicant is faced with this situation, two different applications must be filed and each must be examined separately by the PTO.

Foreign-Based Application.[18] Any foreign applicant that has either filed an application or obtained a registration for a mark in a foreign country may apply for a federal registration for that same mark in the United States based on both the foreign application or registration and the foreign applicant's stated bona fide intention to use the mark in the United States. Ultimately, to obtain the U.S. federal trademark registration, the foreign applicant can *either* simply submit a copy of the foreign registration or actually begin to use the mark in the United States in interstate commerce.

(ii) Trademark Searches Prior to Registration

Once a trademark owner determines that he or she wishes to obtain a federal registration for a particular mark used in connection with specific goods and/or services, it is typically recommended that the trademark owner have a trademark search conducted to evaluate whether there are already existing marks used on similar goods and/or services that could ultimately preclude the owner from obtaining a registration for his or her mark. If the trademark search report reveals that there is a preexisting registration or application so similar to the applicant's mark and the applicant's goods that consumers would likely be confused by the simultaneous existence of both marks, then it is unlikely that the PTO will issue a registration for the applicant's proposed mark. Making this determination prior to filing a trademark application for a mark can ultimately save an applicant the costs associated with filing and "prosecuting" a trademark application.

Moreover, obtaining an early preliminary determination with respect to the availability of a proposed mark has the added advantage of saving a company the time and expense associated with the adoption and advertising of a new mark. This saving can be quite significant in light of the fact that many companies spend tens of thousands of dollars when introducing a new trademark to the relevant public.

---

[18] 15 U.S.C. §1126(d).

Finally, at least one court has indicated that in some circumstances, a company has a duty to conduct a trademark search before adopting and advertising a new mark. In *Sands, Taylor & Wood v. Quaker Oats Co.*,[19] a trademark infringement case, the district court in Illinois determined that the failure of the defendant company to conduct a basic trademark search prior to its adoption and launching of a particular mark was inexcusable. The court stated that the defendant, "[a]s a highly sophisticated national marketer [with] access to every imaginable resource to avoid the slightest possibility of confusion . . . indicate[d] a complete indifference to plaintiff's federal trademark rights [and] suggest[d] calloused indifference which is a factor favoring relief."[20] Accordingly, in some instances, conducting a preliminary trademark search before adopting a new mark may not only be prudent, but also mandatory.

(iii) Prosecuting a Federal Trademark Application for Registration

Prosecuting a trademark application refers to the examination process that occurs between filing an application for a mark and ultimately receiving a federal registration for that mark. During the examination process, the PTO will often issue Office Actions in which the examining trademark attorney may refuse to register the mark for a variety of reasons. It then becomes necessary for the trademark applicant to file a response to the Office Action and persuade the examining attorney that the mark is entitled to registration. If the examiner does not agree, an administrative appeal to the Trademark Trial and Appeal Board and, ultimately, an appeal to the Court of Appeals for the Federal Circuit is available. If the examining attorney ultimately agrees that the mark is registrable on the Principal Register, the mark will then be published in the "Trademark Official Gazette" for a period of 30 days to give any third party who may be damaged by registration of the mark the opportunity to oppose the mark. Trademark oppositions are discussed in Chapter 5, section 5.6(a).

Assuming no oppositions are filed, the next step depends upon whether the applicant has begun actual use of the mark in connection

---

[19]18 USPQ2d 1457, 1472–73 (N.D. Ill. 1990), *aff'd in part and rev'd in part on other grounds*, 978 F.2d 947, 24 USPQ2d 1001 (7th Cir. 1992).

[20]*Id.* at 1473.

with the goods or services set forth in the application. If use has begun, a registration for the mark will be issued by the PTO in due course.

If, however, the application was filed pursuant to the intent to use provisions of the Trademark Act and use of the mark has not yet begun, a Notice of Allowance will be issued in place of a registration. Once the Notice of Allowance is issued, the applicant has six months to file a verified statement indicating that the applicant has begun use of his or her mark on the goods and/or services indicated in the Notice of Allowance. If, after those six months, the applicant still has not begun using his or her mark in interstate commerce, an automatic six-month extension of time is available upon payment of the required fee and a statement that the applicant still has a bona fide intent to use the mark in the United States. Further extensions of time (in six-month intervals) are available provided certain statutory requirements are met. Altogether, extensions of time may be obtained for a total of three years from the issuance of the Notice of Allowance.

(iv) Advantages of Registration

Once a federal registration for a mark issues on the Principal Register, the owner of the registration obtains certain procedural and substantive legal advantages simply by virtue of having that registration. The procedural advantages include a trademark registrant's right to bring an infringement action in federal court without having to satisfy any specific amount in controversy and may entitle a registrant to treble damages and attorneys' fees, not otherwise available, if successful in proving infringement.

Substantively, a federal registration on the Principal Register is prima facie evidence of a registrant's ownership of a mark and the exclusive right to use the mark throughout the United States.[21] It is very important to recognize that this exclusive right to use the mark throughout the United States exists even if the trademark owner is not using the mark in certain states. Thus, in a priority battle over who has the exclusive rights to a particular mark, having a federal registration for the mark can be extremely advantageous to the registrant. For example, Company A begins use of a mark in Maryland and Virginia on January 1, 1993, but does not file a federal trademark application. Company B then begins use of the same mark on February 1, 1993, in West

---

[21] 15 U.S.C. §§1057(b), 1115(a).

Coast states. In this example, Company A would have the exclusive right to use the mark in Maryland and Virginia, but Company B would have the exclusive rights in the West Coast states. If, however, Company A had also filed a federal trademark application on January 1, 1993, it would have obtained exclusive rights throughout the United States and would have been able to prevent Company B from using the mark anywhere in the United States.

A registration on the Principal Register provides other substantive advantages. It can provide prima facie evidence that a mark is entitled to exclusive protection either because it is inherently distinctive or, in the case of a descriptive mark, has acquired secondary meaning pursuant to §2(f) of the Trademark Act. It also can be prima facie evidence that the mark is not confusingly similar to other registered marks.

Once a mark has been registered on the Principal Register for a period of five years and has been continuously used throughout that period, and other statutory requirements have been met, a registrant can file an affidavit of incontestability for a mark. When this occurs and the affidavit is accepted by the postregistration section of the PTO, the registration becomes conclusive proof of the registrant's exclusive right to use the mark subject only to a small number of specific defenses.[22]

Another substantive advantage to registration is the fact that registration is considered constructive notice that the registrant is the owner of the mark.[23] Because a federal registration gives a trademark registrant the right to use his or her mark exclusively throughout the United States, and puts all trademark users on notice of that right, federal registration eliminates any defense by an infringer of not knowing that the mark existed.

Finally, as discussed more fully in Chapter 5, a federal registration may be used to prevent articles bearing an infringing mark from being imported into the United States.[24]

Certain marks that are not eligible for registration on the Principal Register may nevertheless be registrable on the Supplemental Register provided the mark is capable of distinguishing an owner's goods or services. For example, noninherently distinctive marks (see section 4.1(e)) can typically be registered on the Supplemental Register. A supplemental registration is not as strong as a registration on the Princi-

[22]15 U.S.C. §§1065, 1115(b).
[23]15 U.S.C. §1072.
[24]15 U.S.C. §1124.

pal Register because such a registration does not give the owner prima facie evidence of the exclusive right to use the mark. Nonetheless, a trademark owner with a supplemental registration should be able to prevent others from obtaining a federal registration, may well discourage others from using the same or similar term for their products, and has prima facie evidence that the mark is not confusingly similar to other registered marks. Furthermore, after five years of continuous, exclusive, and substantial use of a mark, a trademark owner may be able to convert a supplemental registration into a registration on the Principal Register.[25]

(i) State Registration

Most states have adopted provisions for registration of trademarks used within that state. Often, trademark owners who cannot avail themselves of federal trademark law due to nonuse of their mark beyond a state's limits will turn to whatever protections are afforded by the state. A state registration may have little legal significance other than proving that the registrant filed a claim that it was using a particular mark in connection with particular goods or services and, in some circumstances, providing priority of use for the entirety of a state, rather than just the part of a state where the mark is actually used. On the other hand, state registrations are a matter of public record and will be found by others who conduct a nationwide search of marks before selecting their own mark. It is possible that the existence of a state registration will prevent others from using or attempting to register a similar mark on the federal level.

State registrations are generally based on actual use of a mark. Thus, a trademark owner cannot obtain a state registration until the mark has actually been used in connection with the sale of goods or services within that state.

If state trademark law conflicts with federal trademark law, the federal law preempts the state law. In other words, a state trademark registration does not prevail over the rights provided by federal law and a federal registration. Moreover, although a state registration may give the registrant limited rights to exclusive use of a trademark for particular goods within the respective state, if that registration conflicts

---

[25]Unlike applications for registration on the Principal Register, marks on the Supplemental Register are not published for opposition.

with another owner's prior federal registration for the same or similar mark in connection with similar goods, the owner with the federal registration will have priority in the mark even if that owner does not actually use the mark within the state. Consequently, if possible, it is much more advantageous for a trademark owner to obtain a federal registration for a mark rather than merely a state registration.

(j) Foreign Registration

As indicated previously, if a foreign trademark applicant's country of origin is a party to certain international treaties signed by the United States and the applicant has, or will obtain, a trademark registration in the foreign country, the foreign applicant is entitled to a U.S. trademark registration based upon the registration from the foreign applicant's country of origin. Similarly, if a U.S. citizen or company has filed an application, or obtained a registration for a mark in the United States, that U.S. citizen can file a foreign application for the same mark in any of the "treaty countries" and obtain special benefits in those countries.

If a company in the United States has filed a trademark application in the United States based either on actual use of the mark in interstate commerce or on a bona fide intent to use the mark in interstate commerce and intends also to use the mark in any foreign country that is a party to certain treaties, it is recommended that the U.S. company file a trademark application in those foreign countries within six months of the date on which the U.S. application was filed. The advantage this provides is that the U.S. company will be given an effective filing date in the foreign country that is the same as the filing date in the United States. This can be beneficial if, during those six months, another company files an application for the same mark in the foreign country. Despite actually filing later, the U.S. company would have priority rights in the mark.

Finally, it is often very wise for U.S. trademark owners to file applications for their marks in foreign countries because in many foreign countries, the first applicant to file is entitled to registration of the mark. Thus, if a U.S. trademark owner neglects to file in a foreign country (or countries) and someone else decides to file an application for the same or similar mark in a first-to-file country before the U.S. trademark owner, then that other entity is entitled to the registration even if the U.S. trademark owner used the mark in that foreign country first.

4.2 Trade Dress

(a) Types of Protectable Trade Dress

Names and symbols are not the only methods to identify the source of a product or service. Sometimes, the packaging or even the total image of the product itself can serve as a source identifier. This type of source identification is called trade dress. Protection of trade dress began as a concept to protect the packaging of a product, including the size, shape, configuration, color, and texture of the packaging. Today, trade dress protection has been expanded to include the configuration of the product itself, as well as any other aspect of a business that serves to identify that business. For example, the decor of a restaurant can be protectable trade dress if it is distinctive and is identifiable with the restaurant owner.

(b) Basis of Protection

In much the same way that the Trademark Act protects inherently distinctive words, slogans, symbols, etc., used as trademarks, §43(a) of the Act also protects the distinctive trade dress of a product or service.[26] Thus, when the total image or overall appearance of a product is inherently distinctive, that trade dress is entitled to protection against infringement by others. The Lanham Act prohibits anyone from unfairly competing in the marketplace by adopting a trade dress so similar to an existing trade dress that a consumer will be confused as to the origin of the product.

Much like trademarks, the trade dress of a product or service can be registered in the PTO as a trademark. For example, the shape of the Coca-Cola® bottle is a particular type of trade dress for which a U.S. federal trademark registration has been obtained. Although

---

[26] 15 U.S.C. §1125(a).

registering a trade dress can often be more complex than registering a more traditional-type trademark, it is often worth the effort since a registration for the trade dress of a product provides all the same procedural and substantive advantages of registration afforded a trademark (see section 4.1(h)(iv)).

Generally, trade dress protection under federal law is greater than that afforded by state law. In 1964, in the *Sears–Compco*[27] cases, the Supreme Court held that federal patent and copyright laws prevent states from applying their own unfair competition laws that hold one liable for copying a product shape not protected by federal laws. While the *Sears–Compco* rule does not preclude all state law remedies for trade dress infringement, federal protection under the Lanham Act is broader and eliminates questions of federal preemption.

Not all trade dress can be protected. To be eligible for protection, the trade dress must (a) be nonfunctional, and (b) be inherently distinctive or have achieved secondary meaning.

(c) Functionality

Trade dress that is deemed "functional" is not entitled to protection under the Lanham Act. If a particular trade dress is functional, it must be available to everyone so that they can compete in the marketplace. To preclude others from using a functional feature could effectively keep competitors from producing a particular product. Such an expansive preclusion policy does not comport with the purpose underlying the Lanham Act. This prohibition against protection of functional trade dress controls even if the trade dress is otherwise distinctive and even if there is a likelihood of confusion.

(i) Proving Functionality

It is useful to recognize that although every trade dress has a function and serves a purpose, this is not what courts mean when they speak in terms of the "functionality" of trade dress. For example, a bottle that is typically made of glass serves the function of holding liquid. That does not mean, however, that all bottles are functional

[27]Sears, Roebuck & Co. v. Stiffel Co., 376 U.S. 225, 140 USPQ 524 (1964); Compco Corp. v. Day-Brite Lighting, 376 U.S. 234, 140 USPQ 528 (1964).

and, hence, incapable of trade dress protection. In fact, there are many bottles with shapes and characteristics that have entitled them to trade dress protection, such as the Coca-Cola® bottle example mentioned above.

The relevant inquiry is whether the trade dress has to have a particular design to be sold effectively. If so, the trade dress is considered functional. Although various courts have established different criteria for proving functionality, the Supreme Court recently cited the Fifth Circuit and stated that to prove functionality, one must demonstrate that the design is "one of a limited number of equally efficient options available to competitors and free competition would be unduly hindered by according the design trademark protection."[28]

The functionality inquiry is a question of fact and the Court of Customs and Patent Appeals (the predecessor to the Court of Appeals for the Federal Circuit) set forth four factors relevant to this inquiry.[29] First, the existence of a utility patent that identifies the utilitarian advantages of the design of a product is evidence that the design is functional. Second, product advertising that promotes the utilitarian advantages of the product design is also evidence of functionality. Next, the availability of alternative designs that perform the utilitarian task as well as the design in question is evidence of nonfunctionality. Finally, if the design in question is the result of a relatively simple, inexpensive, or superior method of manufacturing, then this fact will serve as evidence of functionality.

(ii) Overall Design

Typically, the focus on functionality is whether the overall design of the trade dress is functional. For example, if a specific product is in a particular shape for utilitarian reasons, then the overall design of the product may be functional. The inquiry is not whether the product itself is useful, but whether the specific overall design of the product is necessary to use the product. If so, the trade dress is functional and cannot be protected.

It is also possible to protect the overall design of a product's trade dress even though the product consists of a combination of individually

---

[28]Two Pesos, Inc. v. Taco Cabana, Inc., 112 S. Ct. 2753, 2760, 60 USLW 4762, 4765, 23 USPQ2d 1081, 1086 (1992).

[29]*See* In re Morton-Norwich Prods., 671 F.2d 1332, 1337–41, 213 USPQ 9, 12–16 (C.C.P.A. 1982).

functional features. For example, the trade dress of a restaurant that consists of numerous functional features can still be protected when the particular random combination of the individual features is not functional. The inquiry in this instance is on the overall design of the restaurant, not on its individual parts.

(iii) Functionality of Individual Features

In addition to the fact that the overall design of a product may be functional, it is also possible that one or more features of a product may be functional. When a particular feature is claimed as a protectable trade dress, the functionality inquiry should focus only on the utility of that feature and not on the utility of the overall design of the product. This is due to the fact that individual design features of a product may be nonfunctional, even though the product itself may be functional. Thus, the individual nonfunctional features can be protectable trade dress.

(iv) Burden of Proof

Courts are generally split on the issue of whether functionality is a defense to be proven by the defendant, or whether nonfunctionality is an element of a trade dress claim to be established by the plaintiff. At present, a majority of circuit courts have determined that the plaintiff should bear the burden of proving that the trade dress is nonfunctional. These courts include the Courts of Appeals for the Third, Sixth, Eighth, Ninth, Tenth, Eleventh, and District of Columbia Circuits.

A minority of courts, on the other hand, maintain that once a plaintiff demonstrates that (1) its trade dress has acquired secondary meaning or is inherently distinctive, and (2) there is a likelihood of confusion between its trade dress and the trade dress of the allegedly infringing product, the defendant must establish that the copied features are functional to avoid liability. Both the Courts of Appeals for the Second and the Seventh Circuits have adopted this approach. In 1985, the Second Circuit explained the rationale for its view by quoting a law review note:

> Requiring the plaintiff to prove nonfunctionality in order to prevail might "defeat[] the Lanham Act's purpose of enabling a purchaser to distinguish one product from another, . . . because a plaintiff unable to prove that the features copied are nonfunctional will not prevail, no matter how

compelling the evidence that purchasers are confused as to product source."[30]

Although the Supreme Court may one day resolve this split in the courts, until that day arrives, one must look to where the case is being litigated to determine whether a plaintiff or a defendant has the burden of proving functionality (or nonfunctionality) in a trade dress case.

(v) Aesthetic Functionality

Not only can a utilitarian design be deemed functional and hence not protectable under the law of trade dress, but some courts have accepted the notion that even a mere aesthetic design can be functional. This has become more commonly known as "aesthetic functionality."

In 1952, the Court of Appeals for the Ninth Circuit used the theory of aesthetic functionality to permit a defendant to copy floral designs that existed on the china dishes of the plaintiff.[31] The Ninth Circuit concluded that the floral designs were functional because they satisfied "a demand for the aesthetic as well as for the utilitarian."[32] Hence, the court concluded that the floral designs were not a protectable trademark and could be copied by Wallace China's competitors.

Since 1952, courts have wrestled with the task of applying the aesthetic functionality theory, causing some courts to instead redefine the theory and causing others to simply reject the theory outright. For example, the Second Circuit redefined aesthetic functionality to mean features that are purely ornamental,[33] while the Federal Circuit has consistently refused to accept the notion of aesthetic functionality. Finally, the trademark owner or applicant should be aware that although utilitarian functionality is alive and well, the aesthetic functionality concept is not applied in the PTO.

(d) Secondary Meaning

As stated in section 4.1(g), a trademark that has acquired secondary meaning indicates that a nondistinctive mark has, through use,

---

[30]LeSportsac, Inc. v. K Mart Corp., 754 F.2d 71, 76, 225 USPQ 654, 657 (2d Cir. 1985) (quoting Note, *The Problem of Functional Features: Trade Dress Infringement Under Section 43(a) of the Lanham Act,* 82 COLUM. L. REV. 77, 87n.78 (1982)).

[31]Pagliero v. Wallace China Co., 198 F.2d 339, 95 USPQ 45 (9th Cir. 1952).

[32]*Id.* at 344, 95 USPQ at 49.

[33]*See* Wallace Int'l Silversmiths v. Godinger Silver Art Co., 916 F.2d 76, 16 USPQ2d 1555 (2d Cir. 1990), *cert. denied,* 111 S. Ct. 1622, 59 USLW 3724 (1991).

become uniquely associated with a specific source. This concept applies equally to trade dress, although until mid-1992, courts were split on the question of whether secondary meaning was required in all trade dress cases—even where a trade dress had previously been found to be inherently distinctive.

(i) Secondary Meaning No Longer Required in All Cases

With its decision in *Two Pesos v. Taco Cabana,*[34] the Supreme Court ruled unanimously that trade dress that is inherently distinctive is protectable under the Trademark Act, even though the trade dress lacks secondary meaning. Holding that trade dress can be protected if it is either inherently distinctive or has acquired distinctiveness through secondary meaning, the Court explicitly rejected the notion that inherently distinctive trade dress also requires a showing of secondary meaning to be protected.[35]

The Supreme Court's decision brings the law with respect to trade dress more in line with general trademark law. The Court noted that inherently distinctive trademarks do not require a showing of secondary meaning and discerned no reason to treat trade dress differently. The fact that owners will now receive immediate protection for an inherently distinctive trade dress without a showing of secondary meaning should greatly discourage potential infringers from copying the trade dress.

(ii) Inherently Distinctive Trade Dress

Even with the decision in *Two Pesos,* the Supreme Court provided no guidance with respect to what constitutes "inherently distinctive" trade dress. Although the Court noted that merely descriptive marks (or trade dress) are not inherently distinctive because they identify a product rather than the source of the product, no further elaboration was provided.

In the future, courts will undoubtedly attempt to define inherently distinctive trade dress more fully. Until then, however, a couple of observations can be made. First, the more unique and arbitrary the features of a particular trade dress, the greater the likelihood that the trade dress will be deemed inherently distinctive. For example, unusual

---

[34]*Supra* note 28.

[35]*Id.* at 2760–61, 60 USLW at 4765–66, 23 USPQ2d at 1085–86.

colors or shapes comprising a trade dress could be considered inherently distinctive. Second, if the features of a trade dress serve to describe a product or service being offered in connection with the trade dress, a court is unlikely to find that the trade dress is inherently distinctive. This latter point is consistent with the policies that are applied to merely descriptive trademarks. (See section 4.1(e).)

4.3 Dilution

(a) Definition and Basis of Protection

Dilution is a type of trademark infringement where the mark is used in a way that causes a "gradual diminution in the mark's distinctiveness, effectiveness and, hence, value. This kind of infringement corrodes the senior user's interest in the trademark by blurring its product identification or by damaging positive associations that have attached to it."[36] Unlike traditional trademark infringement, dilution does not require a showing of likelihood of confusion. To the contrary, as explained in section 4.3(c), dilution usually exists in the absence of a likelihood of confusion.

Courts have generally recognized two types of dilution—dilution by blurring and dilution by tarnishment. Dilution by blurring occurs when others attempt to use an owner's mark on goods and/or services that are unrelated to the goods or services that consumers associate with the mark. Permitting others to use the mark, although not likely to cause confusion in the marketplace, can blur the distinctive identity of the mark. For example, even if the mark Exxon® on stereo speakers is not likely to cause confusion with Exxon® gasoline, Exxon Corporation may still be able to prevent someone else from using its mark on stereo speakers under a dilution theory.

Dilution by tarnishment, on the other hand, occurs when the unauthorized use of a mark results in the tarnishment, degradation, or dilution of the distinctive quality of a mark. Generally, it is accepted that no dilution by tarnishment will be found when a defendant uses

---

[36]Ameritech, Inc. v. American Information Technologies Corp., 811 F.2d 960, 965, 1 USPQ2d 1861, 1865 (6th Cir. 1987).

the mark on goods that are of a higher price and quality than the plaintiff's goods.

Very often, plaintiffs that allege trademark dilution are met by defendants that assert a parody defense. This occurs because courts have recognized parody as a defense to trademark infringement and trademark dilution actions. For example, in *Eveready Battery Co. v. Adolph Coors Co.*,[37] the defendant had been running a beer commercial featuring the comedian/actor Leslie Nielsen dressed like the Energizer Bunny. Eveready brought a preliminary injunction action against Coors, seeking to enjoin Coors' use of the beer commercial, alleging trademark infringement under the Lanham Act and trademark dilution under the Illinois Anti-Dilution Act.[38] Coors asserted a defense of parody. The court denied Eveready's preliminary injunction motion and concluded that Coors' television commercial did not dilute or infringe Eveready's Energizer Bunny trademark. Note, however, that a parody defense will only carry a defendant so far, and courts have consistently found in favor of plaintiffs when defendants use a plaintiff's mark in a crude, degrading, or unsavory manner.

The protection given to trademarks pursuant to a dilution theory has its basis in state law. Despite attempts to pass a federal antidilution law, the dilution theory never materialized into part of the Lanham Act. Accordingly, neither the courts nor the PTO will entertain an action based on a dilution theory brought under the provisions of the Lanham Act because, quite simply, no such federal cause of action is viewed to exist. As a result, plaintiffs must turn to individual states to determine whether an antidilution statute has been enacted. As of 1990, 26 states had adopted such statutes.

(b) Elements of Dilution

In order to identify the elements necessary to sustain a cause of action for dilution, one must turn to the appropriate state's antidilution statute. For example, under the New York statute, the Second Circuit set forth the following elements: (1) the mark must be strong and distinctive; (2) there must be a likelihood of dilution by whittling down, blurring, or tarnishing a plaintiff's reputation; and (3) predatory intent

---

[37] 765 F. Supp. 440, 19 USPQ2d 1265 (N.D. Ill. 1991).

[38] ILL. REV. STAT. ch. 140, para. 22 (1986).

is a relevant factor to consider in determining whether to grant equitable relief.[39] Although it is not clear that all states require the same elements to prove dilution, it does appear clear that neither competition between the parties nor confusion as to the source of products is necessary to state a cause of action for dilution.

(c) Relationship to Likelihood of Confusion

The dilution doctrine is based on a type of infringement that goes one step beyond traditional trademark infringement based on a test of likelihood of confusion. Whereas the Lanham Act prohibits defendants from using a plaintiff's mark on goods or services likely to cause confusion in the marketplace, the dilution doctrine prohibits defendants from using a well-known mark even when consumers are not likely to be confused by the defendant's use. Of course, for the plaintiff to prevail, the result of the defendant's use must be likely to result in lessening or diluting the strong identification value of the plaintiff's mark.

In explaining the difference between dilution and likelihood of confusion, a well-known trademark treatise states the following:

> For dilution to occur, the relevant public must make some connection between the senior user's mark and the junior user's unauthorized usage of it. But that connection is not the kind of mental link that triggers the classic likelihood of confusion test. Rather, the assumption is that the relevant public sees the junior user's use, and intuitively knows, because of the context of the junior user's use, that there is no connection between the owners of the respective marks. However, . . . the ability of the senior user's mark to serve as a unique identifier of the plaintiff's goods or services is weakened because the relevant public now also associates that designation with a new and different source.[40]

(d) Strength of the Mark

Generally, only strong, distinctive, and well-known marks will be protected under a theory of dilution. Clearly, nationally recognized

---

[39]*See* Sally Gee, Inc. v. Myra Hogan, Inc., 699 F.2d 621, 625–26, 217 USPQ 658, 661–62 (2d Cir. 1983).

[40]2 J.T. McCarthy, McCarthy on Trademarks and Unfair Competition §24.13[1][b], at 24–107 (3d ed. 1992).

marks such as McDonald's® and Kodak® should be protected pursuant to antidilution statutes, but as marks become less famous, the chance of prevailing on a cause of action for dilution decreases significantly.

In the well-publicized LEXIS case,[41] the owner of the "LEXIS" mark for a computerized legal database sued Toyota under a dilution theory for its use of the mark "Lexus" covering an expensive, high-quality automobile. Concluding that the plaintiff had not established its dilution case, the Second Circuit stated, among other things, that the "LEXIS" mark did not have the requisite degree of strength and fame among the likely consumers of the "Lexus" automobile to result in dilution of the mark. The court found that the "LEXIS" mark did not possess a distinctive quality capable of dilution since it was not well known to the general public.

---

[41]Mead Data Cent. v. Toyota Motor Sales, U.S.A., 875 F.2d 1026, 10 USPQ2d 1961 (2d Cir. 1989).

5

Enforcing Trademarks

5.1 Likelihood of Confusion

The U.S. Patent and Trademark Office (PTO) does not permit the registration of marks that so closely resemble a mark previously registered with the PTO, or previously used by another in the United States, "as to be likely, when used on or in connection with the goods [and/or services] of the applicant, to cause confusion, or to cause mistake, or to deceive."[1] This notion of "likelihood of confusion" is not only used by the PTO in determining whether a mark is registrable, but is also applied by the courts when considering claims of infringement of federally registered marks, state registered marks, and unregistered common law marks. In a trademark infringement action, the court must determine whether the defendant's mark is likely to be confused in the marketplace with the plaintiff's previously used mark.

(a) Factors for Determining Confusion

Both the PTO and the Court of Appeals for the Federal Circuit have established 13 factors that must be considered in determining whether a likelihood of confusion exists between marks. These factors include the following:

---

[1] 15 U.S.C. §1052(d).

(1) The similarity or dissimilarity of the marks in their entireties as to appearance, sound, connotation, and commercial impression.
(2) The similarity or dissimilarity and nature of the goods or services as described in an application or registration or in connection with which a prior mark is in use.
(3) The similarity or dissimilarity of established, likely-to-continue trade channels.
(4) The conditions under which and buyers to whom sales are made, i.e., "impulse" vs. careful, sophisticated purchasing.
(5) The fame of the prior mark (sales, advertising, length of use).
(6) The number and nature of similar marks in use on similar goods.
(7) The nature and extent of any actual confusion.
(8) The length of time during and conditions under which there has been concurrent use without evidence of actual confusion.
(9) The variety of goods on which a mark is or is not used (house mark, "family" mark, product mark).
(10) The market interface between applicant and the owner of a prior mark:
    (a) a mere "consent" to register or use.
    (b) agreement provisions designed to preclude confusion, i.e., limitations on continued use of the marks by each party.
    (c) assignment of mark, application, registration, and good will of the related business.
    (d) laches and estoppel attributable to owner of prior mark and indicative of lack of confusion.
(11) The extent to which applicant has a right to exclude others from use of its mark on its goods.
(12) The extent of potential confusion, i.e., whether *de minimis* or substantial.
(13) Any other established fact probative of the effect of use.[2]

Although no one of these factors is controlling in determining likelihood of confusion, some of the factors may be more relevant than others in certain circumstances. For example, if two marks are similar and used in connection with nearly identical goods, the trier of fact will probably conclude that consideration of these two factors alone is sufficient to conclude that there is likely to be confusion between the simultaneous use of the marks. For example, simultaneous use of the marks "City Girl" and "City Gal" covering magazines and books, respectively, is likely to create confusion in the marketplace as to the

---

[2]In re E.I. DuPont DeNemours & Co., 476 F.2d 1357, 1361, 177 USPQ 563, 567 (C.C.P.A. 1973). Each Court of Appeals has developed its own list of factors to be considered in a "likelihood of confusion" analysis. Likewise, each state has its own list of factors. Although there is substantial overlap in the factors considered by the various courts, parties should be familiar with the relevant factors when litigating in different circuits or state courts.

source of each trademark owner's goods. In addition, some factors may be important to the PTO in determining the registrability of a mark, but may be of little relevance in a court proceeding. For example, the presence of a consent agreement can have a significant impact on the PTO in assessing the registrability of a mark, but will have virtually no impact in a court proceeding since it is unlikely that such an agreement would even exist between parties involved in a trademark infringement action in the courts. The factors most often present are discussed below.

(i) Similarity of the Marks

The degree of similarity that must exist between marks to constitute a likelihood of confusion is a fact-sensitive, highly subjective determination that varies from case to case. It is quite clear, however, that two marks need not be identical to be considered confusingly similar. Where the goods are identical or competitive, the degree of similarity necessary to establish a likelihood of confusion is less than in a case where the goods are different. Conversely, as explained in Chapter 4, section 4.1(a), even identical marks may not be confusingly similar since the fact-finder must consider the marks in terms of the similarities or differences in the goods and/or services covered by the marks. Thus, there can be no confusion between the same or similar marks for very different goods.

In looking at the marks themselves, the court in *DuPont* noted that similarities or dissimilarities of marks must be viewed "in their entireties as to appearance, sound, connotation and commercial impression."[3] Similarity of appearance is typically based on nothing more than a side-by-side comparison of two marks. This factor is particularly relevant when comparing design marks (as opposed to word marks) since the conclusion regarding the similarity of the marks will be based primarily, if not fully, on how the designs or logos look to the viewer. Of course, the very nature of such a comparison is inherently subjective.

Other types of marks that may be considered similar are those that sound the same, but look different. For example, the marks "Arrow" and "Air-O" look very different, but were considered confusingly similar based in part on their phonetic equivalence.[4] In determin-

---

[3]*Id.*

[4]*See* Cluett, Peabody & Co. v. Wright, 46 F.2d 711 (C.C.P.A. 1931).

ing phonetic similarity, courts pronounce a mark in a way that is consistent with the pronunciation given the mark by the average consumer who may purchase the product bearing the mark. For example, the marks "Apple" and "AP-Pull" may be considered phonetically similar if the consuming public pronounces the mark "AP-Pull" as "apple." If, however, consumers pronounce "AP-Pull" as "A. P. Pull," then the marks would not likely be considered confusingly similar based on phonetic equivalence.

Finally, there are some marks that look and sound different, but are still considered confusingly similar by virtue of the similar commercial impression created by the marks. For example, "Crocodile" on shoes is likely to be found confusingly similar to "Alligator" on shoes because the mental image associated with these terms is essentially the same. Because the two words have similar meanings in the ordinary consumer's mind, it is likely that a purchaser would confuse the terms when used in connection with similar goods. Thus, the commercial impression created by a mark can have a significant impact upon a likelihood of confusion analysis.

(ii) Similarity of the Goods

As indicated above, a likelihood of confusion analysis must consider whether two marks, when used in connection with particular goods or services, are likely to confuse the consumer as to the source of the goods or services. In determining similarity of goods, products need not be identical or even competitive to be considered similar. Of course, if the goods are the same or competitive, this "similarity of goods" factor will weigh more strongly in favor of a finding of likelihood of confusion.

In some cases, goods that are merely related may provide enough of a nexus to be deemed similar. For example, "Henckel" is a mark used in connection with very high quality knives and blades. If a consumer were to go to a housewares department of a store and see the mark "Henckel," "Hanckel," or some other substantially similar term on a set of cookware, that consumer might very well assume that the cookware emanated from the same source as the knives. Although knives and cookware are neither competitive nor functionally equivalent, the fact that they are related goods typically used in the kitchen and located in the same areas of stores may be enough of a relationship to cause a likelihood of confusion among consumers when similar marks are used on these different goods.

Of course, there comes a point when a relationship between particular goods becomes so tenuous that it is no longer likely that consumers would believe that the source of Product "A" is probably also the source of Product "B." For example, if a consumer purchases an air-conditioning unit from a hardware store and it bears the mark "Henckel," the consumer is probably not likely to be confused into thinking that the source of the air conditioner is the same as the source of the "Henckel" brand knives. A closer question, however, exists where the consumer goes into the same hardware store and purchases an electric saw bearing the mark "Henckel." In this situation, ordinary consumers could conclude that since both knives and electric saws have blades, the manufacturer of "Henckel" brand knives is also the manufacturer of electric saws. If this occurs, there may be a likelihood of confusion between the simultaneous use of the marks. Consequently, use of the "Henckel" mark on electric saws would be an infringement of the "Henckel" mark for knives.

(iii) Similarity of Trade Channels

Another factor considered when determining whether a likelihood of confusion exists is the similarity or dissimilarity of respective trade channels. In other words, how and to whom are companies' goods sold? If a company sells its goods to a particular group of purchasers through a specific trade channel, it is less likely that those purchasers will be confused by similar trademarks used in connection with similar goods sold through a different channel of distribution. For example, the mark "Puritan" for laundry and dry cleaning services offered to consumers is not likely to cause confusion with the same mark for commercial dry cleaning machine filters sold to professionals in the dry cleaning industry. The rationale for this conclusion is premised on the notion that consumers purchasing "Puritan" dry cleaning services are not likely to ever encounter the "Puritan" dry cleaning machine filters.

The types of stores in which various goods are sold are often indicative of the particular channels of trade for those goods. For example, an electric air purifier for a room in one's home can probably be purchased in department stores or hardware stores. However, an air purifying system for one's entire home or for an office building will likely have to be purchased from a company or store that specializes in the installation of such units. Although each of these goods performs a similar function, they travel in completely different channels of trade.

Sometimes, different price ranges of particular goods are considered relevant in establishing that the goods travel in different channels of trade. For example, toy boats that cost $3.00 to $10.00 likely travel in different channels of trade from yachts that cost tens of thousands of dollars. Thus, the same or similar mark on each of these goods is probably unlikely to cause confusion in the marketplace.

(iv) Impulse Versus Careful and Sophisticated Purchasers

The price of a product may not only have a bearing on trade channels, but may also affect the amount of care a purchaser will use in choosing the product. For example, a 75¢ item, such as a pack of gum found in a checkout line, is the kind of item that is purchased on impulse. "Impulse" purchases are typically purchased with little care and without much thought to the purchase. Conversely, a purchaser buying a very expensive item such as an automobile has often researched the item and selected the product only after very careful consideration of a number of factors. Generally, courts recognize that when more care is taken to select a particular item, the purchaser of that item is less likely to be confused as to the source of the product. Thus, a greater showing of the other likelihood of confusion factors must be present when the goods are expensive than when goods are inexpensive and bought on impulse.

With respect to certain types of items, the relevant purchasers are often very sophisticated and knowledgeable about the purchases they make. For example, physicians who purchase complex technological medical equipment for their practices are typically sophisticated consumers who choose to purchase a piece of medical equipment only after careful consideration of the product. Consequently, sophisticated consumers are generally less likely to be confused as to the source of goods at issue, and are more likely to appreciate smaller differences between two marks.

(v) Fame of the Prior Mark

Marks that are famous and widely known in the marketplace are often afforded a broader degree of protection than other marks. The rationale for affording a famous mark broader protection is based on the notion that because the public expects to see famous marks used in connection with a variety of products, they will assume that new uses of a mark must be affiliated with the same source that produces the goods usually connected to the mark.

For example, Nike® is a famous trademark used in connection with sneakers. If the "Nike" mark were suddenly to appear on a restaurant as a service mark used in connection with restaurant services, it is entirely possible that the public would believe that the source of the restaurant services was somehow affiliated with the source of Nike® sneakers. Because the Nike® mark has instant nationwide recognition, courts will be more likely to afford the mark protection for goods and/or services completely unrelated to those goods for which the mark is typically known.

(vi) Number and Nature of Similar Marks in Use on Similar Goods

The existence of a large number of similar marks used in connection with similar goods indicates that the marks are relatively weak when used in connection with those particular goods.[5] Marks that are weak are generally afforded very narrow protection.

When the common element of conflicting marks is a term that is weak, this decreases the likelihood of confusion between the marks as a whole. For example, the mark "Salon Innovations" for hair care products may initially seem confusingly similar to "Salon Styles" for hair care products. However, when one considers that the term "Salon" for hair care products is commonly used by many sellers in the hair care market and is, thus, a weak term for hair care products, the likelihood of confusion decreases between the marks "Salon Innovations" and "Salon Styles." Accordingly, while there may be a slight advantage (in terms of registration) to selecting a new mark similar to many already existing marks, the disadvantage is that the new mark will not be afforded broad protection.

(vii) Actual Confusion

Any evidence of actual confusion that has occurred between marks is strong evidence of a likelihood of confusion. Although instances of actual confusion are not necessary to establish a likelihood of confusion,

---

[5]Note that the marks must be owned by a variety of companies or individuals to be considered relatively weak marks.

the presence of such instances of confusion is substantial proof of a likelihood of confusion. The evidence of actual confusion must be significant, however, to be given substantial weight in the likelihood of confusion analysis. Isolated instances of confusion that are explainable by the submission of other evidence will probably be insufficient to result in a finding of likelihood of confusion.

The lack of any actual confusion may also be considered by the trier of fact. If allegedly conflicting marks have been used simultaneously for an extensive period of time without any instances of actual confusion, this fact should be considered when conducting a likelihood of confusion analysis.

(viii) Family of Marks

Sometimes, a trademark owner will attempt to develop a "family" of marks whereby the trademark owner uses some distinctive common element within a series of marks such that the common element becomes recognizable by the public as an indication of source. When a trademark owner successfully develops a family of marks, it is often afforded broad protection with respect to other marks that incorporate that same element.

One of the most prominent examples of a family of marks is owned by McDonald's Corporation. This company successfully used the prefix "Mc" to create an entire family of "Mc" marks. Such marks include Chicken McNuggets, Egg McMuffins, McChicken Sandwiches, and McLean Sandwiches. Because of McDonald's widespread use of the "Mc" prefix followed by other terms, the consuming public has come to associate such marks with McDonald's. Consequently, McDonald's has had great success in preventing others from using the "Mc" prefix to create new marks such as McTeddy for teddy bears and McSleep for a chain of motels. Of course, it is possible to create a family of marks that is not as recognizable to the public as the "Mc" family of marks. When this occurs, the family of marks will still be considered in a likelihood of confusion analysis, but will be afforded less weight than if the family were highly recognizable to the relevant public.

(ix) Consent Agreements

When the PTO refuses registration of an applicant's mark on the grounds that it is likely to be confused with a prior existing mark, the applicant may attempt to overcome the examiner's objection by obtaining a consent agreement from the owner of the cited mark whereby that owner consents to the registration of the applicant's mark. In *DuPont,*[6] the court specifically addressed the question of how much value a consent agreement ought to be given. Then Chief Judge Markey explained that while a "naked 'consent' may carry little weight . . . [t]he weight to be given more detailed agreements . . . should be substantial."[7]

In drafting consent agreements, it is important that the parties set forth factors that lead them to conclude that the simultaneous use of the marks at issue is not likely to cause confusion in the marketplace. These factors may include some, or all, of those that have been discussed in this chapter.

Recently, the Federal Circuit emphasized the prominent role that consent agreements play in a likelihood of confusion analysis.[8] In the *Four Seasons* case, the Trademark Trial and Appeal Board refused registration of the applicant's mark on the grounds that it was likely to be confused with the registrant's mark. The court, concluding that the Board had failed to give substantial weight to the parties' consent agreement, reversed the Board's determination. The court explained:

> [T]he PTO's role is to protect owners of trademarks by allowing them to register their marks. Denial of registration does not deny the owner the right to use the mark, and thus, will not serve to protect the public from confusion. "No government could police trademark *use* so as to protect the public from confusion. It must count on the self-interest of trademark owners to do that."[9]

Thus, detailed consent agreements can have a substantial impact on a likelihood of confusion analysis.

(x) Other Factors

Both the courts and the PTO view the defendant's (or the applicant's) intent in selecting the mark at issue to be relevant in determining

---

[6]In re E.I. DuPont DeNemours & Co., *supra* note 2, at 1362, 177 USPQ at 568.

[7]*Id.* As indicated above, although the existence of a consent agreement is relevant in a proceeding to determine the registrability of a trademark, it is not typically relevant in a lawsuit for trademark infringement.

[8]*See* In re Four Seasons Hotels, 987 F.2d 1565, 26 USPQ2d 1071 (Fed. Cir. 1993).

[9]*Id.* at 1566, 26 USPQ2d at 1072 (quoting In re National Distillers & Chem. Corp., 297 F.2d 941, 950–51, 132 USPQ 271, 279 (C.C.P.A. 1962)).

likelihood of confusion. While a showing of unlawful intent is not a requirement to establishing likelihood of confusion, evidence that demonstrates that a defendant began using a mark in bad faith with the intent to trade upon and benefit from the good will already developed by a senior user will be considered in a likelihood of confusion analysis. If the accused infringer believed that adopting the mark at issue would confuse the public into believing that it had some affiliation with the senior user, then the trier of fact is entitled to reasonably infer that confusion resulted.

(b) "Reasonably Prudent" Consumer

In determining whether a likelihood of confusion exists, both the PTO and the courts will resolve the issue in terms of an appreciable number of "reasonably prudent" consumers in the relevant public. Thus, if two potentially conflicting marks are used on medical equipment that is sold to physicians, the trier of fact must determine whether a reasonably prudent physician is likely to be confused by the simultaneous use of the marks.

Unfortunately, there is no simple definition as to what constitutes the reasonably prudent consumer. In fact, courts have described the reasonably prudent consumer as anything from one who is reasonably intelligent and discriminating to one who is hasty, heedless, and easily deceived.[10] Generally, it appears that the "reasonably prudent" consumer is someone who is an average purchaser exercising an ordinary amount of care for the purchase being made.

As stated above, there is likewise the requirement that there be a likelihood of confusion among "an appreciable number" of consumers. Thus, a showing of likelihood of confusion among only a few reasonably prudent consumers is not sufficient.

(c) Consumer Surveys

In both trademark prosecution cases before the PTO and trademark infringement cases before the courts, consumer survey evidence can

---

[10] *See* 2 J. T. McCarthy, McCarthy on Trademarks and Unfair Competition §23.27[2], at 23-170 to 23-171 (3d ed. 1992).

be a useful tool in determining whether an appreciable number of consumers will likely be confused by simultaneous use of the marks at issue. Surveys are particularly common in trademark infringement actions, and a party may be at a significant disadvantage if it does not present a survey.

Survey evidence is circumstantial, rather than direct, evidence of likely confusion. A person conducting a survey will normally set up an experimental environment in which he or she will ask consumers to answer questions, the results of which can be used by the trier of fact to draw inferences as to whether a likelihood of confusion exists. For example, relevant consumers may be stopped in a shopping mall, shown the defendant's product, asked whether they know the name of the company that is the source of the product and, if so, asked to provide the name of that company. If consumers are almost always correct, the results may be presented by the challenger to show that confusion does not exist and, therefore, is not likely. On the other hand, if many consumers incorrectly name the plaintiff as the source of the defendant's product, these results can be presented to show that there is a likelihood of confusion.

Survey results can be attacked by the party opposing the results. For example, the challenger may attack the methodology used in the survey on the grounds that it was designed to yield particular subjective results. Obviously, greater weight will be afforded surveys that are perceived to have generated objective results.

Finally, in creating a consumer survey, it is very important to define the relevant public or "universe" to whom the survey should be administered. Likelihood of confusion is considered in terms of the relevant public; therefore, surveys must be administered to members of that particular group. For example, if the relevant purchasing public of the goods bearing the cited marks is physicians, the survey needs to be administered to physicians. Again, a survey that does not define the proper universe is subject to attack and may be completely discounted.

5.2 Procedures in Infringement Cases

(a) Jurisdiction

Actions that are brought pursuant to the Lanham Act (including a claim for infringement of a federally registered mark or an unregistered mark or trade dress used in interstate commerce) may be initiated in either federal court or state court.[11] A suit brought in state court for a Lanham Act violation is, however, removable to federal court upon motion by the defendant. Any federal district court in the United States can entertain an action arising under the federal Lanham Act. This is due to the fact that such a claim constitutes a federal question and, thus, gives the federal courts subject matter jurisdiction over the case.[12]

Even infringement cases that do not arise under the federal Lanham Act can be brought in federal court if certain conditions are satisfied. For example, although a state unfair competition claim, a claim for infringement of a state registered mark, or violation of a common law trademark used only in one state does not set forth a federal question, the case can be brought in federal district court if the matter in controversy is greater than $50,000 and if all plaintiffs are citizens of states different from those of all defendants.[13] This type of federal subject matter jurisdiction is called diversity jurisdiction since the citizenship of *all* plaintiffs must be "diverse" from the citizenship of *all* defendants. Where there are multiple plaintiffs and defendants, if even one plaintiff has the same citizenship as one defendant, diversity is destroyed for all the parties to the action.[14] A federal court must have subject matter jurisdiction over an action in order to have the power to hear a particular case. Thus, if subject matter jurisdiction does not exist, the court can dismiss the case upon its own motion.

Not only is a federal court required to have subject matter jurisdiction over a case, but the particular district court where the action has been brought must also have personal jurisdiction over the defendant. Courts are concerned with having personal jurisdiction over a defendant because that party did not choose the court where the action was filed and fairness dictates that it should not be completely unreasonable to expect the defendant to defend an action in that court.

Generally, there are two ways to obtain personal jurisdiction over a defendant. First, if the defendant is personally served with notice of the lawsuit while within the territorial limits of the court, the requirements of personal jurisdiction will be satisfied. Second, if the defendant

---

[11]Both copyright and patent infringement actions must, however, be brought in federal court due to the exclusive jurisdiction given to federal courts to hear these types of cases.

[12]*See* 28 U.S.C. §1338(a).

[13]*See* 28 U.S.C. §1332(a).

[14]For purposes of determining citizenship, a corporation is deemed a citizen of both its state of incorporation and the state where it has its principal place of business.

has minimum contacts with a particular state, any federal district court within that state will have personal jurisdiction over the defendant. Generally, minimum contacts with a state are satisfied by any defendant who purposefully avails itself of the privilege of conducting activities within that state. If a defendant wishes to take advantage of the laws of a particular state, then it is reasonable for the defendant to expect that it will be subject to personal jurisdiction within that state.

A majority of states have enacted long-arm statutes consisting of enumerated activities which, if conducted by the defendant, are adequate to subject the defendant to personal jurisdiction within the state. A federal court will apply the relevant state's long-arm statute to determine whether the court has personal jurisdiction over a defendant corporation.

(b) Venue

Trademark suits are governed by general federal venue rules. Thus, where an action in federal court is based solely on diversity of citizenship, the general venue rules provide that the action may only be brought in

> (1) a judicial district where any defendant resides, if all defendants reside in the same State, (2) a judicial district in which a substantial part of the events or omissions giving rise to the claim occurred, or a substantial part of property that is the subject of the action is situated, or (3) a judicial district in which the defendants are subject to personal jurisdiction at the time the action is commenced, if there is no district in which the action may otherwise be brought.[15]

Where an action in federal court is not based solely on diversity of citizenship, the action may be brought in either of the judicial districts listed in (1) and (2) above. In addition, the action may also be brought in any judicial district in which any defendant may be found, if there is no district where the action could otherwise be brought.[16] Pursuant to the venue rules, a defendant corporation is deemed to reside in any judicial district where it is subject to personal jurisdiction at the time the action was initiated.[17]

---

[15]28 U.S.C. §1391(a).

[16]*See* 28 U.S.C. §1391(b).

[17]*See* 28 U.S.C. §1391(c).

Any defendant who wishes to challenge venue (or personal jurisdiction) must do so through either a motion to dismiss the action or by objecting in the answer to the complaint. If no such objection is made, the defendant is deemed to have waived any objections it may have had.[18] Upon a proper objection by the defendant, or upon the court's own motion, the court may either dismiss a case for improper venue or transfer it to another judicial district where the action could have been brought.[19]

(c) Standing

Section 32(1) of the Lanham Act provides a cause of action for trademark infringement against any party that uses a mark without the consent of the registrant. Any plaintiff that initiates a trademark infringement action pursuant to §32(1) must, therefore, be the federally registered owner of the mark. In such actions, only the registrant has standing to sue for infringement of its federally registered mark.

Pursuant to §43(a) of the Lanham Act, even plaintiffs who do not own federally registered marks have standing to initiate a cause of action in federal court for both infringement of unregistered marks and infringement of unregistered trade dress, provided the marks or trade dress are used in commerce. Because the Act defines "commerce" as all commerce that may be lawfully regulated by Congress, the "commerce" referred to in §43(a) typically means interstate commerce or commerce between a foreign country and the United States. Section 43(a) also states that any person who violates the statute's provisions "shall be liable in a civil action by *any* person who believes that he or she is likely to be damaged by such act."[20] Consequently, it appears that in appropriate circumstances, even a nonowner of a mark may have standing to sue.

(d) Jury Trials

In a federal trademark infringement case, the right to a trial by jury is guaranteed with respect to certain claims. Specifically, a party

[18] *See* FED. R. CIV. P. 12.
[19] *See* 28 U.S.C. §1406.
[20] 15 U.S.C. §1125(a) (emphasis added).

may demand a jury trial for legal claims. The party is not, however, entitled to a jury trial for equitable claims. For example, when it is clear that the only issue in a case is whether an injunction should be granted, this is an equitable issue and there is no right to a trial by jury. Thus, a plaintiff that seeks only equitable relief cannot ask for a jury trial and, therefore, prevents a defendant from the opportunity to have a trial by jury. When both legal and equitable claims are presented in federal court, the rule typically is that the legal issues will be tried first before a jury, followed later by the court's resolution of the equitable claims. Of course, the parties can always waive the right to a jury trial and allow the judge to decide all issues.

In state court, when the issues presented are either purely legal or purely equitable, the rights of the parties are similar to those provided by federal court. If, however, the issues presented in state court are mixed, the trend of the courts is to look at the paramount issue in the case and proceed on that basis. If the paramount issue is deemed to be a legal claim, the parties are typically entitled to a trial by jury. If, however, the paramount issue is of an equitable nature, there is no right to a trial by jury.

(e) Appeals

Appeals from trademark infringement cases in federal court are typically filed in the Court of Appeals for the circuit where the federal district court sits. Very often, however, a case involving a claim for trademark infringement also includes a claim for patent infringement. When this occurs, an appeal of the case must be filed in the Court of Appeals for the Federal Circuit due to that court's exclusive jurisdiction over appeals for all cases arising under a federal patent statute.[21] Although the Federal Circuit will apply federal patent law to substantive patent issues, it applies the law of the regional circuit where the district court sits to the substantive trademark issues. Appeals from trademark infringement cases filed in state court follow the normal appellate procedures that have been designated for that jurisdiction.

---

[21]*See* 28 U.S.C. §§1295, 1338.

5.3 Defenses

There are a host of defenses that may be asserted by a defendant in a trademark infringement action. Some of these defenses (see section 5.6 of this chapter) are also available in interpartes proceedings before the PTO. This section discusses a number of the defenses that are available to a defendant when sued for trademark infringement.

(a) Abandonment

When a party claiming exclusive rights in a mark is found to have abandoned that mark, the party loses all rights to the mark and the mark becomes part of the public domain. When this occurs, the public is free to use the mark.

The most common way in which a party can abandon its mark is by not using the mark. Thus, if a trademark owner fails to use its mark for a certain period of time without exhibiting any actions that indicate an intention to resume use, that party may lose any rights it had to exclusive use of the mark. Similarly, if the trademark owner takes explicit actions that indicate it has no intention of resuming use of the mark at issue, the owner may be deemed to have abandoned its mark.

Under the majority rule, clear and convincing evidence of abandonment is required for the courts to find abandonment. Even in cases where an inference of abandonment can be drawn, the inference may be rebutted by the trademark owner if the period of nonuse of the mark can be explained. For example, a trademark owner that encounters significant delay in restarting a company after a move or a natural disaster may be able to explain an extended period of nonuse. If successful, a court will not find that the plaintiff has abandoned its rights to exclusive use of the mark at issue.

Under the Lanham Act, proof of nonuse of a mark for at least two years creates a presumption of abandonment. The Act specifically provides:

> A mark shall be deemed to be "abandoned" . . . (1) When its use has been discontinued with intent not to resume such use. Intent not to resume may be inferred from circumstances. Nonuse for two consecutive years shall be *prima facie* evidence of abandonment. "Use" of a mark means the bona fide use of that mark made in the ordinary course of trade, and not made merely to reserve a right in a mark.[22]

---

[22] 15 U.S.C. §1127.

As with most presumptions, once the defendant meets its burden of proof with respect to the presumption, the burden shifts to the plaintiff to rebut the presumption. Provided the plaintiff presents evidence challenging the presumption, the presumption will effectively be eliminated. Ultimately, the burden of persuasion is on the party claiming that the mark has been abandoned.

One way in which a party may rebut a presumption of abandonment is to establish that the good will of a mark continues to be strong even though the trademark owner may not currently be using the mark. Courts have generally recognized that the good will associated with a mark does not disappear immediately upon the cessation of using the mark. In one fairly recent case, the Court of Appeals for the Fourth Circuit affirmed a district court's holding that due to the continuing good will of a mark, there was no abandonment even though the mark had not been used for five years and was then sold to another party who reused it on the same product.[23]

A trademark owner that does not take proper actions against infringers of its mark can be found to have abandoned its rights to exclusive use of the mark. If a trademark owner continuously fails to enforce its trademark rights against others such that the owner's mark is being widely used by others, the mark may lose any distinction it once had and may ultimately result in an abandonment of the mark.

(b) Mark Is or Has Become Generic

As indicated in Chapter 4, section 4.1(f), the generic term for a product cannot function as a trademark for that same product. As a result, if an entity's trademark becomes the generic term for the product covered by the mark, the entity loses whatever trademark significance the mark once had as an indication of source. In a trademark infringement action, a defendant that asserts and proves that the plaintiff's mark is or has become generic not only proves its lack of any liability in using the generic term, but also precludes the plaintiff from continuing to claim any trademark rights to the term.[24]

---

[23]*See* Seidelmann Yachts Inc. v. Pace Yacht Corp., 14 USPQ2d 1497 (D. Md. 1989), *aff'd*, 13 USPQ2d 2025 (4th Cir. 1990).

[24]The test for determining whether a mark is or has become generic is discussed in Chapter 4, section 4.1(f).

(c) Uncontrolled Licensing

The law permits a trademark owner to license its mark to others as long as the owner maintains sufficient control over the nature and quality of the goods bearing the mark that are sold by the licensee. In other words, a trademark owner can license a trademark to another provided he or she retains the right to control the quality of the goods sold under the mark by the licensee. A licensee who disregards the trademark owner's quality specifications can be liable for both trademark infringement and breach of contract. When a trademark owner does not exercise the requisite amount of quality control over the goods sold by another under the licensed trademark, the mark can lose its trademark significance because the level of quality associated with the mark may no longer be accurate. This is known as uncontrolled licensing of a mark and is a valid defense to a trademark infringement claim.

The Lanham Act provides that any mark shall be deemed abandoned when the owner engages in acts of omission as well as commission that cause a mark to lose its significance as a mark.[25] Uncontrolled licensing is an act that has not only resulted in a mark losing its trademark meaning, but has also been found to be a fraud on the public. As explained in Chapter 4, consumers come to associate and expect a certain level of quality with products that bear particular trademarks. When a trademark owner licenses its mark to others without maintaining control over the quality of the products produced by the licensee, it is possible that the products will be below the level of quality that consumers associate with the mark. When this occurs, consumers are deceived because they believe they are purchasing a product that meets a certain quality level when in fact the quality level may be much lower than the consumers expect. This is clearly not fair to the public. Proof of uncontrolled licensing can, therefore, result in a trademark's ceasing to function as such and, thus, cause a trademark owner to lose its trademark rights in the mark.

(d) Assignment of Mark Apart From Good Will

A trademark owner who assigns its rights in a trademark to another, apart from the good will associated with the mark, does not pass any

[25]*See* 15 U.S.C. §1127.

right to the "assignee." This rule stems from the fact that the public associates the good will developed by a company with that company's trademarks. If a trademark owner were free to assign a mark apart from the good will associated with the mark, the public would be deceived by the assignee's use of the mark. Consequently, an assignment of a mark apart from the good will associated with the mark is an invalid assignment that can result in a mark's losing its trademark significance.

In spite of the invalidity of this type of assignment, the assignor typically stops using the mark after the assignment is effected. Because, however, no valid rights in the mark actually pass to the assignee, the assignee has no right to use the mark. Consequently, no party with recognized rights in the mark (i.e., the trademark owner/assignor) is using the mark; therefore, the mark can be deemed to have been abandoned by the trademark owner.

Even if there is an invalid assignment, all may not be lost. The new owner is entitled to begin development of its own good will in the mark. The major element that is lost by an invalid assignment is the assignee's right to rely upon the previous owner's priority date. If there is no intervening user, that is, an entity that began use of the mark after the previous owner but before the invalid assignment, then there is no entity with rights more superior than that of the assignee. If, however, there is an intervening third party, a significant problem will occur because the intervening user will be considered the first user. Not only will the intervening user have a valid defense, such a user may also be able to prevent use of the mark by the recipient of the invalid assignment.

(e) Laches and Estoppel

Laches and estoppel are equitable defenses asserted by a defendant who believes that the plaintiff acted in a manner that, in turn, induced the defendant to act to his or her prejudice. When a plaintiff fails to assert or enforce its rights in a timely manner, the defendant may be induced to act in a way that is ultimately prejudicial to his or her interests. Thus, if a plaintiff knowingly fails to act for a sufficiently long time before deciding to assert his or her rights against a defendant, the defendant may be able to prove a laches or estoppel defense.

To prove a laches defense, a defendant must demonstrate, first, that the plaintiff delayed filing suit for an unreasonable and inexcusable length of time from the date the plaintiff knew or reasonably should have known of his or her claim against the defendant, and second, that the delay operated to the prejudice of the defendant. For example, a plaintiff that whiles away an extended period of time, while a junior user incurs substantial expense in the adoption and advertising of a mark, may have to defend himself or herself against an assertion of laches. In this example, the plaintiff's delay in initiating his or her lawsuit caused the junior user to suffer economic prejudice. As a result, the defendant has a valid laches defense.

An estoppel defense is similar to a laches defense. In a defense of estoppel, the defendant must plead that the plaintiff communicated something in a misleading way that was then relied upon by the defendant to the detriment of the defendant. For example, if a trademark owner affirmatively indicates that he or she does not intend to press an infringement claim against another, that person has a right to rely on that representation and continue to both use a mark and develop good will associated with the mark. If the trademark owner were subsequently permitted to assert a claim inconsistent with his or her earlier assurance, the junior user would be detrimentally harmed. When this occurs, the defendant has a valid estoppel defense.

(f) Fair Use

A junior user who uses a descriptive term in its descriptive sense cannot be precluded from doing so by a trademark owner. Although a trademark owner can preclude others from adopting and using a confusingly similar trademark, he or she is not permitted to prevent others from "fairly using" the same term in a nontrademark descriptive sense. This concept is known as "fair use" and, in appropriate circumstances, is a defense that can be asserted in a trademark infringement action.

A fair use defense is available only against a descriptive trademark. As indicated in Chapter 4, section 4.1(e), a descriptive mark is one that describes or identifies an ingredient, quality, characteristic, function, feature, purpose, or use of the goods or services to which the mark is applied. For example, the mark "Little Tavern" for use in connection with restaurant and bar goods and services is a descriptive mark. If that mark achieves secondary meaning[26] in the marketplace, it is entitled

---

[26]*See* Chapter 4, section 4.1(e) for the discussion on Noninherently Distinctive Marks.

to protection, and the owner is entitled to preclude others from adopting and using a trademark confusingly similar to its "Little Tavern" mark. If, however, the owner also tries to preclude others from using the term "Little Tavern" in a nontrademark descriptive sense, he or she will likely have to overcome a fair use defense. In other words, the registrant cannot prevent someone from using the term "Little Tavern" to describe the nature or size of his or her drinking and eating establishment.

For a party to assert a successful fair use defense, the term must be actually used in its ordinary descriptive sense and not in a trademark sense. If the term is used in a way that calls special attention to the words, there is a risk that the fair use defense may not be available. Finally, the "fair user" must be acting in good faith. If the defendant is intending to capitalize on the plaintiff's good will, the fair use defense is not available.

(g) Other Defenses

There are a number of other defenses available to an alleged infringer in a trademark infringement action. For example, a defendant may assert that the plaintiff lacks standing to bring the lawsuit or that the tribunal does not have jurisdiction to hear the case. In addition, a defendant is entitled to claim that the mark at issue is not entitled to protection because it is not capable of registration for many of the grounds set forth in the Lanham Act.[27] With respect to the defense of fraud, any challenger should be aware that he or she must plead the defense with particularity to withstand a motion for dismissal. Finally, any challenger who used his or her mark prior to the plaintiff's use of his or her mark or prior to the plaintiff's filing an intent-to-use application for the mark can assert prior use as a valid defense to a trademark infringement action.[28]

---

[27]*See* 15 U.S.C. §§1052, 1064. *See also* Chapter 4, section 4.1(f), for a discussion of the grounds for which a mark is not capable of registration.

[28]It should be noted, however, that it *generally* is not a good defense to a claim of trademark infringement that someone other than the defendant is a prior user of a mark that is confusingly similar to the plaintiff's mark. Such a defense can, however, be asserted in a proceeding to cancel a plaintiff's federal registration if such a proceeding is brought within five years of the date of registration.

5.4 Remedies

(a) Injunctions

The Lanham Act provides that infringement of federally registered marks may be remedied by the courts through their "power to grant injunctions, according to the principles of equity and upon such terms as the court may deem reasonable."[29] An injunction against further infringement by the defendant is a primary remedy issued in trademark infringement cases since monetary damages alone would typically be inadequate to compensate the plaintiff if the defendant were allowed to continue its unlawful acts of infringement.

Balancing the equities in a case often affects the scope of an injunction by limiting the injunction in certain circumstances and broadening it in others. For example, the fame of a mark may significantly broaden the scope of an injunction. Infringement of the mark McDonald's®, for instance, is likely to result in a permanent injunction prohibiting use of the mark on a wide range of products and services. Conversely, if a mark is relatively weak and unknown, an injunction may be limited only to the specific goods or services at issue.

The good or bad faith of an infringer is another factor that can affect the scope of an injunction. For example, a court may permit an innocent infringer to sell its remaining inventory, while ordering the destruction of all infringing goods in a case where the defendant intended to trade upon the good will developed by the trademark owner. In still other cases, a court may issue an injunction that orders the defendant to advertise that it has no connection with the plaintiff to ensure that the public is not confused about the source of the defendant's products.

Where a plaintiff seeks an injunction against a defendant for trademark infringement, the plaintiff need not establish actual injury to prevail. The mere threat of injury as a result of the defendant's impending action is sufficient to warrant the issuance of an injunction. In order to establish liability, a plaintiff must demonstrate that based on the defendant's imminent actions, there is a likelihood that confusion

---

[29] 15 U.S.C. §1116(a).

will develop in the marketplace. Thus, a plaintiff may obtain injunctive relief even if the defendant has not yet sold any infringing products.

Oftentimes, prior to a final determination of the merits of a case, a plaintiff may wish to attempt to prohibit a defendant from continuing its alleged unlawful acts. In this situation, a plaintiff will seek preliminary injunctive relief from the court. If successful, the plaintiff has effectively gained much of the relief it will presumably request after a trial on the merits. Because preliminary injunctions are such extraordinary remedies, courts are cautious about granting this relief.

In order to prevail on a motion for a preliminary injunction, the plaintiff has the burden of meeting several criteria. First, the court must be convinced that the plaintiff is likely to prevail at a trial on the merits. Second, the plaintiff has to demonstrate that he or she will suffer irreparable harm if the preliminary injunction is not granted. Third, the court must determine whether a preliminary injunction will restore the original status quo. Finally, the court will consider whether the hardship to the plaintiff of not granting the requested relief is greater than the hardship that will result to the defendant if the requested relief is granted. Although each of these criteria will undoubtedly be considered by the court, no one criterion is more significant than any other. In fact, a plaintiff's presentation of very strong evidence with respect to one factor may compensate for a weaker showing with respect to another factor.

Once a preliminary injunction (or an injunction after a trial on the merits) is granted, the court issues a detailed order setting forth the scope of the injunction. Once the injunction is issued, the defendant must abide by the terms of the injunction or risk finding himself or herself in contempt of the court's order. If a defendant violates the order, both federal and state law provide that he or she is punishable by fine or imprisonment or both.

(b) Seizure of Counterfeit Goods

In certain cases of trademark infringement, injunctions (even preliminary ones) are inadequate. For example, if vendors on the streets of New York City who sell counterfeit goods are served with a summons to appear at a preliminary injunction hearing, they tend to disappear. Recognizing that blatant counterfeiting was becoming an increasing problem of trademark owners, Congress enacted §34(d) of the Lanham

Act in 1984. This statute explicitly authorizes federal courts to issue immediate ex parte orders for the seizure of counterfeit goods without notice to the defendant.[30]

These special seizure provisions apply only to a counterfeit mark. A counterfeit mark is defined by the Act as a spurious mark used in connection with goods or services that is identical to or substantially indistinguishable from a mark registered for those goods or services on the federal Principal Register in the PTO and still in use.[31] For example, a street vendor who sells watches that look like "Gucci" brand watches and bear the Gucci® mark on the face of the watches is selling counterfeit goods that bear a counterfeit mark if, in fact, the watches are not genuine Gucci® watches.

In order to convince a court that an ex parte seizure order is warranted, the plaintiff must demonstrate that the defendant is likely to flee or dispose of the counterfeit goods if notice is given. If the plaintiff meets his or her burden, the court will issue a seizure order specifying the time period in which the seizure must occur and indicating the date on which the postseizure hearing will take place. Typically, ex parte seizure orders are valid for 7 days and will specify that the hearing occur sometime between 10 and 15 days after issuance of the order. In addition, the order will specify that the plaintiff provide a bond in the event that a remedy for wrongful seizure becomes necessary.[32]

United States marshals are responsible for carrying out the provisions of the seizure order and actually conducting the seizure. Very often, the plaintiff's attorney accompanies the marshals in an effort to provide assistance in identifying the counterfeit items subject to seizure.

Once the seizure has occurred, a postseizure hearing is conducted. At the hearing, the plaintiff is required to establish that the seized goods bear counterfeit marks. In addition, the plaintiff must convince the court that returning the seized articles to the defendant would likely result in destruction of the items. If the plaintiff prevails, the court will retain the seized goods pending a trial on the merits. If the plaintiff prevails at trial, the counterfeit goods are typically destroyed.

---

[30] 15 U.S.C. §1116(d).

[31] 18 U.S.C. §2320(d)(1)(A)(ii).

[32] *See* 15 U.S.C. §1116(d).

(c) Monetary Relief

A successful plaintiff in a trademark infringement action is not automatically entitled to monetary relief. In fact, many courts are reluctant to award monetary relief in cases where the defendant is an innocent infringer or where there has been no actual confusion or damage to the plaintiff. Conversely, however, if the plaintiff demonstrates actual damages resulting from a defendant's intentional wanton conduct, courts and juries appear very willing to award the plaintiff substantial monetary relief.

(i) Plaintiff's Actual Damages

One way of measuring a defendant's monetary liability in a trademark infringement case is by determining the plaintiff's actual business damages and losses caused by the defendant's illegal act. In order to recover these damages, most courts require the plaintiff to establish that there was actual confusion in the marketplace as a result of the defendant's infringement. Generally, if a plaintiff can demonstrate that the defendant's actions were deliberate and intentionally designed to take advantage of the good will developed by the plaintiff, a strong inference can be made that the defendant caused confusion in the marketplace. Once the plaintiff has successfully established that the defendant acted deliberately, the burden shifts to the defendant to show that no consumer confusion actually occurred.

The plaintiff may also present other types of evidence that show the existence of confusion in the marketplace. Such evidence may consist of either consumer surveys or testimony of consumers who were actually deceived by the defendant's conduct. Unlike other types of monetary relief, no wrongful intent on the part of the defendant is necessary for the plaintiff to be awarded his or her actual damages. In other words, even an innocent infringer can be liable for the loss incurred by a plaintiff as a result of the defendant's actions.

Establishing a monetary amount to compensate a plaintiff for his or her actual damages is often difficult and courts tend to be rather liberal with respect to the latitude given to a plaintiff attempting to justify his or her damages claim. The most common type of recovery of a plaintiff's actual damages is his or her lost profits on sales lost due to the defendant's infringement. Another type of recovery is an award of a reasonable royalty. In such a case, courts will determine what the defendant would have paid to the plaintiff as a royalty for a license that would have given the defendant the right to sell the infringing goods.

ii) Defendant's Profits

Another way to measure the monetary recovery awarded to a plaintiff in a trademark infringement case is through an accounting of the profits made by the defendant as a result of the infringing acts. Before an accounting of the defendant's profits is granted, the courts almost invariably require that the plaintiff establish a wrongful intent on the part of the defendant. Where the defendant did not intentionally infringe the plaintiff's mark, an accounting of the defendant's profits is not a proper monetary remedy.

Once the court determines that an accounting of the defendant's profits is the appropriate measure of monetary relief to be awarded to the plaintiff, it becomes the defendant's burden to establish what percent of his or her profits was generated by factors other than his or her own misconduct. In addition, the defendant has the burden of proving any deductions from gross sales that should be considered by the court. Typically, the accounting period will be for the same time frame as the infringement period.

(iii) Increased Damages

Pursuant to §35 of the Lanham Act, a court has the discretion to increase actual damages by three times the amount awarded, and it can also modify an award of profits if it concludes that the award is excessive or inadequate.[33] The discretionary power to increase damage awards is typically invoked by the courts when an adjustment is necessary to compensate for difficulties in proving an amount of damages. Although the statute specifically states that an increased damage award shall constitute compensation and not a penalty, courts seem more likely to find that an adjustment in damages is needed where the defendant's infringement was deliberate and willful.

In counterfeiting cases, the court is required to award treble damages unless it finds that there are extenuating circumstances for not

[33] 15 U.S.C. §1117.

doing so.[34] In these cases, Congress has deemed it appropriate to award treble damages as a penalty to the counterfeiter.

(d) Punitive Damages

Pursuant to state law, punitive damages are permitted in many jurisdictions for trademark infringement in appropriate cases. Typically, punitive damages are awarded to deter the defendant from repetitive misconduct and to provide a warning to others that such conduct will be penalized. While the standard for awarding punitive damages varies state by state, most states require that the defendant's conduct be malicious, wanton, fraudulent, or reckless.

Punitive damages are not available under federal law. As indicated above, however, courts have the judicial authority to increase damages or profits when warranted.

(e) Attorneys' Fees and Costs

In 1975, Congress amended the Lanham Act to provide for the award of reasonable attorneys' fees to the prevailing party in exceptional cases.[35] The Senate Judiciary Committee determined that an exceptional case is one where the act of infringement is malicious, fraudulent, deliberate, or willful. Where there is no proof of willful infringement, an award of attorneys' fees is not appropriate.

In certain cases, an award of attorneys' fees to the defendant may be justified. For example, where a trademark infringement action is initiated in bad faith for purposes of harassment or delay, the defendant is entitled to an award of attorneys' fees.

Typically, reasonable attorneys' fees are calculated by determining the number of hours worked on the litigation and multiplying that number by a reasonable hourly rate. The party seeking the award of attorneys' fees should provide the court with evidence of the number of hours spent on the litigation and the rates claimed.

Rule 54(d) of the Federal Rules of Civil Procedure provides that costs shall be awarded to the prevailing party unless the court otherwise

[34] *See* 15 U.S.C. §1117(b).
[35] 15 U.S.C. §1117.

directs. The party claiming costs is required to provide an affidavit to the court asserting that the costs are correct, that the costs were necessary, and that the services warranting the costs were actually performed.

5.5 Preventing Importation of Goods

(a) Infringing Goods

Federal law provides that no article may be imported into the United States if it bears a trademark or trade dress that infringes another's federally registered mark or trade dress. To benefit from this provision, the trademark owner must comply with the regulations of the U.S. Customs Service.[36] These regulations are designed to exclude infringing goods from entry into the United States, subjecting them instead to seizure and forfeiture. Although forfeited articles are typically destroyed, seized articles may be returned to the country of origin whenever it is shown to the satisfaction of the district director of U.S. Customs that the importer had no reasonable grounds for believing that his or her actions constituted a violation of the Lanham Act. In addition, seized articles may be released to the importer provided the importer removes or obliterates the infringing marks in a manner acceptable to the Customs officer examining the articles.

To implement the seizure provisions, a trademark owner must record his or her federally registered mark[37] with the Customs Service. An application for recordation must include, among other things, a certified copy of the certificate of registration on the Principal Register, five photocopies of the registration, and the required filing fee, which is currently $190 per mark, per class. Once recorded, a trademark owner's claim is valid for the duration of the certificate of registration. The recordation can be renewed concurrent with renewing the trademark registration.

When a claim is recorded, the district director of Customs is put on notice that a particular trademark registration exists and shall with-

---

[36]*See* 19 C.F.R. §133.0 *et seq.*

[37]Only marks federally registered on the Principal Register may be recorded with the Customs Service. Marks registered on the Supplemental Register are not entitled to protection against importation.

hold any imported article that is deemed to "copy or simulate" the registered mark. The test used to make this determination is very similar to the likelihood of confusion test discussed in section 5.1 of this chapter. If Customs determines that a particular shipment of goods should be detained, the district director is required to notify the importer of the action taken by Customs and must advise the importer that it has 30 days in which to contest the detention. If the importer does not respond within 30 days, the imported goods shall be deemed infringing copies and shall be subject to forfeiture. As indicated previously, once forfeited, the infringing goods are typically destroyed.

If, on the other hand, the importer files a denial of infringement with the Customs Service, the district director must then provide the registered trademark owner with a sample of the imported article and advise the trademark owner that the article will be released to the importer within 30 days unless the trademark owner files a written demand for the exclusion from entry into the United States of the detained imported article. Following the filing of briefs by both parties, the Commissioner of Customs will resolve the dispute by determining whether the imported articles infringe the registered mark. If the claim of infringement is sustained, the district director will seize the articles and institute forfeiture proceedings. If, however, the claim of infringement is not sustained, the district director will release the detained goods to the importer.

As a practical matter, simply registering a trademark with the Customs Service may not ensure that infringing goods will be denied entry into the United States. Rather, additional measures are often necessary. If an owner suspects that a foreign manufacturer is importing infringing goods into the United States, the owner may hire a private investigator to determine which U.S. ports of entry are being used for shipment of the infringing goods. Once this information is obtained, the Customs Service can be alerted, thus significantly decreasing the possibility that infringing goods will be permitted entry into the United States without first being detained.

(b) Counterfeit Goods

Counterfeit goods, like infringing goods, are subject to restriction by the Customs Service. Counterfeit goods bear a counterfeit mark, which is defined in the Lanham Act as "a spurious mark which is identical with, or substantially indistinguishable from, a registered mark."[38] Counterfeit marks are applied to goods without any authorization from the rightful trademark owner. Once a counterfeit mark is applied to a product or a portion of a product, the entire product is deemed counterfeit and subject to seizure. Whether a mark on imported goods is in fact counterfeit will be determined from the viewpoint of an average consumer, rather than an expert.

Pursuant to Customs Service regulations, articles bearing a counterfeit mark are seized immediately at the U.S. port of entry. The trademark owner is notified of the seizure and given an opportunity to consent to the importation of the goods. Absent the trademark owner's written consent, the counterfeit goods are forfeited. Unlike the case of infringing goods, counterfeit goods will not be released to the importer upon the satisfactory removal or obliteration of the counterfeit marks. In addition, counterfeit goods will not be returned to the country of origin in any circumstance, even if the importer can demonstrate it had no knowledge that its actions constituted a violation of the Trademark Act. Simply put, an importer's lack of intent to infringe is not a valid defense to a charge of importing counterfeit products.

Once the counterfeit articles are forfeited, the counterfeit mark is removed from the imported goods by Customs. The Customs Service then disposes of the goods by destroying them or by giving them to a federal agency or a charity so that these institutions can put the articles to a beneficial use.

(c) Gray-Market Goods

Gray-market goods are a third category of goods that Customs has identified as being subject to restriction. A gray-market good is a "foreign-manufactured good, bearing a valid United States trademark, that is imported [into the United States] without the consent of the United States trademark holder."[39] In other words, the mark is validly placed on the goods by the foreign manufacturer with the consent of the trademark owner, but is then imported into the United States without the consent of the trademark owner. Because these goods actually bear a valid trademark, they are called gray-market goods.

---

[38] 15 U.S.C. §1127. *See also* section 5.4(b) of this chapter.

[39] K Mart Corp. v. Cartier, Inc., 486 U.S. 281, 285, 6 USPQ2d 1897, 1899 (1988).

Shipments believed to be gray-market goods are typically detained by Customs upon entry into the United States. The importer of the goods is notified of the detention and is given 30 days to demonstrate that the goods are exempt from seizure. Because Customs regulations permit goods manufactured abroad to be imported into the United States by any person who is subject to common ownership or control with the trademark owner, an importer that can establish, for example, a parent-subsidiary relationship between the foreign manufacturer and the U.S. trademark owner will be permitted to import gray-market goods into the United States. If the importer is unable to establish that the goods are exempt from seizure, Customs will initiate forfeiture proceedings in accordance with Customs regulations.

(d) ITC Proceedings

The International Trade Commission (ITC) is that branch of the government having the authority to issue orders against imported goods whenever it finds "[u]nfair methods of competition and unfair acts in the importation of articles . . . into the United States."[40] Unfair methods of competition and unfair acts in the importation of articles include both infringement of registered trademarks and unregistered common law marks, as well as copying protectable trade dress.

The ITC conducts a preliminary investigation of any allegation of unfair competition once a complaint is filed with the agency. When the preliminary investigation is concluded, the investigators will advise the ITC whether a formal investigation and proceeding should be initiated. If the ITC decides to pursue the complaint, the investigators become neutral parties to the proceeding. Once the notice of investigation is published, the ITC has 12 months to conclude the case. As a result of this statutory deadline, the ITC has its own rules of pretrial motions and discovery.

The ITC proceeding is essentially held before an administrative law judge (ALJ). The ALJ holds prehearing conferences and presides over the hearing itself. When the hearing is concluded, the ALJ makes a recommendation to the ITC with respect to whether an ITC violation has occurred and if so, recommends an appropriate remedy. If the ITC agrees with the ALJ's determination and remedial recommendation,

[40] 19 U.S.C. §1337(a).

the decision is submitted to the President of the United States, who then has 60 days to exercise his or her veto power over the decision on the grounds that it could negatively affect U.S. foreign relations. If the president permits the decision to stand, the infringer's only recourse is to file an appeal with the Court of Appeals for the Federal Circuit.

Asserting a trademark infringement complaint with the ITC can have certain procedural advantages that the complainant would not otherwise have in an action brought in federal court or with the Customs Service. Specifically, in an ITC proceeding, the complainant does not have to establish personal jurisdiction over the allegedly infringing importer. Moreover, the ITC can issue in rem exclusion orders that prevent infringing articles from entry into the United States. The Customs Service is the agency responsible for enforcement of the ITC's exclusion orders.

5.6 Inter Partes Proceedings in the PTO

The trademark rules provide for three types of proceedings between opposing parties ("inter partes proceedings"), which take place before the Trademark Trial and Appeal Board (TTAB). These proceedings include opposition proceedings, cancellation proceedings, and concurrent use proceedings. The purpose of each of these proceedings is to determine if, and under what circumstances, a mark is entitled to a federal registration. These are usually internal proceedings within the PTO, and the determinations (subject to court appeal) are made by the TTAB. Each is discussed in detail below.

(a) Opposition Proceedings

As discussed in Chapter 4, section 4.1(h)(iii), provided a trademark applicant's mark successfully passes through the examination process of the PTO, the mark will be published for opposition in the PTO's Trademark Official Gazette. The Official Gazette is published weekly and contains actual illustrations of the published marks, the goods and/or services used or intended to be used with the mark, the date of first use of the mark (if applicable), and the name and address of the applicant trying to register the mark. Once the mark is published, a potential opposer has 30 days to file a notice of opposition (along with the required fee) or a request for an extension of time to file a notice of opposition with the TTAB. Any notice or request not timely filed will be dismissed.

The Lanham Act provides that any person who believes that he or she would be damaged by the registration of a particular mark on the Principal Register may oppose registration by filing a notice of opposition with the TTAB.[41] To be successful, an opposer must plead and prove that he or she has standing to oppose the mark at issue. Provided the opposer can demonstrate that he or she is likely to be damaged by the registration of the applicant's mark, the opposer will have satisfied the standing requirement. In the opposition, the opposer must also set forth a short and plain statement of the grounds for opposition. Among the most common grounds for opposition are a likelihood of confusion with the opposer's previously used mark, or contention that the applicant's mark is functional, merely descriptive, primarily a surname, or generic. The opposer may also assert any other reason that the mark is not entitled to registration.

The trademark rules state that, except as otherwise provided, the procedure and practice in PTO inter partes proceedings are governed by the Federal Rules of Civil Procedure.[42] In an opposition proceeding, the opposer is deemed to be the plaintiff, while the applicant is in the position of the defendant. The notice of opposition and answer thereto correspond to the complaint and answer in a court proceeding. After the notice of opposition is filed, the TTAB mails notice to the applicant of the opposition and sets a time period by which the applicant must file an answer. Like an answer in a court proceeding, the answer may contain denials, defenses, and/or counterclaims. Depending on the circumstances of the case, the defenses may include, among other things, abandonment, laches, and/or estoppel. A counterclaim will typically seek cancellation of the opposer's federally registered mark. An opposition may be withdrawn without prejudice before an answer is filed. Once the answer is filed, however, the opposition may not be withdrawn without prejudice except with the written consent of the applicant.[43]

---

[41] 15 U.S.C. §1063. Applications for registration on the Supplemental Register are not subject to opposition proceedings, although such registrations can be the subject of a cancellation proceeding after registration.

[42] *See* 37 C.F.R. §2.116.

[43] 37 C.F.R. §2.106(c).

Pleadings in a notice of opposition may be amended in the same manner as pleadings filed in a civil action in a U.S. district court.[44] Once the pleadings in any PTO inter partes proceeding have been filed, the TTAB sets forth deadlines for discovery, testimony, submission of briefs, and oral arguments. These deadlines can be extended when necessary upon motion by a party to the proceeding.

Generally, the discovery provisions of the Federal Rules of Civil Procedure apply to the discovery period in PTO inter partes proceedings. The trademark rules set forth specific provisions relating to discovery depositions, interrogatories, requests for admissions, motions, sanctions, and telephone conferences with the TTAB.

In all PTO inter partes proceedings, the TTAB is responsible for issuing a trial order assigning to each party time for taking testimony.[45] A period of 30 days is assigned for the opposer to take testimony, followed by another 30 days in which the applicant can take testimony. The opposer then has an additional 15 days for rebuttal.[46] These time periods can be extended by agreement of the parties or by a motion to the TTAB. This assignment of testimony period corresponds to setting a case for trial in a court proceeding.

Testimony during the testimony period is obtained by taking depositions upon oral examination or by depositions upon written questions. Within 30 days of the completion of each deposition, one copy of the transcript of testimony, together with documentary exhibits, must be served on each adverse party. In addition, one certified transcript with exhibits must also be filed with the TTAB.[47]

The Federal Rules of Evidence govern evidentiary questions and issues in inter partes proceedings.[48] If a party in such a proceeding wishes to rely on particular documentary evidence or on portions of previously taken depositions, the party should prepare a notice of reliance. A notice of reliance sets forth the specific document (or portion thereof) that the party intends to rely upon and also specifically states the relevance of the material being offered into evidence. Once the notice of reliance is prepared, it is served on all other parties to the proceeding and then submitted to the TTAB during the offering party's assigned testimony period.

---

[44]37 C.F.R. §2.107.

[45]*See* 37 C.F.R. §2.121.

[46]There are 30-day intervals between each testimony period to permit each party to obtain and submit the transcripts.

[47]*See* 37 C.F.R. §2.125.

[48]*See* 37 C.F.R. §2.122.

Following the close of the testimony period, the party in the position of the plaintiff has 60 days in which to submit his or her brief to the TTAB. The party in the position of the defendant then has 30 days from the due date of the first date to submit his or her brief. If the party in the position of the plaintiff wishes to file a reply brief, he or she must do so within 15 days after the due date of the defendant's brief. Within 10 days of submission of the reply brief, any party desiring an oral argument must file a notice with the TTAB requesting such an argument. The argument will be heard by at least three members of the TTAB at the time specified in the notice of the hearing. Any party who appears at the hearing will be heard by the TTAB.[49] An oral hearing is the final phase of a PTO inter partes proceeding prior to issuance of a decision by the TTAB and, thus, corresponds to oral summation in a court proceeding.

Any final decision of the TTAB may be appealed to either the Court of Appeals for the Federal Circuit or to any district court in which the requirements of jurisdiction and venue are satisfied. In an appeal to the Federal Circuit, the court will review the TTAB's decision based on the evidence presented to the TTAB. An appeal to a district court, on the other hand, will be treated as a trial de novo.

(b) Cancellation Proceedings

Cancellation proceedings are initiated in the PTO by a party that wishes to contest the registration of a mark that has been registered on either the Principal Register or the Supplemental Register. The contesting party must timely file a petition for cancellation, together with the required fee, with the TTAB.[50]

The Lanham Act allows "[a]ny entity which believes that it is or will be damaged by a registration [to] file a petition . . . to cancel the registration in whole or in part."[51] A petition for cancellation of a registration on the Supplemental Register may be filed at any time. Although a petition seeking to cancel a registration on the Principal

---

[49]37 C.F.R. §2.129.

[50]*See* 37 C.F.R. §2.111 *et seq*. A party cannot initially file a cancellation proceeding in a federal district court. If, however, a plaintiff initiates a lawsuit for infringement of a federally registered trademark, the defendant can then include a count for cancellation of the registration as a counterclaim.

[51]37 C.F.R. §2.111(b).

Register can also be filed at any time, the grounds for seeking cancellation are significantly reduced unless the cancellation petition is filed within the first five years following the registration of the mark at issue.

During the first five years, any grounds that could have been submitted to oppose registration can be asserted as grounds to cancel the mark. When a petition to cancel, however, is filed more than five years after registration, the registration can be canceled only on certain grounds as set forth in the Lanham Act. These grounds are limited to the following:

1. The registered mark has become the generic term for all or some portion of the goods or services covered by the registration;
2. The registered mark has been abandoned by its owner;
3. The registration was obtained fraudulently;
4. The registration consists of immoral, deceptive, or scandalous matter, or falsely suggests a connection with living or dead persons, institutions, beliefs, or national symbols;
5. The registration consists of the flag or coat of arms of the United States, or of any state, municipality, or foreign nation;
6. The registration consists of a name, portrait, or signature of a living individual or of a deceased President of the United States during the life of his or her widow; or
7. The registered mark is being used by, or with the permission of, the registrant in a way that misrepresents the source of the goods or services covered by the mark.[52]

Thus, many of the most common grounds for cancellation (such as likelihood of confusion with a prior owner's mark or a merely descriptive objection) cannot be raised after five years. Similar to a notice of opposition, a petition for cancellation must set forth a short and plain statement showing why the petitioner believes he or she is or will be damaged by registration of the mark, state the specific grounds for cancellation, and indicate the name and address of the current owner of the registration.[53] In a cancellation proceeding, the petitioner is analogous to the plaintiff in a court proceeding and the registrant is analogous to the defendant. Once the petitioner files the petition for cancellation, the TTAB provides notice to the registrant of initiation of the cancellation proceeding and sets a time period in which the

---

[52] 15 U.S.C. §1064(3).

[53] *See* 37 C.F.R. §2.112.

registrant must file an answer to the petition. The answer may contain denials, defenses, and/or counterclaims. The Lanham Act specifically allows the defenses of laches, estoppel, and acquiescence to be asserted in all PTO inter partes proceedings.[54] As in opposition proceedings, a petition for cancellation may not be withdrawn without prejudice after an answer is filed unless the registrant provides its written consent for the withdrawal. If the registrant does not consent, the dismissal of the action will be with prejudice. Assuming the petition is not withdrawn, once the pleadings have been filed, the cancellation proceeding progresses in the same manner as in an opposition proceeding (see section 5.6(a)).

(c) Concurrent Use Proceedings

A basic concept of trademark law has always been that the first party to adopt and use a trademark has a right to continued exclusive use of that mark.[55] Thus, the first user is able to prevent subsequent use by others of marks confusingly similar to the first user's mark. Often, however, the first user only uses its mark in a limited manner such as in a geographically restricted territory or in a specific channel of trade. When this is the case and the second user innocently adopts a confusingly similar mark and starts to use the mark in a different territory or in a different market, it may be possible for both users to legally use their respective marks concurrently. A successful concurrent use proceeding allows both users to federally register their similar marks by limiting each registration in a way that is designed to prevent confusion arising from the concurrent use of the marks.

A concurrent use proceeding is commenced by an applicant (i.e., the second user of a mark) who files a trademark application for registration of a mark on the Principal Register as a lawful concurrent user of the particular mark. In addition to the routine statutory elements that must be included in any application, a "concurrent use application"

---

[54]*See* 15 U.S.C. §1069.

[55]This aspect of trademark law was limited to a certain degree in late 1989 with the introduction of "intent-to-use" trademark applications (*see* Chapter 4, section 4.1(h)(i)), because an applicant who files such an application, although not yet using a mark, will have priority in the mark over someone who starts using the mark after the application is filed. In this specific instance, therefore, it is possible for the later user of a mark to have priority in the mark.

must also indicate the territory in which the mark will be used, describe the concurrent lawful use of the mark by others, and list any registrations issued to or applications filed by others, the additional territories of use of the mark, the goods covered by the mark, and the time periods of use of the mark.[56]

Once an application for registration as a lawful concurrent user is filed, the application will be examined in the same manner as other applications for registration. Once the PTO determines that the mark is registrable, except for the issue of concurrent territorial rights, the mark is published for opposition. If no notices of opposition are filed within the requisite statutory time period, the TTAB then mails notices to all the parties named in the application notifying them of the "concurrent use application."[57]

Notices that are received by registrants or applicants named as concurrent users in the application do not have to be answered by the parties, although an answer may be filed if desired within 40 days after the mailing of the notice. Conversely, any other party specified as a concurrent user in the application must file an answer to the notice within 40 days after the notice is mailed.[58] Any party not filing a required answer will be precluded from claiming any right to the mark at issue that is more extensive than that acknowledged in the application for concurrent use registration.[59]

The burden of proving entitlement to registration is on the applicant who filed the application for concurrent use registration. The applicant will attempt to meet this burden during the concurrent use proceedings that follow submission of the pleadings. Like opposition and cancellation proceedings, a concurrent use proceeding follows the same PTO inter partes procedures. Ultimately, the TTAB will determine whether a mark is entitled to concurrent use registration.

---

[56] *See* 37 C.F.R. §2.42.
[57] *See* 37 C.F.R. §2.99.
[58] 37 C.F.R. §2.99(d)(2).
[59] *See* 37 C.F.R. §2.99(d)(3).

6
False Advertising

6.1 Introduction

Once a little known and little used aspect of the common law of business torts and of some state statutes, the law of false advertising has become an increasingly potent form of protection against unfair and untrue claims of competitors. Although it cannot be used against every type of untrue claim, it can be used to stop a wide variety of false claims, invidious comparisons, and product disparagement. This chapter addresses some of the basic aspects of this area of the law.

Originally, the common law action against a false advertiser required relatively strict proof of a number of elements and included stringent requirements for standing. In its first form as a federal law,[1] it was an obscure provision that was almost never used. Enacted as §43(a) of the 1947 Lanham Act,[2] it was still considered a relatively minor part of the statute. Beginning in the 1960s, however, judicial interpretations of §43(a) made the law of false advertising more applicable and more effective. Most recently, through passage of the Trademark Law Revision Act of 1988, effective November 16, 1989,[3] the

[1]Section 3 of the Act of 1920 included a prohibition against false advertising, but required proof of willfulness and intent to deceive.

[2]15 U.S.C. §1125(a).

[3]Pub. L. No. 100-667, 102 Stat. 3935 (1988) (amending certain sections of 15 U.S.C. §§1051–1128).

law has been rewritten to codify existing case law and to expand its scope even further to include product disparagement and trade libel.

Both federal and state courts have concurrent jurisdiction over allegations of false advertising, provided the challenged advertising or representations were made in or affect interstate or foreign commerce. A §43(a) claim that satisfies this requirement may be brought in either forum and can be accompanied by any appropriate parallel state law claims. A §43(a) claim initiated in state court, however, can be removed to federal court by the defendant. If the challenged advertising was made in and affects intrastate commerce only, a plaintiff must initiate its false advertising claim in state court, unless diversity of citizenship is established.[4]

6.2 Common Law

Although formulations of the common law prohibition against false advertising differ, the essence of the law came from the long-standing prohibition against passing off one's goods as another's. In advertising, this took the form of falsely ascribing qualities to "A's" goods in an attempt to equate them in the consumer's mind with "B's" usually superior product. While theoretically effective, use of the common law was severely curtailed by strict requirements as to standing and proof.

Because the common law in this area evolved in the context of property law, not fraud, a prospective plaintiff was required to prove some economic injury to its business, rather than that the trade or the consumer was being defrauded by the false advertising. Proving actual injury to the plaintiff[5] was always difficult and, in a multisupplier market, could well be viewed as virtually impossible. The common law also did not allow the competitor-plaintiff to act as a "vicarious avenger," that is, one who claims to have standing for the purpose of

[4]Diversity of citizenship establishes jurisdiction of the federal courts between citizens of different states, where the party on one side is a citizen of one state, and the other party is either a citizen of another state or an alien. In addition, a minimum amount in controversy must also be met.

[5]To demonstrate actual injury, the plaintiff had to prove that, but for the defendant's false advertising, a consumer would have bought from the plaintiff rather than the defendant.

protecting the consumer. This resulted in a dilemma: the competitor could not sue without proving actual economic injury and lacked standing to sue on behalf of the consumer; yet the consumer could not sue because the tort was not considered a fraud.

In recent years, courts have increasingly lessened the ban imposed by the vicarious avenger theory in order to allow more actions against false advertisers. One avenue around the problem of standing was to institute a class action on behalf of all sellers against the false advertiser. This solved the problem of proving injury and enabled the entry of an injunction. Proof of actual damages, however, remained a problem, as did apportionment of any damages recovered.

There is one major and one relatively minor exception to the vicarious avenger bar—the "single-source" exception and the "false representation of geographic origin" exception. The single-source exception is applicable where the plaintiff is the only source of a particular set of goods, and the defendant can sell its goods only by misrepresenting them. This occurs in either a two-supplier market, or where the plaintiff's goods are unique. For example, goods may be unique when they are patented, copyrighted, or trademarked. If the defendant falsely advertises its goods as created or produced by the plaintiff, then the single-source exception is applicable.

At least one court has taken an expansive view of the relief that can be afforded in a two-supplier market. In *Electronics Corp. of America v. Honeywell, Inc.*,[6] the court considered a two-supplier market for replacement programmers for the plaintiff's power plant controllers. Although the court acknowledged that in this situation, other courts might require the plaintiff to show that the defendant falsely advertised its products as having the qualities of the plaintiff's products, the First Circuit determined that *any* material misrepresentation was actionable.[7]

With respect to the false representation of geographic origin exception, some courts have held that any competitor actually associated with the geographic region, or selling goods associated with the region, has standing to sue a seller who falsely advertises that it or its goods are also associated with the particular region. Other courts, however, require that the plaintiff also be the single source of the particular goods from the relevant geographic region.

---

[6]428 F.2d 191, 165 USPQ 674 (1st Cir. 1970).

[7]*Id.* at 194 n.3, 165 USPQ at 676–77 n.3.

While the common law afforded an avenue to prevent false advertising, it also made that way a narrow, rocky path. Fortunately, as discussed below, the prohibition against false advertising was codified and expanded. Thus, it is now easier to invoke and much more effective.

6.3 Protection Under the Lanham Act

Today, the major vehicle to redress false advertising claims is §43(a) of the Lanham Act. Section 43(a), as amended in the late 1980s, currently reads as follows:

> (a)(1) Any person who, on or in connection with any goods or services, or any container for goods, uses in commerce any word, term, name, symbol, or device, or any combination thereof, or any false designation of origin, false or misleading description of fact, or false or misleading representation of fact, which—
>
> > (A) is likely to cause confusion, or to cause mistake, or to deceive as to the affiliation, connection, or association of such person with another person, or as to the origin, sponsorship, or approval of his or her goods, services, or commercial activities by another person, or
> >
> > (B) in commercial advertising or promotion, misrepresents the nature, characteristics, qualities, or geographic origin of his or her or another person's goods, services, or commercial activities,
>
> shall be liable in a civil action by any person who believes that he or she is or is likely to be damaged by such act.

The late 1980s amendment to §43(a) was expressly intended to codify existing law and expand the coverage provided by the section. In particular, the section now covers product disparagement and trade libel. The revision also codified a majority of decisions regarding damages and now expressly provides that all of the Lanham Act remedies for infringement of registered trademarks are available to plaintiffs asserting violations of §43(a). The courts are split in considering whether §43(a) should be applied retroactively. Some courts have held that where the confusion or deception resulting from the false advertising remains or arises after the effective date of the revision, the current version of the statute is applicable even if the misleading activities occurred prior to the effective date.

6.4 The Parties

(a) Plaintiffs—Standing to Sue

Section 43(a) has been construed as creating a completely new federal cause of action for false advertising. Unlike the common law, which arose from property law and developed to protect a small range of direct competitors, §43(a) of the Lanham Act was enacted with the express purpose of protecting consumers. It also protects against a wider range of false representations, including representations that have a tendency to deceive or mislead. The courts have therefore discarded most, if not all, of the common law restrictions on standing, making relief under §43(a) available to anyone, whether or not in competition with the defendant, provided the plaintiff can show that it "is or is likely to be damaged."

Standing requires a greater showing of likelihood of damage than a plaintiff's wholly subjective belief, but a lesser showing, at least for establishing liability, than actual damage such as lost sales. The added element of consumer protection has encouraged the courts to establish a relatively low threshold for finding that standing is satisfied. For example, direct competitors have standing to protect their own reputations or the reputation of the product. In addition, trade associations and cooperatives have standing to protect the reputation of an entire industry or a special segment thereof. Authors of creative works or designs have standing to prevent advertising that falsely attributes, overattributes, or omits to attribute creative credit to the author. In at least one instance, a court has held that an investor in a business alleged to have been damaged by false advertising had standing to bring an action under §43(a) against the advertiser.[8]

Standing does require some nexus between the allegedly false advertising and the damage to the plaintiff. Mere "gadfly" litigation is not permitted. A competitor may sue an advertiser for its own damages, but does not have standing to bring suit on behalf of other competitors whose products also were falsely compared with the defendant's products. Likewise, lack of standing has been found where the damage or likelihood thereof is too remote. Thus, for example, a manufacturer of cameras designed to use conventional film lacked

---

[8]Thorn v. Reliance Van Co., 736 F.2d 929, 222 USPQ 775 (3d Cir. 1984).

standing to sue an advertiser of cameras using instant film under §43(a).[9] In general, however, it is clear that the courts will err, if at all, in favor of liberal standing requirements in order to best effectuate the purpose of the statute.

(b) Defendants

Not only may a plaintiff sue the party that is directly responsible for the false advertisement or misrepresentation, but the plaintiff may also join other parties as defendants in the case. Where the plaintiff can show that such parties knowingly aided the defendant by, for example, selectively analyzing or editing data to be used to substantiate an advertisement's claims, those parties may be joined as defendants in a §43(a) case.

An important exception to this general rule is where the other party is a communications medium or a publisher. A newspaper or printer is not required to test each product advertised in its pages to ensure that all claims are true. Thus, as long as the medium or printer is an innocent violator, the medium carrying the false advertisements or misrepresentations is not liable for damages under §43(a).[10] The medium or printer can, however, be enjoined from future dissemination of the false material. Even this remedy is limited because no injunction can be issued against a publication if it would cause a delay in the normal delivery or transmission.

The carrier will be subject to suit, of course, not only when it is the carrier, but also when it is the source of the advertisement. A publication may also subject itself to liability if it undertakes to endorse, certify, or guarantee a particular product advertised in its pages.

6.5 False or Misleading Advertising

The "false advertising" prohibition set forth in §43(a) is concerned with misrepresentations of "the nature, characteristics, qualities, or

---

[9]Pignons S.A. de Mecanique de Precision v. Polaroid Corp., 657 F.2d 482, 212 USPQ 246 (1st Cir. 1981).

[10]*See* 15 U.S.C. §1114(2).

geographic origin" of goods, services, or commercial activities in commerce within the regulation of Congress. Prior to the 1988 revision of the section, the prohibition was directed only at misrepresentations of the goods and services of the defendant. The revision, however, expanded the scope to include "another person's" goods or services. Thus, §43(a) has also become an effective vehicle for asserting claims of disparagement and trade libel.[11]

In considering cases of false advertising, courts must address a number of issues. Courts have to determine whether the defendant's accused activities had an impact on commerce. Next, courts consider whether the defendant's challenged activities consisted of commercial advertising and, if so, whether that advertising contained false or misleading statements, representations, or facts. Whether the defendant's conduct is likely to deceive consumers is a further issue that arises in a false advertising case. These issues are discussed more fully below.[12]

(a) In Commerce

In order to be actionable under §43(a), a defendant's accused activities must have some impact on commerce regulated by Congress (typically, interstate or foreign commerce with the United States). Earlier §43(a) cases required that the representations in question had to concern the defendant's own goods or services, and these goods or services had to be in commerce. As the case law developed, the emphasis shifted from a requirement that the goods or services be in commerce to a requirement that the challenged advertising or representations be made in interstate or foreign commerce. It is not required that the goods or services be in interstate commerce, or that they even exist at the time the challenged representations are made. For example, the Second Circuit has held that the improper use of a mark by a saloon is actionable under §43(a) when there is significant advertising of the

[11]There are some limits to the activity covered by §43(a). For example, a defendant is not liable for material omissions, but rather, only actual false or misleading representations. Evidence of omissions, however, may help prove that the representations actually made were false or misleading.

[12]Courts must also address whether the plaintiff has demonstrated that it has suffered, or is likely to suffer, harm. This final issue is the same one that arises in a standing analysis and is, therefore, discussed in section 6.4(a).

saloon in travel guides and brochures that have interstate circulations.[13] Some courts have expanded this even further, holding that for purposes of §43(a), it is sufficient that there be an effect or likely effect on the plaintiff's sales in interstate commerce, even if the defendant's sales and advertising are wholly intrastate.

(b) Advertising

The definition of "advertising" for purposes of §43(a) is very broad. It includes well-known avenues of advertising such as print and broadcast media. It also includes a variety of items such as catalogs, brochures, fliers, in-store displays, and exhibits at trade fairs and trade shows. The dividing line between "commercial advertising and promotion" subject to §43(a) and activities that are not subject to the section is unclear. At least one court, however, has denied a motion to dismiss a §43(a) case where the activity in question consisted of telephone calls by the defendant to friends and business associates.[14]

False advertising and false statements, however, must be "commercial" to be actionable under §43(a). The term "commercial activity" was included in the 1988 revision for the express purpose of ensuring that §43(a) could not be used to curtail political speech, opinion, editorial comments, or other types of noncommercial publications or representations. Even where the activity does not fit directly within the categories of political or opinion speech, it still will be outside the purview of §43(a) so long as its use is for a noncommercial purpose.

(c) Falsity

The most basic element of any false advertising case is proof that the advertising is in fact false. The plaintiff has the burden of proving

---

[13]Lobo Enters. v. Tunnel, Inc., 822 F.2d 331, 3 USPQ2d 1446 (2d Cir. 1987).

[14]National Artists Mgmt. Co. v. Weaving, 769 F. Supp. 1224, 20 USPQ2d 1113 (S.D.N.Y. 1991). The court found that, at least in the relatively small theater management and booking industry, such oral telephone contacts were indeed the means of promoting one's services.

falsity. Thus, there is no legal requirement under the law of false advertising that a party have studies to prove that its claims are true before making them.[15] Of course, it is always prudent for an advertiser to have good reason to believe that statements are true before they are made. In addition to helping to protect an advertiser's credibility, development of proof that a claim is accurate can help avoid inadvertent false statements that could lead to legal liability and help provide the necessary proof to defeat an allegation of false advertising.

(i) Literal Versus Implicit Falsity

Statements that are literally false, as well as those that are implicitly false, are actionable under the Lanham Act. There is, however, a difference in the proof depending on whether the misrepresentation is considered literally or implicitly false. If literally false, the "falsity" requirement is satisfied simply by proof that the statement is false. Where, however, the advertising is only implicitly false, proof that consumers were actually misled is generally required. Such proof is usually supplied by a properly conducted consumer survey or by market research.[16] Sometimes, direct testimony of consumers stating that they were misled will suffice.

Although the ease of proving literal falsity will vary from case to case, the question is quite simple: Is what the defendant said true or not? Examples of false statements are as numerous as the cases in which the statements are attacked. Such statements include untrue claims for "lowest tar" cigarettes,[17] advertisements falsely referring to the employment history of an actress,[18] and false assertions of fiber content in garments.[19]

---

[15]Other statutes, such as Food and Drug Administration requirements, may require substantiation before statements are made or a product is marketed.

[16]*See* Chapter 5, section 5.1(c), where consumer surveys are discussed.

[17]American Brands, Inc. v. R.J. Reynolds Tobacco Co., 413 F. Supp. 1352 (S.D.N.Y. 1976).

[18]Dallas Cowboys Cheerleaders, Inc. v. Pussycat Cinema, Ltd., 467 F. Supp. 366, 201 USPQ 740, 4 Media L. Rep. 2325 (S.D.N.Y.), *aff'd,* 604 F.2d 200, 203 USPQ 161, 5 Media L. Rep. 1814 (2d Cir. 1979). In a thorough and thoughtful opinion, the district court found, among other violations, that the advertisement's claim that the actress was a past member of the Dallas Cowboys Cheerleaders was literally false. The court enjoined the advertising and the showing of the film *Debbie Does Dallas.*

[19]Camel Hair & Cashmere Inst. of Am. v. Associated Dry Goods Corp., 799 F.2d 6, 231 USPQ 39 (1st Cir. 1986).

Implicit falsity exists where the statements made, although not literally false, become deceptive or misleading when considered in their complete context. The fact that the statements, considered alone, are literally true will not be a sufficient defense if the overall effect is or is likely to be deceptive.

In *Vidal Sassoon, Inc. v. Bristol-Myers Co.*,[20] the court found that Bristol-Myers' advertisements implied that each participant in its touted survey was in a certain age group and had conducted comparative tests of its products as well as the products of others. In fact, each participant had rated only a single product. In addition, a significant number were not within the implied age group. Other examples of falsity include misleading statements regarding the availability of guaranteed seating on aircraft flights[21] and the false implication that products sold by the defendant were warranted by the manufacturer.[22] The range of prohibited conduct is very broad, extending, as one court has stated, to "clever use of innuendo, indirect intimations, and ambiguous suggestions," which in context are misleading or deceptive.[23]

Omitting a fact from an advertisement is not itself considered actionable under §43(a). Although it is not a universally accepted standard, many courts have held that omission of a material fact may be actionable where the failure to state the fact makes the advertising as a whole misleading. In *Performance Industries v. Koos, Inc.*,[24] for example, the court held that Performance Industries' omission of information regarding price was misleading in light of its statements that its product was more economical than its competitors' products. Another type of misleading omission is the failure to state that a product has been made in a foreign country where the implication of the representation as a whole is that the product is domestic. Courts have also considered it misleading to promote creative works and neglect to mention the contributions of co-creators.[25]

---

[20]661 F.2d 272, 213 USPQ 24 (2d Cir. 1981).

[21]Eastern Air Lines v. New York Air Lines, 559 F. Supp. 1270, 218 USPQ 71 (S.D.N.Y. 1983).

[22]Seiko Time Corp. v. Alexander's, Inc., 218 USPQ 560 (S.D.N.Y. 1982).

[23]American Home Prods. Corp. v. Johnson & Johnson, 577 F.2d 160, 165, 198 USPQ 132, 137 (2d Cir. 1978).

[24]18 USPQ2d 1767, 1771 (E.D. Pa. 1990).

[25]Lamothe v. Atlantic Recording Corp., 847 F.2d 1403, 7 USPQ2d 1249 (9th Cir. 1988).

(ii) False Comparative Advertising

False "comparative" advertising cases involve a special application of the rules of literal or implicit false advertising. Although §43(a) does not prohibit a competitor from referring to or showing another's products in its advertising in order to compare them, it does prohibit the making of false statements that mislead or deceive consumers.[26] Comparative advertising includes statements of equivalence between the defendant's product and another's product.[27]

Performance Industries[28] is an example of a comparative advertising case in which several comparisons were found to be either literally false or implicitly false. The advertising falsely implied that Performance Industries had completed direct comparison tests between its products and Koos' products when in fact no such tests were done. Performance Industries had instead relied upon general studies for the class of compounds within which Koos' products fell. In addition, Performance Industries falsely stated that its product had the approval of the Environmental Protection Agency (EPA), when, in fact, the EPA had no applicable standards at the time. Moreover, Performance Industries represented its product as more economical because it could achieve the same effect as Koos' by using half as much of the product. Performance Industries neglected, however, to include the fact that its product cost about eight times more than Koos' product.

Because §43(a) focuses on the advertising representations themselves, most courts do not require that an advertiser substantiate its comparison claims before making the claims. The issue of liability will rest on whether preexisting substantiation is correct and sufficient, or whether later tests confirm the claims made in the advertising. In other words, in order to obtain relief, the burden is on the plaintiff to establish that the comparison is false.

Where, however, a defendant claims that "tests prove" that its product is superior to the plaintiff's product, it may not be necessary for the plaintiff to prove that the underlying claim (i.e., that the defendant's product is superior) is in fact false. Rather, liability can be shown

---

[26]Likewise, when a competitor uses another's trademark or trade name in its advertising, it must do so in a way that does not create a likelihood of confusion as to source, association, or sponsorship. *See* Chapter 5, section 5.1.

[27]Tyco Indus. v. Lego Sys., 5 USPQ2d 1023 (D.N.J. 1987), *aff'd*, 853 F.2d 921 (3d Cir.), *cert. denied*, 488 U.S. 955 (1988).

[28]Performance Indus. v. Koos, Inc., *supra* note 24, at 1770–71.

simply by attacking the tests and demonstrating that the defendant's tests, properly interpreted, do not support the defendant's claim that "tests prove" the superiority of its product.

(iii) Puffing

Neither a comparative advertiser nor a noncomparative advertiser will be liable under §43(a) for representations that are "merely puffing," even though such representations technically may be false. The classic example of puffing is the assertion that a used car is a "peach" when, in fact, it is a "lemon." More specifically, puffery consists of exaggerations or statements that either are so generalized that it is impossible to label them true or false, or are such that no reasonable consumer would rely upon them. Vague claims that one's product is "new" and "better" are not actionable. Similarly, fanciful advertisements that imply that wearing a particular cologne or drinking a certain beer will make one irresistible to members of the opposite sex are not actionable claims.

The reason why "mere puffing" is not a violation of §43(a) is because the nature of the exaggerated or fanciful claims is such that few consumers would believe them. It is for this reason, however, that the line between "mere puffing" and actionable false representations may be a vague one. Thus, words that appear to be mere puffing may turn out in fact to be false or misleading if consumers are likely to believe the claims. For example, the claim that a particular product was "new" and was "immediately" effective was held to be false where the ingredients were actually well known and the effect was not immediate.[29]

(d) Deception

Liability under §43(a) does not depend on the defendant's willfulness or intent to deceive,[30] although proof of bad intent may have an effect on the amount of damages or other relief granted. In this

[29]American Home Prods. Corp. v. Abbott Lab., 522 F. Supp. 1035, 214 USPQ 351 (S.D.N.Y. 1981).

[30]This is another distinction from common law false advertising. In many states, intent to deceive is still required.

context, the misrepresentations must be deemed material, which requires proof that the misrepresentations deceive or at least have the tendency to deceive consumers in their buying decisions.[31]

Proof of this deception element may depend upon whether the statement is literally or implicitly false. Where a statement has been shown to be literally false, many courts find that there is no need for independent proof that the false statement does, or tends to, deceive or mislead the intended consumer. Deception will be presumed from proof of the falsity. Where, however, the advertisement is only implicitly false, proof of a tendency to deceive, usually in the form of a consumer survey or market research, is required. A defendant met with a charge of false advertising may present proof that the alleged falsity does not affect consumers' buying habits and, hence, is not material.

There are several reasons why a plaintiff may want to present proof of actual deception even if it is presumed. First, it is often not clear at the outset of a case whether a statement will be considered literally false (where proof of deception is not required) or only implicitly false (where proof of deception is required). Second, proof of actual deception may be helpful to combat assertions from a defendant that, in fact, there was no material effect on consumers' buying habits. Finally, evidence of actual consumer deception may be necessary to prove, or to augment, a claim for damages.

6.6 Remedies

(a) Injunctive Relief

Injunctive relief available under §43(a) encompasses temporary restraining orders, preliminary injunctions, and permanent injunctions. To obtain a temporary restraining order or preliminary injunction, the plaintiff must meet traditional equitable standards for receiving such relief. There must be a showing of irreparable harm, likelihood of

[31]Some courts hold that the misrepresentations must be in regard to the inherent qualities or characteristics of the relevant product, service, or activity. These courts reason that false statements that do not concern a product's inherent qualities or characteristics may not be actionable because the statements are not material to a consumer's buying decision.

success on the merits, or balancing of hardships as determined by the law of the forum. Where the parties are direct competitors, irreparable harm will often be presumed and a preliminary injunction will issue upon a requisite showing of falsity. The defendant may, of course, present evidence that tends to rebut the existence of irreparable harm.

After trial, a successful plaintiff typically will be awarded a permanent injunction. The successful plaintiff need not establish any actual deception or actual damage, although at least a tendency to deceive must be shown. As explained above, in cases where the accused advertising was literally false, courts have found that this alone justified an injunction. In cases where the accused advertising is false by implication or by omission, courts typically require some proof of a capacity to deceive, which can take a variety of forms such as expert testimony, market surveys, or testimony of consumers.

The type of injunctive relief available to a successful plaintiff, subject to various equitable considerations, can be quite broad. For example, a primary remedy is an order for immediate cessation of the false advertising. In addition, the court may order the recall of all the false advertising or require a campaign of corrective advertising. A court may also require a defendant to recall its products and refund money to buyers. A defendant may likewise be required to include disclaimers in its future advertising or on product containers, especially where the harm from the advertising is a false statement or an implicit endorsement of a product by the plaintiff.

These various injunctive remedies are not automatic. Which injunctive remedy will be granted is fact specific and will differ from case to case. In general, the injunctive relief should be devised to remedy the harm suffered by the plaintiff. Likewise, the nature of the defendant's conduct will be taken into account. If the defendant acted willfully, a court is more likely to order stringent injunctive relief. Finally, as explained in section 6.8, First Amendment concerns also may need to be considered.

(b) Monetary Relief

Prior to the 1988 revision, courts used different methods for measuring the amount of monetary damages that should be awarded to successful plaintiffs in §43(a) cases. Most courts, however, applied the measures set forth in §35 of the Lanham Act, even though at the time, the express language of §35 restricted it to trademark infringement cases. The Trademark Law Revision Act of 1988, however, amended the preamble language of §35 to make clear that it represented a remedy for all actions under §43(a). In appropriate circumstances, a plaintiff may recover any or all of the following: the plaintiff's lost profits, the plaintiff's actual business damages and losses attributable to the false advertising, the defendant's profits, and attorneys' fees.[32] Courts have frequently included at least some measure of the cost of corrective or counteradvertising campaigns as a remedy in false advertising cases.

Monetary relief is not automatically awarded to a successful plaintiff in a false advertising case. The standard of proof that must be met in order to obtain monetary damages from a false advertiser is higher than that required to obtain an injunction. To obtain monetary relief, a plaintiff must generally show that at least some consumers were actually deceived and acted in reliance on the deceit. Stated another way, a right to monetary damages requires a showing of actual deception and actual damage. A mere tendency to deceive or likelihood of damage is not sufficient. Although there is no requirement that each individual lost sale be shown, there must be sufficient evidence of sales diversion from which the plaintiff's losses can be reasonably calculated. The plaintiff must also establish a reasonable connection between the challenged advertising and the loss. Losses due to other factors may outweigh alleged losses or make it impossible to determine that the losses were a result of the false advertising.

The general requirement that actual deception must be shown has been softened, or more liberally construed, by some courts. Deception is usually proved by market surveys, with concomitant statistical interpretation of the results. Courts do not require a showing that each customer who bought elsewhere did so on the basis of the false advertising. Other courts have, in a sense, balanced the degree of falsity against the showing needed to establish actual deception or confusion. For example, when the representations were "patently fraudulent," no proof of actual deception was required. In at least one court, a defendant's deliberate use of false advertising has created a presumption that actual deception occurred.[33]

---

[32]For a more detailed discussion of the types of monetary relief available under §35 and the circumstances under which each type of relief may be awarded, see Chapter 5, section 5.4(c). These considerations generally apply to false advertising cases.

[33]U-Haul Int'l v. Jartran, Inc., 793 F.2d 1034, 230 USPQ 343 (9th Cir. 1986).

6.7 Other Protection Under the Lanham Act

Other types of misuse of advertising, though not technically "false advertising," are also actionable under §43(a). For example, it can be a violation to copy or imitate a successful advertising campaign. In essence, it is the concept or feel of the advertisement that is protected. To establish liability, however, there must be a likelihood of confusion, at least as to affiliation, connection, or association with the source of the advertisement. Similarly, there must be a showing that the advertising concept is distinctive.

Unauthorized use of celebrity likenesses, whether real or fictional, may also be actionable under §43(a), as is use of a celebrity's name in an advertisement in such a way as to falsely imply an endorsement by the celebrity.[34] The underlying rationale for these prohibitions is usually cited as being a likelihood of confusion as to the celebrity's endorsement of the particular product. Some courts also consider potential damage to the celebrity's reputation.[35] For example, a magazine may not put a well-known celebrity name on its cover in such a manner as to imply an endorsement by the celebrity, even if the magazine contains an article or other news concerning the celebrity.[36]

A growing number of cases reflect attempts to sell a now-famous performer's or author's early, or even disowned, works accompanied by advertising or representations showing the performer as he or she is today.[37] Similarly, a claim for a violation of §43(a) can also be made against "look-alikes," "sound-alikes," or "act-alikes" advertisements.[38] Again, the rationale for liability is that there may be a false belief that the celebrity endorses the product. A proper and conspicuous disclaimer, however, may be sufficient to escape liability.

Section 43(a) may also be extended to cover a variety of other misrepresentations, especially in creative and entertainment settings.

---

[34]White v. Samsung Electronics America, Inc., 971 F.2d 1395, 23 USPQ2d 1583, 20 Media L. Rep. 1457 (9th Cir. 1992), *cert. denied,* 113 S. Ct. 2443 (1993); Culliford v. CBS, Inc., 222 USPQ 497 (D.D.C. 1984).

[35]White v. Samsung Electronics America, Inc., *supra* note 34.

[36]Cher v. Forum Int'l, Ltd., 213 USPQ 96, 7 Media L. Rep. 2593 (C.D. Cal.), *aff'd in part and rev'd in part, modified in part,* 692 F.2d 634, 217 USPQ 407, 8 Media L. Rep. 2484 (9th Cir. 1982), *cert. denied,* 462 U.S. 1120 (1983).

[37]Rich v. RCA Corp., 390 F. Supp. 530, 185 USPQ 508 (S.D.N.Y. 1975).

[38]Tin Pan Apple, Inc. v. Miller Brewing Co., 737 F. Supp. 826, 15 USPQ2d 1412, 17 Media L. Rep. 2273 (S.D.N.Y. 1990); Allen v. Men's World Outlet, Inc., 679 F. Supp. 360, 5 USPQ2d 1850, 15 Media L. Rep. 1001 (S.D.N.Y. 1988).

For example, placing false matter in a copyright designation on an unlawfully copied work or falsely designating the copy as being copyrighted are actionable claims under §43(a). Unauthorized use of a copy of another's copyrighted work bearing even an otherwise correct notice of copyright may also be actionable as containing a misrepresentation that the original author authorized, used, or endorsed the publication. Furthermore, unauthorized editing or other alteration of a copyrighted work may be actionable. Each of the foregoing activities may, of course, also subject the defendant to causes of action for copyright infringement and other misappropriation in addition to a violation of §43(a).

Another type of misrepresentation that may be actionable under §43(a) involves the misattribution of the creative contributions of co-authors or other co-creators. Such misrepresentations have included claiming another's work as entirely that of the false advertiser. More common cases are instances where one performer's contribution is advertised as being greater than it was or, conversely, where the contributions of a performer are completely omitted.[39]

6.8 Parody and First Amendment Concerns

Many of the types of representations discussed in section 6.7 are met by a defense that the advertisement or performance is a parody. The question of whether parody and satire can subject the satirist to liability under §43(a) is heavily dependent on the purpose and use of the satire. Whether a parody defense will be successful needs to be determined on a case-by-case basis. Even a satire or parody that is intended solely for the purpose of amusement or entertainment is actionable if the plaintiff can prove that there is a likelihood of confusion as to the source of the parody. On the other hand, a parody used in an advertisement by a direct competitor may be held to be free from misrepresentation or confusion. In general, however, the more that a "parody" is purely commercial and the more that it ridicules the object

---

[39]PPX Enters. v. Audiofidelity Enters., 818 F.2d 266, 2 USPQ2d 1672 (2d Cir. 1987) (overattribution of Jimi Hendrix's contribution to recordings prohibited); Lamothe v. Atlantic Recording Corp., 847 F.2d 1403, 7 USPQ2d 1249 (9th Cir. 1988) (underattribution of co-authors' contributions prohibited).

of the parody, the more difficult it will be to assert a successful parody defense.

Two cases are illustrative. In *Jordache Enterprises v. Hogg Wyld, Ltd.,*[40] the court readily acknowledged that the defendant's use of the mark "Lardashe" for large-sized women's jeans was intended to, and would, create an association between the famous "Jordache" name and the parody. The court held, however, that this association did not create a likelihood of confusion between the two sources of the products. On the other hand, in *Gucci Shops v. R.H. Macy & Co.,*[41] the court held that the defendant was liable for its parodical use of the Gucci look for a diaper bag because the court acknowledged that consumer confusion as to source was likely. The court based its finding of liability on the plaintiff's right to be protected from ridicule.

First Amendment considerations also should be reviewed. The Supreme Court has held that commercial speech is subject to the freedom of speech protection of the First Amendment.[42] Although this appears at first blush to be at odds with the prohibitions on false advertising found under §43(a), the Supreme Court has explained that only truthful commercial speech is protected.[43] Speech that will, or is likely to, deceive may be regulated. Courts have held that, in First Amendment parlance, §43(a) is "content neutral" and, thus, not subject to First Amendment considerations.[44]

Considerations of the First Amendment do require, however, that the relief fashioned be the narrowest, or least restrictive, to accomplish the objective.[45] For this reason, some courts are more likely to require the positive act of inserting appropriate disclaimers before issuing an injunction against the entire advertisement. Injunctions have had to be modified where the injunction suppressed not only the false portions of an advertisement or advertising campaign, but also prohibited the truthful portions.[46]

---

[40]828 F.2d 1482, 4 USPQ2d 1216 (10th Cir. 1987).

[41]446 F. Supp. 838 (S.D.N.Y. 1977).

[42]Virginia State Bd. of Pharmacy v. Virginia Citizens Consumer Council, Inc., 425 U.S. 748, 1 Media L. Rep. 1930 (1976).

[43]*Id.*

[44]Vidal Sasson, Inc. v. Bristol-Myers Co., 661 F.2d 272, 213 USPQ 24 (2d Cir. 1981).

[45]Carroll v. President & Comm'rs of Princess Anne, 393 U.S. 175, 1 Media L. Rep. 1016 (1968).

[46]U-Haul Int'l, Inc. v. Jartran, Inc., 793 F.2d 1034, 230 USPQ 343 (9th Cir. 1986).

7
Copyrights

7.1 Historical Introduction to Copyright Law

Like many U.S. laws, American copyright originated in England, where the King granted exclusive privileges to publishers of text. The American founding fathers sought to protect those privileges throughout the States, by providing through the Constitution, article 1, section 8, clause 8, authority for Congress to protect the writings of authors. The first federal copyright statute was enacted shortly after the Constitution's birth, in 1790. Additional federal statutes were promulgated throughout the nineteenth century, adding copyright protection in a piecemeal fashion as the industrial revolution spawned new forms of expression for America's authors. Those early enactments coincided with the development of a common law copyright at the state and local levels. The common law of copyright was particularly important for works that were not protected under the federal statutes, such as copyrightable works that were unpublished. As a result of the various enactments, American copyright, by the beginning of the twentieth century, consisted of a patchwork of federal acts, along with a body of judge-made common law that varied from state to state.

(a) The 1909 Act

Recognizing the need to address the confusion and inconsistency resulting from the various federal enactments, Congress enacted a comprehensive copyright statute in 1909.[1] The 1909 law significantly changed the copyright law, to preserve copyright in scope, in effect, and in purpose. Prior to the 1909 Act, registration of a work was required before its publication. Hence, publication without registration effectively eviscerated the copyright, placing the published works in the public domain. For those works that remained unpublished, copyright protection was provided under state common law.

In the 1909 Act, Congress eased the registration requirement. To obtain statutory copyright protection, a proper copyright notice had to be placed on the published work. The author then had to promptly deposit copies of the work in the Copyright Office. Publication without strict adherence to the notice requirements of the Act, including content and location of the notice, resulted in loss of copyright. The 1909 Act specifically did not apply to unpublished works that were still protected under state common law. Hence, the 1909 Act maintained a dual federal/common law structure created in the prior century.

Another aspect of registration under the 1909 Act was that it required renewal after 28 years. The purpose of the renewal requirement was to provide the public with the benefit of use of previously protected but unrenowned works, while at the same time it allowed authors to continue holding their copyrights in valuable works. The 1909 Act renewal provisions also had disadvantages. A copyright assignee had to obtain an assignment of an author's renewed rights. If he or she failed to do so, the copyright during the renewal reverted back to the author. By the 1950s this disadvantage, along with the United States' continuing legal isolation from the rest of the world, brought Congress back to debating the necessity of a new law. That law would not be passed until 1976.

The 1909 Act still applies to works created and published and to acts of infringement that occurred before January 1, 1978, the effective date of the 1976 Act. However, essentially all significant issues encountered by most businesses today are governed by the 1976 Act. Accordingly, a detailed treatment of the 1909 Act is not presented in this book.

(b) The 1976 Act

The 1976 Copyright Act, which became effective January 1, 1978, marked a radical departure from the 1909 Act. The 1976 Act evidenced

---

[1]Ch. 320, 35 Stat. 1075 (1909).

Congress's desire for a less formalistic and less restrictive approach to copyright protection. For example, under the 1976 Act, copyright protection arises automatically when a work is fixed in a tangible medium of expression, such as writing on paper or recording on an electronic medium. The hallmark of the 1976 Act, however, was its preemption of common law copyright for unpublished works. By virtue of the 1976 Act, copyright law became essentially entirely statutory. The law is found in Title 17 of the U.S. Code, section 37 of the Code of Federal Regulations, and in regulations set forth by the U.S. Copyright Office (contained in that Office's Compendium of Copyrights).

(c) The Berne Convention Implementation Act

Despite the above-noted changes, the 1976 Act fell short of providing U.S. authors with automatic copyright protection in foreign countries. At the time the 1976 Act came into effect, an author would have to publish simultaneously in the United States and in another country that subscribed to an international copyright treaty known as the Berne Convention[2] in order to receive an automatic publication in most major U.S. trading partners. As a result, publication became a complicated and expensive affair for those authors with international ambitions.

To address this deficiency, Congress passed the Berne Convention Implementation Act of 1988 (BCIA),[3] which conformed the 1976 Copyright Act to the relatively inflexible requirements of the Berne Convention. This conformation did not come without significant debate or difficult compromise. However, the results of the BCIA were significant: after the BCIA, an author achieves international copyright protection upon fixation of his or her expression in a tangible medium of expression in the United States without any registration. The BCIA also added to U.S. law, although only to a limited extent, the notion of moral rights—rights that are inalienable, and that protect the artistic integrity of the author's works. Finally, the BCIA expanded the scope of copyright in several subject areas, most notably architectural works.

---

[2]*Berne Convention* (Paris text, July 24, 1971), *reprinted in Copyright Laws and Treaties of the World,* 26th Supp. (1989–1990), Item H-1, Vol. 3, Multilateral Conventions (BNA 1990).

[3]Pub. L. No. 100-568, 102 Stat. 2853 (1988).

(d) Summary

The history of American copyright law thus can be divided into four eras: (1) the era prior to the 1909 Copyright Act; (2) the era between the 1909 Act and January 1, 1978 (the effective date of the 1976 Act); (3) the era between January 1, 1978, and March 1, 1989 (the effective date of the BCIA); and (4) the era under the BCIA. These eras play an important role in determining what law to apply to any given work and in determining what rights exist. For example, for a work created in 1976, published in 1978, and infringed in 1990, the 1909 and 1976 Acts would apply along with the BCIA. Each would be pertinent to the existence and validity of copyright and each would relate to defining infringement. Hence, an understanding of the history of copyright becomes critical to properly analyzing its current context.

7.2 Protectable Subject Matter

Section 102 of Title 17 of the U.S. Code (the Copyright Act) provides that:

> Copyright protection subsists, in accordance with this title, in original works of authorship fixed in any tangible medium of expression, now known or later developed, from which they can be perceived, reproduced, or otherwise communicated, either directly or with the aid of a machine or device.

Under the 1976 Copyright Act, copyright arises *automatically* upon the fixation of the author's work in any tangible medium of expression. The copyright protects only the expression of the work, not the underlying idea, process, procedure, concept, system, or discovery.

(a) Works of Authorship

Copyrights apply only to works of authorship. The Copyright Act lists a number of categories included in works of authorship. These categories are: (1) literary works; (2) musical works, including any accompanying words; (3) dramatic works and any accompanying music; (4) pantomimes and choreographic works; (5) pictorial, graphic, and sculptural works; (6) motion pictures and other audiovisual works; (7) sound recordings; and (8) architectural works.[4] These categories are not exhaustive. Any work that is created in a tangible medium of expression can be considered a work of authorship. In 1980, the Computer Software Copyright Act[5] amended the copyright statute to include a definition of computer programs as a set of statements or instructions to be used directly or indirectly in a computer in order to bring about a certain result.[6] Computer programs are protectable as literary works (see Chapter 11, section 11.3).

A work is "created" when it is fixed for the first time.[7] If a work is prepared over a period of time, the fixed portion at any given time constitutes a work as of that time. Different versions constitute separate works. To be entitled to copyright protection, the work must be "created" by a person. Works produced by animals or machines are not eligible for protection.

(b) Originality

The work must be *original,* which means it was created by an author. A work cannot be part of the public domain or a copy of another work. A work can still be original even though it includes parts copied from the public domain or other works, as long as it adds original material. If a prior copyrighted work is copied, however, questions of infringement of that prior copyright may be raised (see Chapter 8 for a discussion of copyright infringement). However, the work does not have to be novel, which means that no such identified work previously existed. Thus, if two people independently produced identical works, each would have a copyright in his or her respective work and neither work would infringe the copyright in the other work. "Quality, aesthetic merit, ingenuity, and uniqueness are not considered in determining the copyrightability of a work."[8] The required amount of originality is minimal, but the copyright protects only the original material. For example, a playwright has a copyright covering the words in a play. The actors could also have a copyright in their specific

[4] 17 U.S.C. §102.

[5] Pub. L. No. 96-517 §10, 94 Stat. 3028, 17 U.S.C. §§101, 117 (1980).

[6] 17 U.S.C. §101.

[7] *Id.*

[8] Copyright Compendium §202.

performance of the play as long as that play remained in a fixed medium, since the "performance" includes original expression. Moreover, since the standard for originality does not include a qualitative judgment, works including original sequences or organization, such as yellow page telephone directories or databases, are copyrightable. Originality does have a minimum requirement. For example, where the author's contribution involves no creativity, such as in the alphabetical listing of names in a phone directory, originality will not be present.[9]

(c) Fixation

Fixation, as defined by the 1976 Act, involves a situation in which the embodiment in a "hard" copy or phonorecord is sufficiently permanent or stable to permit it to be perceived, reproduced, or otherwise communicated for a period of more than momentary duration. "A work consisting of sounds, images, or both, that are being transmitted, is 'fixed' for purposes of [the 1976 Act] if a fixation of the work is being made simultaneously with its transmission."[10]

Federal copyright protection does not arise until the work is fixed in a tangible medium of expression, that is, expression that can be perceived, reproduced, or communicated. Sounds and images must be recorded to be fixed. A live broadcast of a program is not eligible for copyright protection unless it is also recorded so that it becomes fixed (but the script is eligible). Improvisational or impromptu performances that are not recorded are also not protected. The fixed work is not required to be humanly readable. Thus, for some works, such as computer programs, which are not understandable or visible when loaded in the computer, the work is nonetheless considered fixed when it is stored in a memory. However, computer information that is transitory is not considered fixed.[11]

(d) Publication

Under the 1909 Act, copyright protection did not arise until publication of the work. Publication under the 1976 Act is defined as "the

---

[9] Feist Publications, Inc. v. Rural Tel. Serv. Co., 111 S. Ct. 1282, 59 USLW 4251, 18 USPQ2d 1275, 18 Media L. Rep. 1889 (1991).

[10] 17 U.S.C. §101.

[11] Lewis Galoob Toys v. Nintendo of Am., 964 F.2d 965, 967–69, 22 USPQ2d 1857, 1859–60 (9th Cir. 1992), *cert. denied,* 113 S. Ct. 1582, 61 USLW 3651 (1993).

distribution of copies or phonorecords of a work to the public by sale or other transfer of ownership, or by rental, lease, or lending."[12] A public performance or display is not publication. Although the 1976 Act required a copyright notice at the time of publication under the BCIA, the notice requirement is no longer a prerequisite for copyright. Notice still remains critical for enforcement, however, since lack of notice may enable defendants to avoid incurring damages.

(e) Compilations

A protectable compilation is a work formed by collecting and assembling existing materials or data in such a way that the resulting work constitutes an original work of authorship.[13] Collections are also regarded as compilations. The copyright in the compilation covers only the author's original selection and arrangement of materials in the work. The author of the compilation does not have and cannot receive a copyright in the preexisting materials. In fact, the compiler might be infringing the copyrights in the preexisting materials if those copyrights are held by others. Additionally, copyright protection does not extend to facts in the compilation.

(f) Nonprotectable Matter

Copyright is intended to protect the expression of authors, but not the "idea, procedure, process, system, method of operation, concept, principle, or discovery."[14] A discussion of the boundaries of copyrights is important to understanding the scope of the rights available.

(i) Idea/Expression

Copyright protects the way a work is expressed, not the ideas expressed in that work. More critically, expansion of expression protection runs into problems with notions of freedom of expression under

---

[12]17 U.S.C. §101.
[13]*Id.*
[14]17 U.S.C. §102(b).

the First Amendment. Although the principle of expression, and not idea, seems relatively simple, its application, particularly in the context of copyright infringement litigation, has been complex, confusing, and often technically rigorous. This complexity stems, in part, from the difficulty in defining with precision where an idea ends and an expression begins. To best understand the boundary between copyright and idea, it is useful to look at how courts separate the two in copyright infringement actions. Various tests have been developed by courts in order to aid this task. Two tests have been particularly useful: the abstractions test and the successive filtration test.

The abstractions test is valuable for defining infringement. It involves expanding the copyrighted expression beyond its literal form to cover other expressions that are "substantially similar," or close, but not identical. The value of the abstractions test is that it enables courts, and copyright holders, to enforce copyrights against those who change wording, order of sentences, or other trivial parts of the expression in an attempt to design around the author's work. The abstractions test acts thereby to inflate the expression to the point where it becomes idea.

Once the abstracted expression is found, recent court decisions have then applied a "successive filtering" test to that expression to extract the unprotected ideas. Once the expression is "filtered," the copyright can be assessed.[15] The filtering test extracts several different things from the work when the expression and idea are the same. First, it ferrets out merged ideas and expressions. To determine what constitutes merged expressions, a court examines whether the work can be expressed in more than one or a limited number of ways. If it cannot, then the idea and the expression have effectively combined. For example, a court has held that the idea of a jeweled bee pin could only be expressed in a single way.[16]

A second element that is extracted from the expression is stock expressions, that is, elements in a work that can only be shown a certain way dictated by common sense. This type of expression is known as "scenes a faire." Scenes a faire cannot impose copyright infringement liability since it is the only practical way to express the idea. It is impossible, for example, to write about a World War II

---

[15]*See* Computer Assocs. Int'l v. Altai, Inc., 982 F.2d 693, 707 (2d Cir. 1992).

[16]Herbert Rosenthal Jewelry Corp. v. Kalpakian, 446 F.2d 738, 742, 170 USPQ 557, 559 (9th Cir. 1971). *See also* Chapter 8, section 8.1 for a discussion of merger with respect to infringement.

event in Europe without resorting to showing Nazi soldiers wearing swastikas.

A third element that can be extracted involves an expression that can only be expressed efficiently in one way. In other words, even though the expression is not technically merged, it can only practically be expressed in a single manner. In computer programs, often certain steps to be performed by the computer can only be efficiently expressed in a single manner. Other expressions affect the operation of the computer and reduce its speed. Similarly, rules for games often have only one efficient, clear expression.[17]

(ii) Functionality/Useful Articles

The above limits to copyright are based on 17 U.S.C. §102(b), which denies protection to any "idea, procedure, process, system, method of operation, concept, principle, or discovery, regardless of the form in which it is described, explained, illustrated, or embodied." A further basis for exclusion derives from the utilitarian functions of a work. Utilitarian features rest on the separation between patent law and copyright law. In effect, patent law not only protects ideas—it also guards against "uses" of the invention. By contrast, copyright law limits or restricts copying, distribution, publication, etc., but has no basis for restricting the use of an object. If it did, it would provide patent law scope to copyrighted expressions.

The basis for the functionality restriction derives from the Supreme Court case of *Baker v. Selden,*[18] which was later modified by *Mazer v. Stein.*[19] Read together, these decisions hold that copying an idea alone is not copyright infringement, so that the creative expressions of purely functional works may still be copyrighted. Infringement would occur only in the event that those expressions, rather than the ideas underlying those expressions, are copied. Nonetheless, the 1976 Copyright Act has refused to recognize copyright when functional works do not appear to have separable expressions. 17 U.S.C. §101 defines useful articles, which do not qualify for protection, as those having an intrinsic utilitarian function that neither portrays the appearance of the article nor expresses information. Courts have defined this

---

[17]*See* Morrissey v. Procter & Gamble Co., 379 F.2d 675, 678, 154 USPQ 193, 195 (1st Cir. 1967).

[18]101 U.S. (11 Otto) 99 (1880).

[19]347 U.S. 201, 100 USPQ 325 (1954).

intrinsic utilitarian function as one involving "conceptual separability" between the artistic and the utilitarian features.[20] For example, an illustration of an electric circuit schematic cannot qualify for copyright since no other purpose than to portray the working elements of the circuit is expressed. By contrast, a work of applied art, such as a lamp base made in the shape of a human figure, has a separable creative expression, that is, the human figure. As a result, §101 leaves copyright open for a variety of useful articles.

(iii) Factual Works

Although not explicitly stated in §102(b), copyright protection generally precludes the protection of facts. The basis for this preclusion derives from (1) the lack of originality resulting from a mere recitation of facts, (2) the fact that the creation of facts constitutes "discovery" which is precluded by §102(b), and (3) the concern that facts and ideas are often inseparable. However, an accounting of facts in an original form *is* copyrightable. Even more, the level of requisite originality is relatively low. Therefore, reconstructions of actual facts may evidence a sufficient quantum of originality to merit copyright protection.

In *Harper & Row, Publishers v. Nation Enterprises,*[21] the Supreme Court indicated that when an individual quotes his or her own remarks from several years prior, that reconstruction alone constitutes copyrightable subject matter of the facts reported.

Originality extends not only to the expressions of originally written facts, but also to compilations of nonreconstructed facts where originality has been shown in the selection and arrangement of those facts. However, this is an area in flux inasmuch as recent Supreme Court decisions have rendered *some forms* of compilation as not being original.[22] Thus, if facts were arranged merely in alphabetical order or in another preordained mechanical arrangement (i.e., by date or numerically), this "selection and arrangement" would be treated as effectively nonoriginal. A critical caveat, therefore, is that the compilation of facts must be arranged in an original way. A further caveat is to consider the issue of infringement: Can copying of the facts from a plaintiff's work shield the defendant from copyright liability? The answer is that

---

[20]Kieselstein-Cord v. Accessories by Pearl, Inc., 632 F.2d 989, 208 USPQ 1 (2d Cir. 1980).

[21]471 U.S. 539, 225 USPQ 1073, 11 Media L. Rep. 1969 (1985).

[22]*See, e.g.*, Feist Publications, Inc. v. Rural Tel. Serv. Co., *supra* note 9.

it depends on *whether* the copier only took facts or the author's original selection or interpretation of those facts.

(iv) Protectability of Forms

The protection of legal forms such as contracts or insurance policies appears to be available as long as those forms, like other literary works, evidence a degree of originality. The fact that those works are useful should bear no limitation to protection. 17 U.S.C. §113(b) indicates that the owner of copyright in any work that portrays a useful article as such has no greater or lesser rights with respect to the making, distributing, or displaying of the useful article so portrayed than those afforded to such works under the law. In other words, the fact that the work is a form, rather than text, has no bearing on its ultimate protectability or enforceability.

(v) Protection of Architectural Works

Under the 1976 Act, architectural works were recognized as protectable under 17 U.S.C. §102(a) since they were implicitly covered by the definition of pictorial, graphical, and sculptural works under §102(a)(5). The BCIA explicitly added architectural works under §102(a)(8). Beyond definition, several differences concerning the scope of protection for such works exist for pre- and post-BCIA works. If the architectural work was created prior to the BCIA and January 1, 1978, and it was published, then it was divested of protection. Thus, prior to 1978, copyright protection for architectural plans existed only if they remained unpublished. A more difficult question, however, is whether under current law the copyright extends to the building constructed from the architectural plan. The overall preponderance of courts and commentators agree that liability is denied by the 1976 Act. The only instance in which infringement can be found is if there is a separate act other than building from the plan (such as making multiple copies of the architectural plan itself). However, the BCIA appears to complicate this since 17 U.S.C. §101 was amended to include "the design of a building as embodied in any tangible medium of expression, including *a building*" (emphasis added). Thus it appears that copyright protection extends to the impermissible *construction* from plans after the effective date of the amendments to the Copyright Act, that is, after December 1, 1990. However, no court decisions on this issue have yet occurred.

7.3 Exclusive Rights

Section 106 of the Copyright Act defines the exclusive rights conferred to authors. In particular, it provides the author with

> the exclusive rights to do and to authorize any of the following:
>
> (1) to reproduce the copyrighted work in copies or phonorecords;
> (2) to prepare derivative works based upon the copyrighted work;
> (3) to distribute copies or phonorecords of the copyrighted work to the public by sale or other transfer of ownership, or by rental, lease, or lending;
> (4) in the case of literary, musical, dramatic, and choreographic works, pantomimes, and motion pictures and other audiovisual works, to perform the copyrighted work publicly; and
> (5) in the case of literary, musical, dramatic, and choreographic works, pantomimes, and pictorial, graphic, or sculptural works, including the individual images of a motion picture or other audiovisual work, to display the copyrighted work publicly.

These rights, described below, are to a large extent dependent upon the type of work copyrighted. Numerous exceptions to these rights exist for specific technologies. In addition, enforcement of the rights enumerated in §106 is subject to the fair use defense which permits limited use of an author's copyrights (see Chapter 8, section 8.2(b)).

(a) The Right to Make Copies

The copying element of infringement can occur only if the defendant's work copies directly from that of the plaintiff, not from another source. Furthermore, as previously discussed relating to the idea/expression issue, the copying of noncopyrightable elements in a work does not constitute an infringement of this right. Therefore, the act of copying those features to the extent that ideas, or facts, are taken from the work at issue, does not rise to the level of infringement. Another instance where copying is not found to be an infringement is when a "use" of the work occurs, rather than mere copying. Hence, if a work is used as an illustration or example in a commentary or criticism, it is more likely that the act will not be considered impermissible copying, but rather a use of the work for purposes of the commentary or criticism.

The application of the fair use doctrine also limits the scope of copying since it considers the purpose behind the act of copying and the character of the copying. For example, if a single insubstantial portion of a large work is copied, courts sometimes adopt a "fair use" argument as an exemption to infringement (see Chapter 8, section 8.2(b)). The Ninth Circuit recently held in *Sega Enterprises v. Accolade, Inc.*,[23] that the making of a single copy for purposes of reverse engineering a computer program was fair use. However, when the entire work has been copied, in most instances, if it is even once, courts are likely to find liability. The copy must also be fixed for it to incur liability.

(b) Derivative Works

Copyright law permits authors the right to make derivatives of their original work under 17 U.S.C. §106(2). A derivative work is a work "based upon one or more preexisting works, such as a translation, musical arrangement, dramatization, fictionalization, motion picture version, sound recording, art reproduction, abridgement, condensation, or any other form in which a work may be recast, transformed, or adapted. A work consisting of editorial revisions, annotations, elaborations, or other modifications which, as a whole, represent an original work of authorship, is [also] a 'derivative work.' "[24]

(c) Distribution, Performance, or Display

17 U.S.C. §106(3)–(5) provides copyright owners with the exclusive right to distribute, perform, or display their works. The distribution right under §106(3) allows authors to control the sale, publication, or rental of their works. However, this right is subject to control only for the first sale. After the first sale, the author may not thereafter exercise

---

[23] 977 F.2d 1510, 1527–28, 24 USPQ2d 1561, 1568 (9th Cir. 1992).
[24] 17 U.S.C. §101.

his or her distribution right over subsequent purchasers. Thus, the owner of the authorized copy is entitled, without the copyright owner's permission, to further sell or otherwise dispose of his or her possession of that copy or phonorecord.[25] The purpose of the first-sale doctrine is to avoid the implicit danger that §106(3) poses in restraining free trade. With regard to rental, however, the first-sale limitation does not apply.

An author's exclusive performance right is defined in §106(4). The performance right extends to literary, musical, dramatic, and choreographic works along with pantomimes, motion pictures, and other audiovisual works. However, several types of expression are not included in this formulation. For example, pictorial, sculptural, and graphical works are not explicitly included. The reason for some of these exceptions is to avoid duplication. For example, sound recording works are duplicative of the copyrights for the musical works. It would thus be unreasonable to expect the infringer of a musical work to pay damages to both the author of the work and the author of the recording.

Performance of the work means to recite, render, play, dance, or act the work. The performance can also be indirect if it is amplified, reproduced, or transmitted electronically. Typical types of performances include broadcasting a play or showing a motion picture. However, home performances, such as the showing of a television program, are excepted since performances must be "public" under 17 U.S.C. §106(4) to violate the copyright owner's right.

Under copyright law, a "public" performance is a performance or display "at a place open to the public or at any place where a substantial number of persons outside of a normal circle of a family and its social acquaintances is gathered."[26] Difficulty lies, to some extent, in defining a "substantial number" and what constitutes "social acquaintances." Are members of a club who do not pay for the performance considered "social acquaintances?" Is a substantial number of persons those individuals who actually attended the performance, or the total number that were invited regardless of actual attendance? Answers to these questions have resulted in some differences among circuit courts.

Copyright law provides numerous exemptions to the performance right. Generally, a host of fair-use nonprofit performances will not create liability for defendants. Typical fair-use exemptions include:

---

[25]17 U.S.C. §109(a).
[26]17 U.S.C. §101.

religious services or performances having educational purposes. Congress also carved out an exemption to the first-sale doctrine with respect to video game performances (known as the "Red Baron doctrine").[27] Specifically, Congress amended the first-sale doctrine to not apply to rentals of a video game work in a video parlor when the arcade game was legally purchased. This act, known as the Computer Software Rental Amendments Act of 1990,[28] addressed this problem by entitling owners/purchasers of such games to subsequently display them without infringing the author's performance right. Finally, compulsory licensing royalties are applied to certain types of performances which, by virtue of the existence of the compulsory license, obviates infringement. Under 17 U.S.C. §118, and other parts of the 1976 Act, compulsory license rules apply to jukebox operations.

A further issue regarding the performance right relates to transmissions. When a single performance is broadcast and then that performance is retransmitted to a separate entity, such as a cable television operation, does it involve a second performance? Generally, the answer appears to be yes, at least as far as the legislative intent of the 1976 Act. However, some secondary transmissions are exempted, including: hotel or apartment house retransmissions, retransmissions that do not include the entirety of the first transmission, retransmissions in a private lodging, and retransmissions that do not incur any direct charge for the secondary transmissions. Additionally, if the secondary transmissions are made for nonprofit reasons, they are also exempted from being considered as separate "performances." Further exemptions also exist for those cable secondary transmissions that are subject to compulsory licenses.

Finally, the display right enables authors to publicly display certain types of works. In particular, the display right relates to literary, musical, dramatic, and choreographic works and pantomimes, and pictorial, graphic, and sculptural works. Additionally, the display right includes images in a motion picture and other audiovisual works. Moreover, the unauthorized display has to occur publicly.[29] Other aspects affecting whether in fact there has been an infringing display include the substan-

---

[27]The name "Red Baron" derives from the case Red Baron-Franklin Park, Inc. v. Taito Corp., 883 F.2d 275, 11 USPQ2d 1548 (4th Cir. 1989), *cert. denied,* 493 U.S. 1058 (1990), where the court held that the playing of a video arcade game on a machine is an infringement regardless of the first sale of that video game to a video arcade.

[28]17 U.S.C. §§101 note, 109, 109 note, 205 note.

[29]17 U.S.C. §106(5).

tiality of the performance and whether the subject was indeed a "copy" of the work, or was a separate work entirely.

(d) International Rights

As of March 1, 1989, the United States joined the Berne Convention. As a result of that membership, copyright owners/authors now receive full protection in all member countries without having to effect prior registration. All that is required is creation of the work. More critically, the rights received abroad are often greater than U.S. authors receive at home. For example, most Berne Convention member countries provide moral rights for all works. By contrast, moral rights protection extends only to a few works in the United States. (See section 7.3(e) for discussion of moral rights.) For enforcement, most foreign countries have no notice requirements, while in the United States lack of notice can preclude damage awards. A further advantage of the Berne Convention is that it guarantees all the traditional rights defined in 17 U.S.C. §106, that is, the reproduction right, the right to make derivatives, the public performance right, the right of distribution, and the right of public display. Finally, publishers are protected by virtue of their publication in a Berne Convention country. The mere fact of publication *initiates* international Berne Convention protection without a simultaneous publication overseas.

However, works created prior to March 1, 1989, do not fall within the Berne Convention. Instead, they are protected under the Universal Copyright Convention (UCC),[30] which the United States joined several years prior to the BCIA. Unlike the Berne Convention, the UCC confers foreign copyright protection only in the foreign country in which the work was published. Also, although the UCC excuses formalities like the Berne Convention, it requires that a copyright notice be used along with the name of the copyright proprietor and the year of first publication. When these conditions are met, the published works of Berne Convention nationals are protected for the term given to published works of the home nation. That term also must be a minimum of 25 years. The UCC is thereby not automatic from the standpoint of rights creation. Consequently, UCC coverage can be expensive since

---

[30]*Universal Copyright Convention* (Paris text, July 24, 1971), *reprinted in Copyright Laws and Treaties of the World,* 26th Supp. (1989–1990), Item B-1, Vol. 3, Multilateral Conventions (BNA 1990).

it requires publication in the contracting state. From a practical standpoint, UCC membership is of relatively little significance since most foreign markets for U.S. works belong to Berne Convention members. One notable exception, however, is the former Soviet Union, which prior to its breakup belonged only to the UCC. Each of the former Soviet Republics is now deciding whether to join the Berne Convention. The significance of the UCC is thus obviously decreasing.

(e) Moral Rights

During the implementation of the BCIA, one of the main areas of discussion and debate was the inclusion of moral rights. Under the Berne Convention, there is a requirement that Berne Convention member states protect authorship and enable authors to object to "any distortion, mutilation, or other modification of, or other derogatory action in relation to, the said work, which would be prejudicial to his honor or reputation."[31] In attempting to comply with the Berne Convention, Congress effectively avoided the issue. It indicated that domestic U.S. law, in its present form, meets the Berne Convention's moral rights minimum. However, one federal law was proposed in 1990 that provides moral rights to artistic works. Specifically, the Visual Artists Rights Act of 1990 amended the 1976 Act to provide explicit moral rights to cover works of visual art including paintings, drawings, sculptures, prints, and multiple copies of those works, so long as an agreement is signed by the artist. Photographs are covered, but only if they are produced for use in exhibitions.[32] The artist's moral rights in these works are defined under 17 U.S.C. §106A(a). They include two rights: the right of attribution and the right of integrity.

Attribution is defined under §106A(a)(1)–(2) as providing the artist with the right to claim authorship in the work, the right to prevent the use of his or her name as the author of any visual work that the author did not create, and the right to prevent the use of his or her name as an author of the work of visual art in the event that a distortion, mutilation, or other modification of the work would be prejudicial to that artist's reputation and honor.

---

[31]*Berne Convention* Article 6 bis #(1), *supra* note 2, at 3.
[32]17 U.S.C. §101 (see definition of "work of visual art").

The right of integrity is defined under §106A(a)(3) as providing the artist with the right to prevent (i) the destruction of his or her work of recognized stature; (ii) the intentional or grossly negligent destruction of the work; and (iii) any intentional distortion, mutilation, or other modification of his or her work that would be prejudicial to that author's reputation or honor.

Enforcement in ownership of the moral rights will remain only with the author of the work and shall last for the lifetime of the artist. Moral rights are also inalienable, so that subsequent assignment of the copyright does not confer ownership of the moral rights. For a joint work, the rights conferred shall endure for the life of the last surviving author. The moral rights are capable of being waived by the author if the author expressly agrees in a signed written instrument and that instrument identifies the work and uses of that work to which the waiver applies. If one of several authors waives his or her moral rights, the waiver shall apply to all joint authors.

Moral rights contain several limitations. Like other copyrights, fair use limits moral rights under 17 U.S.C. §107. In other words, noncommercial use of copyrighted works may create an exception to moral rights. Exceptions also exist for the use of visual works of art on buildings. Whenever a work of visual art is incorporated into a building's structure, if it is incorporated in such a manner that its removal causes its destruction, then moral rights are unavailable.[33]

7.4 Ownership

(a) Authorship, Joint Works

Copyright in a work initially vests in the author or authors of the work.[34] An author is any person who creates original expressions embodied in a work or his or her employer for a "work made for hire" (see section 7.4(b)). With respect to derivative works, the author is the person who creates the derivative portions of the preexisting work—not the preexisting work itself. Similarly, the creator of a compilation

[33]17 U.S.C. §113.
[34]17 U.S.C. §201(a).

is the person who brings the existing works together. The original authors of each part of a compilation have a copyright in their individual parts, not in the combined whole.

A work is considered a joint work if it is prepared by two or more authors with the intention that their contributions be inseparable or interdependent parts of a unitary whole. For example, a songwriter and a lyricist who work together on the song are joint owners of the words and music together. The copyright in a joint work applies to the whole; it covers only the various contributions as part of the whole work. If there is no intention to combine the individual contributions into a unitary whole, each author has independent rights to his or her own contribution. However, minimal contributions are not sufficient to create a joint work or give the contributor an ownership interest.[35]

Generally, the intention of the authors at the time of the creation of their respective contributions is the key consideration in determining creation of a joint work. The authors are not required to work together in creation of the work to be a joint work. In fact, the authors may not even know each other or their respective contributions. It is sufficient if the contributions are intended to be embodied in a single work. The contributions can be made at different times without knowledge of the actual contributors.[36]

Courts and commentators disagree whether a contribution to a work of noncopyrightable material, such as ideas, qualifies as contribution so as to create a joint work. The trend has been toward requiring independently *copyrightable* contributions for joint authorship.[37]

The authors are co-owners of the joint work, each with an undivided interest. Each author has the right to exploit the copyright by using or licensing the copyright. Therefore, each author has equal rights to perform, display, or make and distribute copies of a work, or to license others to do so. An infringement action cannot be maintained against a co-owner or against a licensee of a co-owner. However, the joint owners must account for any profits derived from use or licensing of the joint work. Unless explicitly agreed otherwise, the authors have equal undivided shares in the copyright, independent of the quantity

---

[35]Picture Music, Inc. v. Bourne, Inc., 314 F. Supp. 640, 167 USPQ 348 (S.D.N.Y. 1970), *aff'd,* 457 F.2d 1213, 173 USPQ 449 (2d Cir.), *cert. denied,* 409 U.S. 997, 175 USPQ 577 (1972).

[36]*See* Edward B. Marks Music Corp. v. Jerry Vogel Music Co., 140 F.2d 266, 60 USPQ 257 (2d Cir. 1944); Donna v. Dodd, Mead & Co., 374 F. Supp. 429, 183 USPQ 166 (S.D.N.Y. 1974).

[37]Ashton-Tate Corp. v. Ross, 916 F.2d 516, 16 USPQ2d 1541 (9th Cir. 1990).

or quality of their respective contributions. Also, each owner can transfer his or her ownership rights independently of the other owners. However, a transferee obtains only the joint ownership rights of the transferor. Therefore, a transfer of one owner's rights in a joint work would transfer only an undivided interest in the whole.

(b) Works Made for Hire

The employer or other person for whom a work is prepared is considered the author of a work for hire and owns all of the rights comprised in the copyright. A "work made for hire" is specifically defined in 17 U.S.C. §101 as:

> (a) a work prepared by an employee within the scope of his or her employment; or
>
> (b) a work specially ordered or commissioned for use as a contribution to a collective work, as a part of a motion picture or other audiovisual work, as a translation, as a supplementary work, as a compilation, as an instructional text, as a test, as answer material for a test, or as an atlas, if the parties expressly agree in a written instrument signed by them that the work shall be considered a work made for hire.

Courts have held that a work that is not of a type listed in subsection (b) of §101 cannot be considered a work for hire even if a written agreement is signed by the parties.[38] The copyright for a work that does not qualify as work for hire is owned by the author or authors. It still can be assigned to the party who commissioned or ordered the work; it just initially vests with the actual creator of the work. (See Chapter 10, section 10.2 for a more detailed discussion of works made for hire.)

7.5 Transfers and Termination

(a) Duration of Copyright

Under the 1976 Act, the term of the copyright was extended to 50 years after the death of the author or last surviving author, if more

---

[38]Community for Creative Non-Violence v. Reid, 846 F.2d 1485, 6 USPQ2d 1990 (D.C. Cir. 1988), *aff'd*, 490 U.S. 730, 10 USPQ2d 1985, 16 Media L. Rep. 1769 (1989) (however, in *Reid* there was no written agreement).

than one.[39] For anonymous works or works for hire, the term is the earlier of 75 years from publication or 100 years from creation.[40] The Copyright Office has a system to record statements as to the date of death of an author or that the author is still living on a specified date. After the earlier of a period of 75 years from publication or 100 years from creation, a person who obtains from the Copyright Office a certification that the records do not indicate that the author is living, or died less than 50 years before, is entitled to a presumption that the term of the copyright has expired. Good-faith reliance on this presumption is a complete defense to any action for infringement.[41]

Prior to the 1976 Act, a copyright endured for a term of 28 years from the date of first publication, and could be renewed for an additional 28 years by the author, or the author's widow or widower, children, executors, or next of kin. The 1976 Act adjusted the term of existing copyrights to a total of 75 years. Copyrights that were in their first term as of January 1, 1978, had to be renewed as before, but for a second period of 47 years. Copyrights in their second term were automatically extended.

(b) Transfers

Ownership of a copyright can be transferred in whole or in part by any means as long as a written instrument, notice, or memorandum of the transfer is signed by the owner. Any of the exclusive rights of the copyright (see section 7.3) or subdivision of the exclusive rights can be transferred and owned separately.

A document transferring or otherwise pertaining to the copyright can be recorded in the Copyright Office. Recordation provides constructive notice to all persons of the facts stated in the recorded document, if it identifies the work and the work is registered. Recordation also provides for priority of conflicting transfers. The first transfer to be executed has priority if it is recorded within one month of its execution (two months if executed outside the United States), or before the second transfer to be executed is recorded. In addition, a nonexclusive license, whether recorded or not, prevails over a subsequent conflicting transfer

---

[39] 17 U.S.C. §302(a), (b).
[40] 17 U.S.C. §302(c).
[41] 17 U.S.C. §302(e).

if it was taken before execution of the transfer or before recordation of the transfer and without notice of it.

(c) Termination of Transfers

The renewal provisions of the 1909 Act were limited to the author or the author's heirs to protect authors from the financial powers of prospective purchasers, such as publishers. Often the value of a work is not determinable at the time of its creation or publication. Therefore, copyright law provided an opportunity to increase the power of the author at a later period, that is, after the first term. An assignee of the copyright could obtain the copyright for the renewal period only if the author renewed the copyright. However, publishers often required an assignment of the renewal term and an agreement by the author to renew the copyright at the time of the original agreement.[42]

To return to the original intention of the renewal requirement, and to reduce the burden on authors and their heirs from ignorant failures to renew the copyrights, the 1976 Act provided a procedure for termination of transfers of a copyright. A transfer executed by the author, other than by will, can be terminated during a five-year period starting 35 years after the grant. If the grant includes the right of publication, the period begins at the earlier of 35 years from the date of publication or 40 years after the grant.[43] Transfers can be terminated by the author, or if the author is dead, by the author's widow or widower, children, and grandchildren. Termination is effectuated by sending notice at least 2 and not more than 10 years before the effective date of the termination. Similarly, a transfer prior to January 1, 1978, can be terminated using the same procedure during the five-year period commencing 56 years after the original copyright date.

Upon termination of a transfer, all rights that were covered by the grant revert to those entitled to exercise the termination. A further grant, or an agreement to make a further grant, is valid only if made after the effective date of the termination. However, a grant or agreement can be made to the same party who had the grant before termination if made after the notice of termination is served.

---

[42]Mills Music, Inc. v. Snyder, 469 U.S. 153, 185, 224 USPQ 313, 326 (1985) (White, J., dissenting).

[43]17 U.S.C. §203(a)(3).

7.6 Formalities

(a) Notice

Works published before January 1, 1978, require a copyright notice upon publication or copyright is lost. From January 1, 1978, to March 1, 1989, copyright is not lost, as long as certain curative measures are followed. Under the Berne Convention (effective March 1, 1989), mandatory notice of copyright has been abolished. However, voluntary placement of a notice is advantageous, since it will defeat a claim of innocent infringement in mitigation of damages under 17 U.S.C. §401(d).

When copyright notice is required, the notice has three necessary parts: First, it must contain the copyright symbol, using the letter "C" in a circle (©), or the word "Copyright," or the abbreviation "Copr."[44] For sound recordings, the first part of the notice is the letter "P" in a circle (℗).[45] Second, the notice should include the year of first publication. Third, the notice should provide the name of the copyright owner, an abbreviation thereof, or a generally known alternative designation. In addition, the phrase "All Rights Reserved" should be added to protect the work in certain foreign countries that require this phrase.

The copyright notice should be positioned in a manner and location to give reasonable notice of the copyright claim to those viewing the work. The Register of Copyrights has provided regulations setting forth examples and methods to locate the copyright notice on various types of works. In some instances, failure to follow the regulations has resulted in a finding of failure of notice, without considering whether the location was reasonable.

There are three situations specified in the Copyright Act when omissions of the copyright notice for works published prior to the effective date of the BCIA (i.e., prior to March 1, 1989) do not invalidate the copyright.[46] First, if the notice was omitted from a relatively small number of copies distributed to the public, the copyright is not invalidated. Second, if the copyright owner has registered his or her copyright claim before the publication or seeks to register the

---

[44] 17 U.S.C. §401.

[45] 17 U.S.C. §402.

[46] 17 U.S.C. §405(a).

copyright claim within five years of the publication without copyright notice, the copyright is not invalidated. Reasonable efforts must be made to add a copyright notice to all copies that are distributed to the public in the United States after the omission has been discovered. Third, if there is an express requirement in writing by the copyright owner that the notice be placed on the work, and that this requirement conditions the authorization for a third party to distribute copies, the omission of notice by the third party does not invalidate the copyright.

Even if the omitted copyright notice is covered by §405(a), enforcement of the copyright can be adversely affected. A person who innocently infringes a copyright, relying on an authorized copy of the work without a copyright notice, incurs no liability for actual or statutory damages for any infringing acts committed before receiving actual notice that the copyright in the work has been registered. The innocent infringer must prove that he or she was misled by the omission of the notice.[47] If the notice was removed, destroyed, or obliterated on a copy without authorization, rather than being omitted, then protection under the statute is not affected, and the infringer is not considered "innocent."[48]

(b) Registration

Many people are confused or mistaken about the difference between obtaining a copyright and registering a copyright. After January 1, 1978, copyright arises and is automatically obtained by the author when the work is created and fixed in any tangible medium of expression. The copyright, which has then been "obtained," *may* be registered with the Copyright Office, but registration is not mandatory. Registration can be sought at any time during the subsistence of the copyright in a published or unpublished work. The owner of the copyright, or the owner of any exclusive right in the work, can register the copyright.

Although registration is not required to obtain the copyright after 1977, it *must* occur before bringing suit for copyright infringement. Only U.S. claimants must register the copyright in order to sue. Works that originated in other countries that belong to the Berne Union are not required to be registered prior to an infringement suit. However,

[47] 17 U.S.C. §405(b).
[48] 17 U.S.C. §405(c).

for foreign works created prior to the effective date of the BCIA, registration still remains a prerequisite. Additionally, statutory damages and attorneys' fees are available as remedies only if registration occurred within three months of the first publication date.

(i) Procedures

Registration occurs by submitting the appropriate application form together with a deposit of one or more copies of the work and the requisite fee to the U.S. Copyright Office. The Register of Copyrights has prescribed five classes of works in which copyright may be claimed: serial works (Form SE), nondramatic literary works (Form TX), works of the performing arts (Form PA), works of the visual arts (Form VA), and sound recordings (Form SR). Each class has a corresponding application form.

Typically, when a work has been published, registration is obtained by depositing two complete copies of the best edition of the published work, the appropriate application form, and a minimal filing fee. For unpublished works, one complete copy must be deposited. The application requires basic information, such as the name and address of the copyright claimant, the name and nationality or domicile of the author, a description of the author's contribution, a statement (if applicable) that the work is a "work for hire," a statement of how the claimant obtained ownership (if not the author), the title of the work or alternative titles, the year of creation, and the date and nation of first publication.

The application is examined to determine whether the work includes copyrightable subject matter and whether the legal and formal requirements have been met. After examination, the Copyright Office registers claims of copyright. It does not *grant* copyrights. The Office does not seek out other prior copyright deposits to determine prior registration or originality. It usually does not make fact findings regarding acts occurring outside the Copyright Office.

(ii) Registration in the Berne Era

Following implementation of the BCIA, the formalities appurtenant to obtaining a copyright registration have completely gone with one important exception: registration is a precondition to filing a copyright infringement lawsuit. United States–authored works must first be registered in order for a lawsuit to proceed. However, if the work is foreign originated, then registration is not required. The reason for this stems from the preclusion of formalities for Berne Union members. However, by forgoing registration, foreigners lose various procedural advantages, such as statutory damages and attorneys' fees.[49]

What if the registration application is unsuccessful? Section 411 allows the court action to continue as long as notice of the action along with a copy of the copyright complaint is provided to the Register of Copyrights. At that point, the Register may, at his or her option, become a party to the action with respect to the issue of registrability.

Several exceptions to the registration requirement exist. For works consisting of sounds or images where fixation occurs simultaneously with the works' transmission, registration is not a prerequisite to filing a lawsuit under 17 U.S.C. §411(b). However, the owner of the work must have previously served notice upon the infringer of his or her intention to obtain copyright and must complete registration within three months after the date of the first transmission of the work.

A further exception relates to moral rights. Since moral rights coexist with an author's personality, rather than being dependent upon the existence of a copyright, enforcement of moral rights does not require prior registration.[50]

---

[49] *See* 17 U.S.C. §§411, 412.

[50] 17 U.S.C. §411(a).

8
Enforcing Copyrights

8.1 Copying

Infringement of copyright is defined under 17 U.S.C. §501 as a violation of "the exclusive rights of the copyright owner." To establish copying, two elements must be shown: (1) ownership of a valid copyright, and (2) copying of the constituent elements of the work that are original.[1] Ownership of a valid copyright will be presumed when a plaintiff submits a copy of his or her copyright registration to the court. As a result, the burden of proof shifts to the defendant to prove that the copyright is not valid or waived.[2]

The copying element can be established by proving through direct evidence that there was copying of the work. Proof is through a preponderance of the evidence. If direct evidence of actual copying is not uncovered, and it frequently is not, copying can be established by two separate and essential components: (1) that the defendant had access to the copied work, and (2) that the defendant's work is a substantially similar copy of the plaintiff's work.

To establish access, most courts accept as sufficient evidence that a defendant had an opportunity to review the work. Successful proof of "opportunity" includes the defendant's possession of a copy of the work, a communication to the defendant of the contents of the plaintiff's

---

[1]Feist Publications, Inc. v. Rural Tel. Serv. Co., 111 S. Ct. 1282, 59 USLW 4251, 18 USPQ2d 1275, 18 Media L. Rep. 1889 (1991).

[2]Oboler v. Goldin, 714 F.2d 211, 220 USPQ 166 (2d Cir. 1983) (*per curiam*).

work, or evidence that the plaintiff's work has been widely disseminated without direct communication between the plaintiff and the defendant. Finally, the plaintiff may not need to prove access where the similarities are so striking (such as evidence of common errors between the plaintiff's and the defendant's works) that it can be reasonably inferred that the defendant could not have made his or her work without access.

Once access is established, substantial similarity must be determined by comparing the two works. Generally, the line marking what constitutes a substantially similar copy exists somewhere between one extreme, in which there are no similarities between the works, and the other extreme, of complete identity. The test is thus by necessity vague.[3]

Prior to making a comparison of substantial similarity, courts typically separate those parts of the plaintiff's work that constitute the copyrighted expression from those parts that represent only the underlying idea. In other words, the court extracts from the work those parts of the expression that can represent only an idea (known as merged idea/expression), which are not copyrightable, from those elements that can express an idea in multiple ways, which are copyrightable.[4]

Once the expression has been separated from the idea, a comparison between the two works involves what is widely known as the "ordinary observer test."[5] Although the test is applied somewhat differently in different circuits, the ordinary observer test typically encompasses two prongs. The first prong, known as the "extrinsic test," looks at the two works analytically, dissects the elements in those two works that are copyrightable, and then compares them. The second prong, known as the "intrinsic test," requires that the fact-finder stand in the place of an ordinary observer in order to decide whether there is substantial similarity in the overall expressions of the works.[6] As a general matter, if both prongs of the test indicate that the points of similarity exceed the points of dissimilarity, and the points of dissimilarity within the context of the plaintiff's work are of minimal importance,

---

[3]Peter Pan Fabrics v. Martin Weiner Corp., 274 F.2d 487, 124 USPQ 154 (2d Cir. 1960).

[4]*See* Atari, Inc. v. Amusement World, 547 F. Supp. 222, 227, 215 USPQ 929, 932–33 (D. Md. 1981).

[5]Dawson v. Hinshaw Music, 905 F.2d 731, 15 USPQ2d 1132 (4th Cir.), *cert. denied,* 498 U.S. 981 (1990).

[6]Sid & Marty Krofft Television Prods. v. McDonald's Corp., 562 F.2d 1157, 1164–65, 196 USPQ 97, 102 (9th Cir. 1977).

then there is infringement.[7] In some circumstances, even when there has been a relatively small amount of similarity, courts have concluded that it was copyright infringement.

8.2 Defenses

A number of defenses exist for defendants in a copyright action. Each of these is discussed below.

(a) Invalidity

A defendant can attack the validity of a copyright belonging to the plaintiff on five basic grounds: (1) that originality does not exist (see Chapter 7, section 7.2(b)); (2) that the subject matter of the work is not one that is protected by the copyright law (see Chapter 7, section 7.2(f)); (3) that the citizenship of the author does not permit a claim of copyright; (4) that Copyright Office formalities were not met (particularly if the work was created prior to March 1, 1989 (see Chapter 7, section 7.6)); and (5) that if the rights were transferred, those rights were not properly established (see Chapter 7, section 7.5). To attack validity, a defendant must overcome the presumption of validity that attaches to a copyright registration accepted by the Copyright Office.

An attack on the validity of copyrights can also occur by licensees under the copyright. This principle flows from patent law, under which licensees can challenge the validity of a license or the patent underlying that license.[8]

(b) Fair Use

Copyright was developed to grant authors the exclusive right to exploit their expressions commercially, including the right to prevent

---

[7] *See* Herbert Rosenthal Jewelry Corp. v. Honora Jewelry Co., 509 F.2d 64, 184 USPQ 264 (2d Cir. 1974) (*per curiam*).

[8] *See* Lear, Inc. v. Adkins, 395 U.S. 653, 162 USPQ 1 (1969) (which has been extended in some states to copyright licensees under Golden West Melodies v. Capitol Records, 79 Cal. Rptr. 442, 163 USPQ 429 (Cal. Ct. App. 1969)).

others from making copies of their works. Not long after the creation of statutory copyright, courts developed an equity doctrine known as "fair use." The policy underlying fair use was to avoid hindrances to society's ability to advance knowledge emanating from an author's copyrighted expressions of that knowledge. Fair use is generally determined under 17 U.S.C. §107 by a consideration of four factors: (1) the purpose and character of the use, including whether such use is of a commercial nature or is for nonprofit educational purposes; (2) the nature of the copyrighted work; (3) the amount and substantiality of the portion used in relation to the copyrighted work as a whole; and (4) the effect of the use upon the potential market for or value of the copyrighted work. The four factors are weighed before a determination of fair use is made.

Meeting the factors of §107 is a relatively difficult hurdle. To establish a §107 fair use, a company needs to prove the first factor by showing that it has transformed the product embodying the work into a "nonsuperseding" use. A nonsuperseding product has been variously interpreted by courts to mean a noncompetitive use, even if commercial. Alternatively, the company can establish that its use is *generally* noncommercial. With regard to the second factor, the nature of the copyrighted work, a successful defense will turn largely on whether the copyrighted work evidences a great deal of creativity or whether its subject matter is largely not creative. If the work implies a minimal level of creative content, such as a factual work or compilation of facts, then the second factor may be established. To meet the third factor, a company needs to show that the amount of material used is relatively small in proportion to the plaintiff's entire work. If the whole work has been copied, courts routinely deny fair use as a defense unless the use is *entirely noncommercial*. Finally, to meet the fourth factor, a defendant must show the negligible effect of its use on the potential market for the copyrighted work. Considerable copying under this factor will be instrumental in creating liability. However, if a minor amount of copying occurs, the effect on a potential market would be minimized—and the last factor is met.

A number of special situations always constitute fair use. For nonprofit libraries that are open to the public, fair use exists and copying is permitted, if the purpose for copying is intended for educational or archival preservation. Fair use for calligraphers and videotaping for private use also is available.

One of the most troublesome areas of fair use relates to photocopying. Section 108 of the Copyright Act provides special exemptions for certain types of photocopying (for qualifying libraries and archives).

Other than the §108 exemption, most forms of copying must meet the above-discussed four factors for fair use under §107; and under recent court decisions, most commercial uses would not appear to qualify.[9]

Parody has historically been given immunity from copyright law as being a fair use, without consideration of the various factors under §107. However, the factors and procedures for a determination of fair use for a parody are currently issues of disagreement and conflict. For now, parodies should be considered in the same manner as other claims of fair use.

(c) Innocent Infringement

Copyright law takes into account the intent of the defendant. While lack of requisite intent does not automatically shield defendants from infringement liability, it may reduce their damages.

Under 17 U.S.C. §405(b), the omission of a copyright notice from any work that was publicly distributed may seriously undermine a plaintiff's infringement claim if the defendant innocently copied from the work having relied upon the lack of notice. In such an instance, the defendant would incur *no liability* for actual or statutory damages for his or her infringing acts committed *before* receiving notice that registration of the work has been made. However, the defendant must still prove that he or she was actually misled by the omission of the notice. Nonmonetary damages will not be affected. Thus, injunctive relief will not be precluded and the innocent defendant can be prevented from committing further acts of infringement.

Other forms of innocent intent also can be established as a defense. For example, if the court concludes that the defendant was not aware that he or she was infringing, only a minimum award may be granted. In cases where the defendant copied from an unauthorized copy omitting the notice, courts have routinely granted minor damages. Other instances of innocent infringement occur when a work is based upon a third-party work and the defendant, in ignorance of the existence of the first party's work, copies. Again, the defendant is liable for infringement, but the damage award may be reduced.

---

[9]*See, e.g.,* American Geophysical Union v. Texaco, Inc., 802 F. Supp. 1, 23 USPQ2d 1561 *amended,* 802 F. Supp. 1, 24 USPQ2d 1796 (S.D.N.Y. 1992); Weissmann v. Freeman, 868 F.2d 1313 (2d Cir.), *cert. denied,* 493 U.S. 883 (1989).

(d) Abandonment, Estoppel, and Laches

A defendant also can establish that the plaintiff deliberately abandoned the copyright. To establish abandonment, evidence of an intent to abandon is necessary. Examples of satisfactory evidence of such intent include publication without notice, failure to prevent an infringement, or destruction of the copyrighted work.

The defendant can also raise estoppel and laches defenses. For estoppel to exist, the defendant must prove (1) that the plaintiff knew about the defendant's infringement, (2) that the plaintiff's failure to enforce the copyright was intentional, (3) that the defendant was ignorant of the plaintiff's true intent, and (4) that the defendant relied on the plaintiff's conduct to his or her detriment. A successful showing of estoppel may result in the abandonment of the copyright. Laches is based on proof of delay on the part of the copyright owner in enforcing his or her copyright and proof of prejudicial reliance on such delay by the defendant. However, unlike estoppel, laches will only prejudice the plaintiff from that defendant who actually raises the defense and may only be effective against an innocent infringer. Moreover, laches is effective only with respect to reducing monetary damages. Laches will not destroy the copyright against other defendants.

(e) Misuse

As in patent law, misuse or overextension of the copyright is a defense to infringement. If the copyright owner extends the copyright to noncopyrighted subject matter, courts will deny relief from an infringement action.[10] Examples of misuse include illegal tying arrangements where noncopyrighted products are tied into the plaintiff's copyright in a license agreement and noncompetition clauses that are unreasonable in scope and in time. The misuse defense renders the copyright unenforceable until the misuse is cured. Thus, even if the activity constituting the misuse does not involve a particular infringement defendant, that defendant can still use misuse as a defense.

---

[10] *See, e.g.*, F.E.L. Publications v. Catholic Bishop of Chicago, 214 USPQ 409 (7th Cir. 1982).

(f) Equitable Defenses

A variety of equity-based defenses exists under the doctrine of unclean hands. For example, claims that the copyright owner withheld information from the Copyright Office on his or her registration which would have affected the registrability of the work, such as facts as to originality, might prevent a damage judgment for infringement. Also, a copyright holder who disseminates false or misleading accusations to customers of an alleged infringer may be denied recovery. However, these situations are extremely serious and are usually only available when there is evidence of fraud or misrepresentation that goes to the essence of the copyright action. If the activities are not directly related to the controversy, a defense of unclean hands will normally be denied.

8.3 Remedies

Remedies for copyright infringement fall into six categories: (1) monetary recovery, (2) statutory damages, (3) injunctive relief, (4) special governmental relief, (5) attorneys' fees, and (6) criminal sanctions. A brief discussion of the various remedies is provided below.

(a) Monetary Recovery

Two types of monetary damages are available as a result of a copyright infringement under 17 U.S.C. §504(b): the actual damages suffered by the plaintiff *and* the defendant's actual profits attributable to the infringement. Nonetheless, the conjunctive language of §504(b) is, in reality, only available if one form of compensation does not compensate adequately for the other. Hence, where actual damages do not include a sufficient measure of profits, then, and only then, will profits become available.[11] Typical computations for actual damages include the injury to the market value of the copyrighted work. One standard measure for determining market value is what the profits for the plaintiff would have been but for the defendant's infringement. In

[11]17 U.S.C. §504(b).

the event that no sales have occurred, then courts will look at other factors, such as the price of the actual infringing products.

With regard to proof of an infringer's profits, §504(b) indicates that the copyright owner is required only to present proof of the infringer's gross revenue. It is the alleged infringer's burden to then prove his or her deductible expenses "and the elements of profit attributable to factors other than the copyrighted work."[12] One issue that arises is whether the profits are directly or indirectly derived from the act of infringement. For example, a person who infringes the copyright in one computer program may be selling additional programs jointly with the infringing program. The infringer indirectly profits from the sales of noninfringing programs to the extent that those sales would not have occurred without the sales of the infringing program. If the profits are indirect, then a plaintiff may have a more difficult time establishing that he or she is entitled to the full amount of the infringer's profits.

(b) Statutory Damages

As an alternative to actual damages and profits, the plaintiff may choose statutory damages under §504(c) at any time before final judgment. The election applies to all infringements in the action. The statutory damages relate to any one work infringed where individual or joint and several liability has been established. The range of statutory damages is from $500 to a maximum of $20,000. Factors that affect the amount of the statutory award include: (1) fair market value of the plaintiff's work, (2) amount the defendant saved by copying, and (3) deterrent value of the award.

If the court finds that the infringement was committed willfully, it has the discretion to raise the award. Willful infringement constitutes a situation in which the defendant has been notified that his or her conduct constitutes copyright infringement and he or she nonetheless continues to infringe without a good-faith belief to the contrary. As a result, the statutory damage award can be raised to $100,000. By the same token, if the infringer sustains the burden of proof that he or she was not aware and had no reason to believe that his or her acts constituted infringement, the court may reduce the award of statutory damages to a minimum of $200. Finally, statutory damages may be remitted if

[12] 17 U.S.C. §504(b).

the infringer reasonably believes he or she has a fair use defense and he or she is (1) an employee or agent of a nonprofit educational institution, library, or archive, and (2) acts within the scope of his or her employment.

Statutory damages are available only for acts of infringement of (a) an unpublished work when infringement occurs after the date of registration, or (b) a published work when (i) infringement occurs after the date of registration, and (ii) the registration is filed within three months after the first publication of the work.[13] As previously discussed, however, registration is not a precondition for statutory damages for violations of the author's moral rights or for certain works whose first transmission occurred prior to copyright registration.

(c) Injunctive Relief

17 U.S.C. §502 provides a plaintiff with injunctive relief for acts of infringement. Section 502(a) states that "[a]ny court having jurisdiction of a civil action arising under this title may . . . grant temporary and final injunctions on such terms as it may deem reasonable to prevent or restrain infringement of a copyright." A successful plaintiff is routinely able to receive a permanent injunction. Injunctions are available against all defendants except the U.S. government.

Generally, preliminary injunctive relief is available if the moving party establishes either the possibility of irreparable injury and a likelihood of success on the merits or sufficiently serious questions going to the merits. The moving party also must establish that the balance of hardships is in his or her favor and that a preliminary injunction is in the public interest.

(d) Other Relief

Beyond monetary awards and injunctions, the court has at its disposal the ability to request impoundment and disposition of the infringing articles. Under 17 U.S.C. §503(a), a court may order impoundment, on such terms as it believes reasonable, of any copies or phonorecords ("copies") that have been made or used in violation of

[13] 17 U.S.C. §412.

the copyright owner's rights. In addition to the copies, the means for making those copies may also be impounded. Section 503(a) states that all plates, molds, matrices, masters, tapes, film negatives, or other articles by means of which such copies may be reproduced can be impounded. Under §503(b), a court may also order destruction of all copies along with the means for making those copies.

The Copyright Royalty Tribunal as well as the U.S. Customs Service can also provide remedies. The Copyright Royalty Tribunal (which is an independent agency in the legislative branch) administers the compulsory licenses imposed on defendants for infringing nondramatic musical works and required for jukebox performances of nondramatic musical works. Also, compulsory licenses may be provided for cable television and educational broadcasts or secondary transmissions by satellite carriers.

As to Customs, the Secretary of the Treasury (which has jurisdiction over the U.S. Customs Service) can make regulations that prohibit the importation of works that would otherwise infringe U.S. law as being made illegally abroad (pirated works). Customs can seize pirated works for two reasons: (1) the copyright owner may file with Customs a certificate of his or her registration that, upon approval, causes Customs, within its discretion, to detain imported works that may infringe a U.S. copyright; or (2) the copyright owner can, upon issuance of a court injunction, obtain assistance from the Customs Service by submitting a certified copy of the work. Customs then uses the submitted work as a template from which to judge potential infringing works.

(e) Attorneys' Fees

Unless plaintiffs receive their copyright registration (under §§411 and 412) within three months of first publication or after registration for unpublished works, they are precluded from seeking attorneys' fees.[14] Even if a plaintiff can seek attorneys' fees, they are not automatically granted. The issue of attorney compensation is a difficult one; however, a typical rule is that such fees are available when the plaintiff can establish a degree of culpability on the defendant's part, such as where the defendant acted in bad faith or where he or she deliberately

---

[14] 17 U.S.C. §505.

and willfully infringed. It appears, however, that attorneys' fees are largely discretionary with each court.

(f) Criminal Sanctions

Section 506(a) of the Copyright Act provides that any person who infringes a copyright willfully and for the purposes of commercial advantage or private financial gain is liable for a criminal offense. The penalty imposed for criminal acts is a fine up to $25,000 and/or imprisonment for not more than two years if the offense involves illegal reproduction and distribution of less than 100 copies (or 7 motion pictures) in 180 days. If more than 100 but less than 1,000 copies (or between 7 and 65 motion pictures) are reproduced or distributed in 180 days, a fine of up to $250,000 and/or a prison term of up to two years can be imposed. However, if more copies are distributed in 180 days, the imprisonment term may be increased to not more than five years.

9

Trade Secrets and Confidential Information

9.1 Protection of Trade Secrets

(a) What Is a Trade Secret?

Trade secret law principles are based upon the common law of torts. Tort law is intended to protect individuals from improper interference by others. With respect to trade secrets, tort law prevents the disclosure and use of information that is discovered by improper means or through a breach of a confidence. The principles of trade secret law are set forth in §757 of the Restatement (First) of Torts (1939), which compiled and condensed the common law basis for tort law. Section 757 states that

> one who discloses or uses another's trade secret, without privilege to do so, is liable to the other if (a) he discovered the secret by improper means, or (b) his disclosure or use constitutes a breach of confidence reposed in him by the other in disclosing the secret to him.

The Second Restatement of Torts did not include a section on trade secrets because it was believed that trade secret law had become based less on tort theories than on general legal principles arising from other statutes. In fact, 34 states and the District of Columbia have adopted the Uniform Trade Secrets Act (UTSA),[1] which codified many of the principles previously found in the common law of trade secrets. The UTSA was approved by the National Conference of Commissioners on Uniform State Laws in 1979. Like the common law protection set forth in §757 of the Restatement, the UTSA prevents misappropriation of trade secrets. Misappropriation is defined as

> (i) acquisition of a trade secret of another by a person who knows or has reason to know that the trade secret was acquired by improper means; or
>
> (ii) disclosure or use of a trade secret of another without express or implied consent by a person who
>
>> (A) used improper means to acquire knowledge of the trade secret or
>>
>> (B) at the time of disclosure or use, knew or had reason to know that his knowledge of the trade secret was (I) derived from or through a person who had utilized improper means to acquire it; (II) acquired under circumstances giving rise to a duty to maintain its secrecy or limit its use; or (III) derived from or through a person who owed a duty to the person seeking relief to maintain its secrecy or limit its use; or
>>
>> (C) before material change of his or her position, knew or had reason to know that it was a trade secret and that knowledge of it had been acquired by accident or mistake.

Misappropriation of trade secrets is not the subject of federal law. Rather, it is covered by common law or state statutory law. Thus, the law of the particular state at issue should be consulted when determining whether there is a misappropriation.

First and foremost, a trade secret is information that is valuable because it is maintained as a secret. Trade secrets are protected only so long as they remain substantially secret.[2] Comment (b) of §757 of the Restatement of Torts sets out a definition of a trade secret to include "any formula, pattern, device, or a compilation of information which is used in one's business and which would give him an opportunity to obtain an advantage over competitors who do not know or use it." The UTSA is somewhat broader in that it removes the limitation that the secret be "used in one's business." The UTSA defines a trade secret as "information, including a formula, pattern, compilation, program, device, method, technique, or a process, that: (i) derives independent

---

[1] 14 U.L.A. 433 (1985).

[2] Houser v. Snap-On Tools Corp., 202 F. Supp. 181, 132 USPQ 368 (D. Md. 1962).

economic value, actual or potential, from not being generally known to, and not being readily ascertainable by proper means by, other persons who can obtain economic value from its disclosure or use; and (ii) is the subject of efforts that are reasonable under the circumstances to maintain its secrecy."[3]

Unlike other forms of intellectual property, the information protected as a trade secret need not be original or novel. Furthermore, trade secret protection does not give the owner the exclusive right to use the information. Others may also obtain and use a secret as long as improper means are not used to obtain it. Indeed, several persons may have identical rights in the same trade secret as long as the information is not generally known.

Furthermore, trade secrets apply to information that is useful in a specific business. Information that is generally known in one area or field may be protectable as a secret in another area. For example, the use of a nonstick substance developed for and generally known and used in the aerospace industry took on a new protectable status when applied to housewares.

(b) Types of Protectable Information

Trade secrets apply to a broad range and many types of information. Any information that has economic value from being maintained as a secret is protectable. Both the Restatement and the UTSA set forth an extensive set of information to which trade secrets are applicable, including: formulas, patterns, compilations, programs, devices, methods, techniques, and processes. The courts have noted that "no category of information is excluded from protection as a trade secret because of its inherent qualities."[4]

Generally, trade secret information relates to the method for production of goods such as a machine or formula for production of an article. However, a large number of other areas are also eligible for protection.

Business-type information such as methods, techniques, know-how, procedures, forms, and programs is protectable in proper circumstances. Methods of doing business are protectable to the extent that

---

[3]UTSA §1(4)(i), 14 U.L.A. at 438.

[4]Clark v. Bunker, 453 F.2d 1006, 1009, 172 USPQ 420, 422 (9th Cir. 1972).

they are not known or visible to others. Internal manuals for operations and procedures relating to the business can be protected. In addition, forms, techniques, and programs used in the operation of the business are eligible for trade secret protection. One court has held that a unique marketing program can be maintained as a trade secret.[5]

Data relating to customers, merchandising, cost, and pricing are also protectable. Although cost and pricing are generally publicly known, in certain industries this information has specific economic value when maintained as a secret. For example, in the financial and insurance industries, where cost and prices are based on statistical assumptions, income from various investments and many other factors, the information and procedures, mathematical models, and statistical assumptions used by a specific company are protectable as trade secrets.[6]

Customer lists are often a closely guarded trade secret to the extent that they are not readily discernible outside the company's business. For example, where a customer must first be sold on a new product or on the concepts and principles of a product, and only a small percentage of potential customers actually purchase a product, the customer list may be protectable.[7] However, customer lists obtained from general advertising or from contacting readily identifiable prospective customers generally are not protected.[8] But even if the customer list itself is not a trade secret, specific information of the customer (such as the important contact in a large company or special customer needs) may be protectable.

Information that is generally known may also be protectable as a trade secret when it is combined in an original manner. The specific implementation involving a particular combination of general concepts can amount to a trade secret.[9] Trade secret protection may be used for knowledge of the best combination of processes, methods, tools, and materials.[10]

Finally, computer software is accepted as a protectable trade secret. (Trade secret protection of computer software is more fully discussed in Chapter 11, section 11.4.)

---

[5]Foods Plus v. Frankel, 387 N.Y.S.2d 450 (N.Y. App. Div. 1986).

[6]In re Belth v. Insurance Dep't, 406 N.Y.S.2d 649 (N.Y. Sup. Ct. 1977).

[7]State Farm Mut. Auto. Ins. Co. v. Dempster, 344 P.2d 821 (Cal. Ct. App. 1959).

[8]Leo Silfen, Inc. v. Cream, 29 N.Y.2d 387, 389 (1972).

[9]Cybertek Computer Prods. v. Whitfield, 203 USPQ 1020, 1024 (Cal. Super. Ct. 1977).

[10]Imperial Chem. Indus. v. National Distillers & Chem. Corp., 342 F.2d 737, 144 USPQ 695 (2d Cir. 1965).

(c) Maintenance of Secrecy

As noted above, the principal identifying element of a trade secret is that the information to be protected is maintained as a secret. The definition of a trade secret, set forth in comment (b) of the Restatement, specifically notes that "[t]he subject matter of a trade secret must be secret." Matters of public knowledge or of general knowledge in an industry cannot be appropriated by one as his or her secret. Matters that are completely disclosed by the goods that one markets cannot be his or her secret.

This does not mean that absolute secrecy is required. Information would have little use if it could not be disclosed to others in a business or organization that could make use of the trade secret information. The UTSA notes that the trade secret need only be subject to "efforts that are reasonable under the circumstances to maintain its secrecy."[11]

Whether measures to maintain the secrecy are reasonable depends upon the necessary disclosure to use the secret adequately, the extent to which the information is disclosed to others and their relationship to the owner, and the measures taken to protect the secrecy. Generally, secrecy is maintained through the use of confidential relationships either expressed or implied (see section 9.2(a)). Thus, information disclosed to others outside the company maintains its protection as a trade secret as long as it is made known that the disclosed information is confidential and cannot be disseminated. In various circumstances, it may be necessary to disclose trade secret information to government agencies when obtaining necessary governmental approvals or seeking to obtain a government contract. The government agencies generally establish procedures to protect a company's trade secrets so that the information is not disclosed to the public. It is important that these procedures be followed carefully. If not, there is a risk that trade secret protection will be lost.

(d) Loss of Trade Secret Protection

Trade secret protection can be lost when the information becomes publicly known either through disclosure by the trade secret holder or by discovery by others. Any public disclosure, even if accidental or inadver-

---

[11]UTSA §1(4)(ii), 14 U.L.A. at 438.

tent, destroys the secrecy and the protection.[12] Therefore, it is important that all disclosures be made only when necessary and within a confidential relationship. One of the factors that courts use to determine whether a trade secret exists is the extent to which the information has been disseminated within a company. Despite the confidential relationship of an employer and employee, indiscriminate disclosure to many employees who have no need for the information can result in a determination that the information is not being maintained in secret. In addition, disclosure even to a couple of people outside of a confidential relationship may result in loss of trade secret protection.

Trade secret protection also can be lost by subsequent knowledge and use by others of the information considered to be secret. Trade secret protection, whether under the common law or under the UTSA, prohibits only the acquisition of information by improper means. The UTSA defines improper means to include theft, bribery, misrepresentation, breach of a duty to maintain secrecy, and espionage. Any other methods of obtaining the information are proper and not prohibited. For example, subsequent discovery and use of the information through independent efforts does not constitute misappropriation. Once others know or use the information, trade secret protection is lost.

Trade secret protection can also be lost through sales of products that embody the trade secret.[13] However, this applies only to trade secrets that can be determined from the actual product being sold. If the trade secret relates to the methods or processes for creating the product, and is not determinable from the final product, then sales of the product do not limit the trade secret.

Reverse engineering constitutes proper means for obtaining trade secret information.[14] Reverse engineering refers to dismantling a product to determine how it is designed, how it operates, and any methods or processes of forming the product. For example, chemical analysis of a material can be used to discover the trade secret makeup of the material. Under federal preemption law, contracts and trade secret law cannot be used to obtain patentlike protection for products by limiting competitors' rights to reverse engineer the products or to copy information in the public domain.[15]

---

[12]Defiance Button Mach. Co. v. C&C Metal Prods. Corp., 759 F.2d 1053, 225 USPQ 797 (2d Cir.), *cert. denied,* 474 U.S. 844 (1985).

[13]Space Aero Prods. Co. v. R.E. Darling Co., 208 A.2d 74, 145 USPQ 356 (Md.), *cert. denied,* 382 U.S. 843, 147 USPQ 541 (1965).

[14]Kewanee Oil Co. v. Bicron Corp., 416 U.S. 470, 181 USPQ 673 (1974).

[15]Bonito Boats, Inc. v. Thunder Craft Boats, 489 U.S. 141, 9 USPQ2d 1847 (1989).

Parties who are accused of misappropriating trade secrets often argue that there should be no liability because it is possible that the trade secret can be discovered through reverse engineering. This argument is generally unsuccessful, particularly where the reverse engineering would take considerable time and effort. A court may, however, consider these circumstances in deciding the duration of an injunction.

Finally, issuance of a patent constitutes public disclosure of all the information contained in the patent. Therefore, any information previously considered to be a trade secret that is disclosed in the patent loses its protection as a trade secret. Under patent law, the inventor is provided with the exclusive right to practice the patent for a 17-year period in exchange for a public disclosure of the information and free access and use of the information at the end of the exclusive period. A patent, however, reveals only the trade secrets that are contained in the patent. Any other trade secret information relating to the product or process that is not disclosed in the patent can still be protected under trade secret law. Likewise, if trade secret information is contained in a patent application, but an actual patent does not issue, trade secret protection is still available because patent applications are not released to the public unless and until the actual patent issues.

(e) Protection of Trade Secrets

Like most forms of intellectual property, trade secrets are protected by suits for infringement or misappropriation. The trade secret owner can obtain damages for losses caused by misappropriation, that is, unauthorized use or disclosure of the trade secret. Damages can include any unjust enrichment received by the misappropriator in addition to losses to a trade secret owner. Under the UTSA, a court may also award up to treble damages for willful and malicious misappropriation of trade secrets. Under the UTSA, the trade secret owner can also obtain attorneys' fees necessary to protect its trade secret rights. Therefore, trade secrets receive much broader protection in those states that have adopted the UTSA.

Oftentimes more important than a damage recovery, the trade secret owner can also obtain injunctive relief against actual or threatened misappropriation of trade secrets. Since the trade secret is protected only so long as it is maintained in secrecy, the ability to prevent others from improperly disclosing the trade secret is an important right for protection of the trade secret. An injunction does not necessarily continue indefinitely. Under the UTSA, once a trade secret becomes generally known, a party subject to an injunction may apply to the court to have the injunction terminated.[16] In addition, if the trade secret could have been obtained by legitimate means, the court can issue an injunction for a reasonable period of time to counter any advantage obtained from the misappropriation. In addition to permanent injunctive relief, preliminary injunctions and temporary restraining orders are available to prevent disclosure of trade secrets during pendency of litigation. The usual elements necessary for a preliminary injunction—likelihood of success on the merits, irreparable harm, balance of hardships, and public interest—need to be established.

In trade secret litigation, the burden is on the plaintiff, that is, the trade secret owner, to show by a preponderance of the evidence that a trade secret exists and that misappropriation has occurred or is likely to occur. In showing the existence of a trade secret, the owner must prove each of the elements of a trade secret. The owner must show that an explicitly defined trade secret has a value because it is not generally known or used, that the information is not generally known or used by others in the field, and that the owner has taken steps to maintain the secrecy of the information. In addition, the owner must show that the trade secret was acquired by improper means or that its disclosure or use would be contrary to a duty to maintain its secrecy or limit its use.

The limitation that the secret be explicitly defined is an important element of trade secret litigation. Trade secrets apply only to specific information that has value from not being generally known. General ideas and concepts cannot be protected. Often, trade secret litigation results from the improper use by departing employees of information that was gained during the employment. In addition to trade secret information, employees gain experience and know-how generally applicable to their profession. As with covenants not to compete,[17] the courts are loathe to prevent or interfere with a person working in his or her profession. Therefore, the court requires that the trade secret be explicitly defined rather than described simply as general concepts.

When a formal confidentiality or licensing agreement exists, trade secret protection may be obtained through a suit for breach of contract in addition to tort claims of misappropriation. Although the UTSA

---

[16]UTSA §2, 14 U.L.A. at 449.

[17]For information on covenants not to compete, see ABA SECTION OF LABOR AND EMPLOYMENT LAW, COVENANTS NOT TO COMPETE: A STATE-BY-STATE SURVEY (P. Jerome Richey, ed., BNA Books, 1991).

explicitly preempted common law trade secret rights, the Act also exempted contractual remedies from its coverage.[18] Therefore, a confidentiality agreement or license can provide additional contractual rights to the trade secret owner in addition to providing a duty to keep information confidential and maintaining the required secrecy. Contractual rights may be a stronger weapon than a tort suit. If two parties mutually agree that certain information will be considered a trade secret, many courts will enforce this agreement even if the trade secret owner does not establish each element of a trade secret.

Since trade secrets are considered a form of property, they are also subject to the prohibitions of the criminal law relating to theft. Nineteen states have passed specific statutes as part of their criminal code that make theft of articles embodying trade secrets a crime. In two other states, the definitions in general theft statutes have been amended to include trade secret materials. Similarly, for the remaining states, the general criminal statutes may be broad enough to cover theft of trade secrets without the need for explicit inclusion. Generally, the criminal provisions are slightly less broad than civil protections. Criminal law does not protect the information, per se, that constitutes a trade secret. Rather, articles embodying the trade secret are protected, but the article itself need not have any real value. Therefore, a person who memorized a secret formula would not be subject to criminal sanctions, but one who stole a copy of the formula would.

Federal criminal law is also applicable to trade secrets. With respect to interstate transactions, federal law prohibits the transportation, sale, or receipt of stolen goods, wares, merchandise, securities, or monies having a value of $5,000 or more.[19] "Goods" is interpreted broadly enough to cover articles embodying trade secret information. Furthermore, the value limitation would be applied to the stolen material, including the trade secret information, rather than to the intrinsic value of the article. One court has explicitly held that with respect to recorded information, "[i]t is the idea, not its material paper embodiment, which is valuable."[20]

Therefore, both state and federal criminal law provide additional protections for physical embodiments of trade secret information. These laws evidence the strong public policy toward protection of trade secrets.

---

[18]UTSA §7, 14 U.L.A. at 463.

[19]18 U.S.C. §§2314–2315.

[20]United States v. Lester, 282 F.2d 750 (3d Cir. 1960), *cert. denied,* 364 U.S. 937 (1961) (stolen geophysical maps).

9.2 Establishing Requisite Secrecy

The single most important element of a trade secret is that it remains secret. The owner must take appropriate steps to prevent public disclosure of the information. The owner must also appropriately notify those to whom the trade secret is disclosed of the nature and extent of the information, that it is trade secret, and that it needs to be maintained in secrecy. Since the information must be disclosed to others for more effective use, such as to employees, licensees, or other business partners, the trade secret owner must control and limit the extent of disclosure. Generally, disclosure is limited through the use of confidential relationships with those receiving the information and through various security measures to prevent disclosure.

(a) Confidential Relationships

Confidential relationships may be created either by express agreement or by the nature of the relationship between the parties. Common law often imposes an obligation to maintain the secrecy of information based upon a duty of good faith. Quite often, the relevant relationship is that of employer and employee. The courts have reasoned that an employer has placed trust in the employee and has provided disclosures of information that allow the employee to operate or complete his or her employment. In exchange for the employer's disclosure of this information, the courts have inferred an obligation to maintain the secrecy of information that extends beyond the term of employment. This obligation prevents the employee from using or disclosing information during or after employment to the detriment of the owner or employer.[21] As explained above, in order to protect the ability of the employee to continue to operate within his or her profession, the courts require that the trade secret be explicitly defined and understood.

There are many other situations where courts will find the existence of a confidential relationship. Directors of corporations, although not employees, have a fiduciary duty to the corporation. This duty serves to create a confidential relationship that protects trade secrets that might

[21]In re Uniservices, 517 F.2d 492 (7th Cir. 1975).

be disclosed to them. Partners or joint venturers also have fiduciary duties that create a confidential relationship.

Similarly, independent sales agents rather than an internal sales organization are sometimes used to market products. As employees, internal sales agents would be limited by their confidential relationship with the employer but the law also implies a relationship with independent sales agents. Confidential information that is provided to them in connection with their sales of the manufacturer's products is also protected.

Often, in the sale of a product or business, some information must be transferred before a formal written agreement is completed. In such situations, the law will infer a confidential relationship and will prevent the recipient from using or disclosing trade secret information. Prospective sales situations include information transferred between a prospective licensor and licensee, between a vendor and vendee of a business, and between a supplier and purchaser of a custom product.

Large corporations often use independent contractors to manufacture portions of a total product. These independent contractors may have a confidential relationship with the corporation that protects any disclosed trade secrets. The independent contractor, however, must know or have reason to know that the information is confidential. Information that is freely provided to the independent contractor becomes publicly disclosed and loses its trade secret protection.

Express confidentiality agreements, even with employees, provide a stronger basis for protecting trade secrets. In addition to explicitly defining trade secrets, the express agreement provides notice to the other party of the nature and extent of a claimed trade secret. Moreover, confidentiality agreements may be important evidence to help establish that a trade secret owner has taken appropriate steps to prevent disclosure of the secret. The owner would be well advised to include in contracts with employees, subcontractors, licensees, and in some cases, depending upon the business, with customers, terms establishing that the information to be provided to the other party or to which the other party will be exposed constitutes a trade secret. Such language can prevent the loss of a trade secret through inadvertent disclosure of information that may not have been necessary to use the information effectively. Such inadvertent disclosure without an express agreement could result in loss of the trade secret if a court determined that inadequate measures had been taken to prevent disclosure of the secret.

In addition to explicit trade secret protection, contracts may include terms preventing the other party from competing with the trade secret owner for some discrete period of time. Courts are not favorably disposed to noncompetition agreements and often do not enforce agreements that are not reasonable in scope or duration. The existence of a confidential relationship and the transfer or disclosure of information that is maintained as a trade secret, however, provide significant support to enforcement of a reasonable noncompetition agreement.[22] Noncompetition agreements are discussed in more detail in Chapter 10, section 10.3(a).

Care should be taken in drafting written confidentiality agreements so that they appropriately define the nature and scope of the confidential information to be protected. As noted above, under the UTSA, contract remedies are not limited by the Act and will govern the rights and obligations of the parties. Failure to provide appropriate protection can result in a conclusion that the protection was not intended. For example, in *Filmon Process Corp. v. Spellright Corp.*,[23] the contract between the parties included a term that the defendant was to "keep the matter confidential." This term was held solely to limit the publication or disclosure of the secret process, and not to constitute a limitation against its use.

In addition, restrictive limitations in an agreement may have unforeseen consequences. For example, a license agreement may be construed to bring a relationship within the scope of a state franchise or dealership statute. This would impose unintended obligations on the licensor and/or licensee. Also, the terms of an agreement may be considered to be so restrictive that it could be construed as an attempt to monopolize a market in violation of §2 of the Sherman Act.[24]

(b) Security Measures

Reasonable security measures must be taken in order to maintain the trade secret nature of information. Security measures need not, however, be extreme. The UTSA clearly states that the information must be subject to efforts that are "reasonable under the circumstances to maintain its secrecy."[25] The courts do not require extreme or unduly

---

[22]E.L. Conwell & Co. v. Gutberlet, 298 F. Supp. 623 (D. Md. 1969), *aff'd,* 429 F.2d 527 (4th Cir. 1970); Foti v. Cook, 263 S.E.2d 430 (Va. 1980).

[23]274 F. Supp. 312, 317, 155 USPQ 635, 640 (D.D.C. 1967), *aff'd,* 404 F.2d 1351, 158 USPQ 533 (D.C. Cir. 1968).

[24]15 U.S.C. §2.

[25]UTSA §1(4)(ii), 14 U.L.A. at 438.

expensive procedures to be taken to prevent or protect against flagrant industrial espionage.[26] While the cost of protection required to maintain the secret will vary relative to the value of the information, the failure to take reasonable security measures compels a conclusion that secrecy was not intended, and will result in loss of trade secret protection.[27]

The most basic security measures relate to exercising care not to reveal information considered to be a trade secret in the ordinary course of business. The information must not be revealed through specification sheets, drawings, or diagrams distributed to customers, advertising copy, information and annual reports, speeches, or articles relating to the business, etc. Public disclosure in these ways may result in loss of the trade secret. However, in at least one case, distribution of a maintenance manual containing these types of information to equipment owners was held not to be a general public disclosure that forfeited protection of trade secret information.[28]

Public disclosure does not mean that the information is generally published or provided to a large number of people. Public disclosure simply means that the information was provided to one or more persons outside of a confidential relationship and/or persons in a confidential relationship who did not require the information. In addition, unrestricted access to information may also constitute a public disclosure. For example, permitting visitors or customers unrestricted access to a location where a trade secret process is being used can be considered a failure to maintain reasonable security measures, particularly if the observer would understand the observed trade secret. Of course, trade secret protection will not be lost if the visitor signs a confidentiality or nondisclosure agreement before access is given.

Frequently implemented security measures include: written security agreements, posted reminders, periodic oral or written reminders of confidential and protected information; posting warnings where secret information is used or stored; restricting access to information or to locations where secret information is stored or used on a need-to-know basis; marking documents containing trade secret information as confidential; dividing a process into various subparts so that only

---

[26] E.I. DuPont DeNemours & Co. v. Christopher, 431 F.2d 1012, 166 USPQ 421, 167 USPQ 1 (5th Cir. 1970), *cert. denied,* 400 U.S. 1024, 168 USPQ 385 (1971).

[27] *See, e.g.,* K-2 Ski Co. v. Head Ski Co., 506 F.2d 471, 183 USPQ 724 (9th Cir. 1974); United States Plywood Corp. v. General Plywood Corp., 370 F.2d 500, 152 USPQ 80 (6th Cir. 1966), *cert. denied,* 389 U.S. 820, 155 USPQ 768 (1967).

[28] Data Gen. Corp. v. Digital Computer Controls, 297 A.2d 437 (Del. 1972).

information relating to the relevant subpart is provided to employees; keeping records, data, information, and formulas in a secure place with limited access; monitoring the use of information; and monitoring speeches, articles, brochures, and other public disseminations of information.

Finally, a trade secret owner must take measures to prevent inadvertent disclosures of information in court proceedings. Care should be taken to limit the scope of discovery and to initiate protective measures such as obtaining a court protective order. In litigation, access to confidential information should be limited to outside counsel or experts and others with a need to know and by explicit agreements that the information shall be used only for purposes of litigation and not disclosed to others.

9.3 Unsolicited Ideas

(a) Risks in Receiving Ideas

Under §757 of the Restatement, a marketing idea or concept was not eligible for trade secret protection. The Restatement required that information be continuously used in one's business for trade secret protection. Therefore, an idea that had not yet been used in business was not eligible for trade secret protection when submitted to another. Under the UTSA, however, the use requirement has been eliminated. Therefore, ideas that are confidentially disclosed may be eligible for trade secret protection.[29] Even in non-UTSA states, a charge of misappropriation may be brought if the company later introduces a product that appears to use the unsolicited idea.

Companies often receive submissions of ideas relating to their business from outside persons, often with an implicit expectation of compensation. Generally, the submitter has developed an idea that he or she is unable to use himself or herself effectively. Therefore, he or she submits it to a corporation doing business in the field. The procedures by which these ideas are received, reviewed, and possibly used can affect

---

[29]American Potato Dryers, Inc. v. Peters, 184 F.2d 165, 86 USPQ 499 (4th Cir. 1950), *cert. denied,* 340 U.S. 930, 88 USPQ 569 (1951).

whether some form of compensation will be due to the submitter. Frequently, the idea is similar to others that have been submitted or to ideas that are already under consideration by the company. Later, when the recipient company begins using its own idea, the submitter sues for wrongful use of his or her idea divulged in confidence and characterizes the idea as a trade secret.

Although it has been suggested that such ideas are more appropriately considered under the separate rubric of "submission of ideas," courts often do not make the distinction, and treat the case as one involving a trade secret.[30] The burden then falls on the recipient to prove that the submitted idea was not used, is not a proper trade secret, or was not submitted under a duty of confidentiality. Proof of independent creation, while a perfectly legitimate defense, is often quite difficult to prove.

In allowing recovery on the basis of a confidential disclosure in these situations, courts tend to look at the following elements: (1) whether the idea was solicited or unsolicited, (2) the novelty or originality of the idea, (3) whether the idea was submitted in concrete form, (4) whether it was submitted in a confidential relationship, and (5) whether the idea was in fact used by the defendant.[31]

(b) Procedures for Receiving Ideas

To prevent application of trade secret law to new developments, some companies automatically return any item suspected of containing submissions of ideas. Others establish a separate department to screen suspect items and return any unsolicited items with a notice that the idea has not been seen by anyone other than the screening department. While this wholesale rejection of submitted ideas, if followed, should insulate a company from liability, it can result in the loss of some truly valuable ideas.

Another method for dealing with unsolicited ideas would be to create a procedure whereby the relationship between the submitter and receiver is carefully defined. Returning the idea with a request that the idea be resubmitted in compliance with certain terms and conditions

---

[30] *See, e.g.*, Grepke v. General Elec. Co., 280 F.2d 508, 126 USPQ 93 (7th Cir.), *cert. denied*, 364 U.S. 899, 127 USPQ 555 (1960).

[31] *See, e.g.*, Marcus Advertising v. M. M. Fisher Assocs., 444 F.2d 1061 (7th Cir. 1971).

can prevent unintended consequences. The courts have dismissed cases when the submitter has signed an express waiver of confidentiality.[32] Once the relationship between the parties is expressly defined, the possibility of implicit confidential relationships, necessary to support a trade secret claim, is eliminated.

The agreement, however, must be carefully drafted to provide adequate protection. Because submissions are generally considered to be subject to confidentiality, any waiver should be explicit and clear. Otherwise, the court may not interpret the agreement in the manner the company intended.

For example, in *Burten v. Milton Bradley Co.,*[33] the court inferred a confidential relationship. Milton Bradley required a disclosure form that stated that the submission was made voluntarily and that " 'acceptance by Company does not, in whole or in part, establish or create by implication or otherwise any relationship between Company and me not expressed herein.' "[34] The court found this language not to be an express disclaimer of confidentiality sufficient to negate an implication of a confidential relationship. Furthermore, the disclosure form included other terms that indicated the confidential nature of the submission. Another firm accepted a submission purportedly "with the understanding that there [was] no obligation" on the corporation's part.[35] The court construed this language only as having created no obligation to use the submission. However, if the submission were in fact used, the corporation was obligated to compensate the submitter.

Therefore, it is important that the terms and conditions under which ideas are accepted be clearly defined and understood. As noted previously, under the UTSA, contract law will prevail over general trade secret principles. Careful drafting of a contract can eliminate any purported intent to purchase an idea regardless of its originality or utility. Furthermore, the contract can set forth the terms that define the rights of the parties in the use of the idea and any compensation therefor.

---

[32]*See* Kearns v. Ford Motor Co., 203 USPQ 884 (E.D. Mich. 1978); Crown Indus. v. Kawneer Co., 335 F. Supp. 749, 171 USPQ 401 (N.D. Ill. 1971).

[33]763 F.2d 461 (1st Cir. 1985).

[34]*Id.* at 464 n.3 (quoting Burten v. Milton Bradley Co., 592 F. Supp. 1021, 1025–26 (D.R.I. 1984)).

[35]Moore v. Ford Motor Co., 43 F.2d 685, 687 (2d Cir. 1930).

10

Employee and Consultant Considerations

10.1 Ownership of Employee Inventions

(a) In the Absence of a Contract

Under U.S. patent law, inventorship determines the initial ownership of patent rights. Subject to the exceptions and/or limitation discussed below, an employee who makes an invention owns the rights to that invention, as well as the right to apply for and obtain a patent on the invention. If two or more employees collaborate to make an invention, they are joint owners of the undivided entire interest in the patent. This rule applies even though the employee or employees make the invention on company time and/or use company equipment and materials to make the invention.

There are three basic exceptions to this general rule. First, an employer owns an employee's invention if the employee has signed a contract assigning his or her inventions to the employer. Second, the employer owns an employee's invention if the employee was hired or directed to make that specific invention for the employer. Finally, an employer may own an employee's invention if, due to the employee's position with the employer, the employee has a fiduciary responsibility to assign his or her inventions to the employer.

(b) Contractual Provisions

The assignment of patent rights from employee to employer is governed by state contract law. The typical contract completely assigns the employee's rights to any invention made during the course of his or her employment. Courts uniformly enforce these agreements unless they are grossly unfair to the employee or violate public policy. Courts also generally will enforce an agreement to assign inventions conceived during the course of employment but not reduced to practice until after the termination of employment if the reduction to practice occurs within a short period after termination.

Some courts will even enforce a "holdover agreement" in which the employee promises to assign to the employer inventions conceived for a short period after the termination of employment.[1] However, these agreements are enforceable only if they are reasonable.[2] Such an agreement is reasonable if it is no more restrictive than necessary to protect a legitimate interest of the employer, is not unduly harsh and oppressive to the employee, and is not injurious to the public.[3] Courts are more likely to enforce such agreements when the invention utilizes the employer's trade secrets or proprietary information.[4] This protection may even extend to "highly specialized, current information not generally known in the industry, created and stimulated by the research environment furnished by the employer, to which the employee has been 'exposed' and 'enriched' solely due to his employment."[5] Courts are also more likely to enforce holdover agreements if the subject invention constitutes an improvement to an invention previously conceived during the period of employment. This is particularly true when the improvement relates to a specific project area to which the employee was assigned or if the improvement or invention is closely related to the employer's line of business. On the other hand, the agreement must neither impose unreasonable restrictions on the employee's employment opportunities, nor violate the public's interest in fostering competition, creativity, and invention.

---

[1] *See, e.g.*, Winston Research Corp. v. Minnesota Mining & Mfg. Co., 350 F.2d 134, 146 USPQ 422 (9th Cir. 1965).

[2] *See* Ingersoll-Rand Co. v. Ciavatta, 542 A.2d 879, 8 USPQ2d 1537, 3 IER Cases 1285 (N.J. 1988).

[3] GTI Corp. v. Calhoon, 309 F. Supp. 762, 965 USPQ 621 (S.D. Ohio 1969).

[4] *E.g.*, Armorlite Lens Co. v. Campbell, 340 F. Supp. 273, 173 USPQ 470 (S.D. Cal. 1972).

[5] Ingersoll-Rand v. Ciavatta, *supra* note 2, at 894, 8 USPQ2d at 1549.

(c) Employed-to-Invent

The employed-to-invent rule is a long-standing exception to the general rule that an employee inventor owns the inventions he or she makes.[6] Under this rule, if an employer hires a new employee or directs an existing employee to solve a specific problem, the employer owns any invention made by the employee directed to solving the problem. This right is dependent solely upon the specificity of the task given to the employee. If the employee is hired to use his or her inventive abilities for a specifically designed purpose, any invention resulting from the performance of that work belongs to the employer.[7] If, however, the employer merely hires the employee as a general researcher, engineer, chemist, or other general technical position, subsequent inventions are the property of the employee, absent one of the other exceptions discussed herein.

(d) Fiduciary Responsibility

When the inventing employee is more than a mere employee, that is, when he or she occupies a special relationship of trust and confidence to the employer's business, some courts have held that the employee's inventions are the property of the employer. Generally, the employees who fit in this classification are high-level executive officers of the employer. This duty usually arises under one of three theories:

1. As an officer of the company, the inventor has a fiduciary duty to act in the company's interest;
2. The inventor is so important to the company as an officer (almost always as president or CEO) that he or she is the "alter ego" of the company; or
3. The inventor leads the company/corporation to believe that the patent is a company corporate asset.

---

[6]*See* United States v. Dubilier Condenser Corp., 289 U.S. 178 (1933); Standard Parts Co. v. Peck, 264 U.S. 52 (1924).

[7]Stranco, Inc. v. Atlantes Chem. Sys., 15 USPQ2d 1704, 1716 (S.D. Tex. 1990), *aff'd*, 960 F.2d 156 (Fed. Cir. 1992).

(e) Shop Rights

Even if the employee remains the owner of the invention, an employer also may obtain a limited license to use the employee's invention under the "shop rights doctrine." If an employee uses a nontrivial amount of his or her employer's time and/or resources to create an invention, the employee must grant to the employer a nonexclusive, nontransferable, royalty-free license to use the invention for the term of the patent.[8] The usual justification for granting the employer a shop right is that the employer's resources have been used by the employee to conceive, develop, or commercialize the invention in question. Because the employer has contributed so much to the invention, courts find it unfair to preclude the employer from making use of that for which it has expended both time and resources.

Although the shop rights license may be used as a defense against a claim of patent infringement, it does not entitle the employer to an ownership interest in the employee's patent. Accordingly, the employer does not have standing to sue third parties for infringement of the patent.

Courts have struggled to define the amount of an employer's time or resources sufficient to entitle the employer to a shop right. The prototypical situation arises when an employee conceives of and develops an idea during work hours and uses the employer's resources to perfect the invention and produce an embodiment thereof. However, courts have extended shop rights to employers for less significant uses of the employers' time and resources. For example, courts have awarded shop rights to employers in cases in which an employee conceived an invention at home but reduced the invention to practice during the course of his or her employment[9] and in which an employer introduced the employee's invention (which may have been conceived and reduced to practice at the employee's home) into commercial practice.[10] Even when the use of an employer's resources does not rise to the level necessary to create a shop right, courts usually require the employee to compensate the employer for the use of those resources.

---

[8] *See, e.g.*, Wommack v. Durham Pecan Co., 715 F.2d 962, 219 USPQ 1153 (5th Cir. 1983).

[9] Consolidated Vultee Aircraft Corp. v. Maurice A. Garbell, Inc., 204 F.2d 946, 98 USPQ 4 (9th Cir.), *cert. denied*, 346 U.S. 873, 99 USPQ 491 (1953).

[10] *See* Wommack v. Durham Pecan Co., *supra* note 8.

An employer's shop right continues until expiration of the patent or the termination of the employer's business, whichever comes first. The shop right does not end with the termination of the inventing employee's employment. Although a shop right is a personal right of the employer and may not be sold to another entity, the shop right may be transferred in the context of a complete succession to the entire business and good will of the licensee, such as by incorporation of a business, purchase of an entire business, or merger into a larger corporation.[11]

Because a shop right license is nonexclusive, the inventing employee is free to license or assign his or her invention to any person or business he or she desires. The employee is thus free to transfer his or her ownership rights in the invention to his or her employer's competitors. Such a license or assignment, however, does not extinguish the employer's shop right. As with an inventing employee's ownership rights, shop rights may be expanded or narrowed by express agreement between the employer and employee. Courts generally apply the shop right doctrine to inventions of employees and generally do not give employers any rights in inventions made by independent contractors.[12]

10.2 Ownership of Works of Authorship

(a) Works Made for Hire[13]

Under the Copyright Act, the author of a work is the initial owner of the copyright for that work.[14] When a work is "made for hire," the employer, rather than the employee, is deemed the author.[15] In

---

[11]*See* Lane & Bodley Co. v. Locke, 150 U.S. 193 (1893); California E. Lab. v. Gould, 896 F.2d 400, 13 USPQ2d 1984 (9th Cir. 1990); Neon Signal Devices v. Alpha-Claude Neon Corp., 54 F.2d 793, 12 USPQ 339 (W.D. Pa. 1931).

[12]*But see* Francklyn v. Guilford Packing Co., 695 F.2d 1158, 217 USPQ 317 (9th Cir. 1983) (granting shop right to employer even though plaintiff may have been an independent contractor).

[13]These rules are a departure from the rules in existence prior to the 1976 Copyright Act and would not apply to any works prepared prior to January 1, 1978.

[14]17 U.S.C. §201(a).

[15]17 U.S.C. §201(b).

determining whether a work of authorship constitutes "work made for hire" under the statute, it is important to determine the nature of the employer's relationship with the person who creates the work. The Act defines as a "work made for hire" any work of authorship:

> (1) prepared by an employee within the scope of his or her employment; or
> (2) specially ordered or commissioned for use as a contribution to a collective work, as a part of a motion picture or other audiovisual work, as a translation, as a supplementary work, as a compilation, as an instructional text, as a test, as answer material for a test, or as an atlas, if the parties expressly agree in a written instrument signed by them that the work shall be considered a work made for hire.[16]

Any work prepared by an employee within the scope of his or her employment qualifies as a work made for hire. The employer is the author of that work and thus the owner of the copyright. The meanings of the terms "employee" and "scope of employment" will largely determine whether a particular work is "made for hire" under the Act. Unfortunately, the Copyright Act does not define these key terms.

The Supreme Court resolved this uncertainty in the case of *Community for Creative Non-Violence v. Reid,*[17] by looking to the general rules of agency law as expressed in the Restatement (Second) of Agency. In that case, the Community for Creative Non-Violence (CCNV), an organization that benefits the homeless, asked Reid, a sculptor, to create a work depicting homeless people in a nativity-like scene. CCNV paid Reid $15,000 to cover his expenses, and Reid donated his efforts. Although CCNV supervised some aspects of Reid's work, Reid generally acted independently in creating the sculpture. When a dispute arose concerning copyright ownership in that sculpture, Reid claimed he was not an employee of CCNV, but an independent contractor fully vested with ownership rights to the copyright in the sculpture.

To decide the case, the Supreme Court applied the general common law rules of agency law to interpret the term "employee" in the Copyright Act. Under these rules, a hired person is an employee of the hiring party if the hiring party has the right to control the manner and means by which the work in question is accomplished. The Court also

---

[16]17 U.S.C. §101.

[17]490 U.S. 730, 10 USPQ2d 1985, 16 Media L. Rep. 1769 (1989).

relied on a list of other common law factors relevant to the determination of whether a hired party is an employee rather than a contractor. Those factors are:

1. The level of skill required to create the work;
2. The source of the instrumentalities and tools used to create the work;
3. The location of the work (i.e., at the hiring party's location or at the hired person's location);
4. The duration of the relationship between the parties (i.e., does relationship extend beyond completion of work?);
5. Whether the hiring party has the right to assign additional projects to the hired party;
6. The extent of the hired party's discretion over when and how long to work;
7. The method of payment;
8. The hired party's role and discretion in hiring and paying assistants;
9. Whether the work is part of the regular business of the hiring party;
10. Whether the hiring party operates a business;
11. Whether the hiring party provides employee benefits to the hired party; and
12. The tax treatment of the hired party's income for the project.[18]

Although CCNV directed some of Reid's work to ensure that he produced a sculpture meeting its specifications, the Court found that this factor was not dispositive. The Court found the remaining relevant factors to weigh against finding an employment relationship between CCNV and Reid. As sculptor, Reid was engaged in a skilled occupation. Reid supplied all of his own tools and worked in his own studio in another city from that where CCNV was located, making daily supervision of his work "practicably impossible." CCNV retained Reid for a short period of time (two months). CCNV had no right to assign other projects to Reid before, during, or after this period. As long as he met the deadline for completing the sculpture, Reid was free to decide when and how long to work. Reid was paid in a manner common to the contractor relationship—he received a lump-sum payment at the completion of a specific task. Reid had discretion in the hiring of assistants. CCNV was not in business and certainly not in the business

---

[18] *Id.* at 751-52, 10 USPQ2d at 1995, 16 Media L. Rep. at 1779.

of creating sculptures. Finally, CCNV paid no payroll or social security taxes, paid no contributions to health insurance or workers' compensation funds, and provided no employee benefits on behalf of Reid.

Even if a person is considered an employee under the Copyright Act of 1976,[19] his or her actions must be within the scope of employment for the employer to be deemed the author of the work under the "work made for hire" provision. The fact that the employee uses his or her employer's facility or works on company time is not necessarily dispositive of copyright ownership. Instead, courts will often look at the overall situation from which the work evolved to determine if the person was acting within the scope of employment.

Under 17 U.S.C. §101, certain specially ordered or commissioned works by independent contractors also will qualify as "works made for hire" if they fall within one of the following nine categories:

1. A contribution to a collective work;
2. A part of a motion picture or other audiovisual work;
3. A translation;
4. A supplementary work;
5. A compilation;
6. An instructional text;
7. A test;
8. Answer material for a test; or
9. An atlas.

However, falling within one of these categories is not, by itself, enough to entitle the hiring party to "work made for hire" ownership of the copyright. Both parties to a commissioned work must specifically agree, in a signed, written instrument, that the work will be "made for hire."

If there is no written agreement between the hiring party and the independent contractor, but the hiring party or one of its employees contributes as an author to the creation of the commissioned work, the hiring party may qualify as a joint author together with the independent contractor. The hiring party would qualify as a joint owner regardless of whether the work falls within the nine categories of commissioned works that qualify as "works made for hire."

(b) Contractual Provisions

An employer and an employee or independent contractor may alter their respective rights under copyright law by entering into written

[19] 17 U.S.C. §101.

agreements. Thus, an employee may acquire from his or her employer the copyrights to any works that the employee authored during the scope of his or her employment. Likewise, an employer may acquire from an independent contractor the copyright to any commissioned work even if it does not fit within one of the nine categories listed in part (2) of the definition of works made for hire.

Although these agreements may transfer ownership of a copyright from one party to another, the agreements may not vary any party's status as author of the work. This distinction between "authorship" and "ownership" was made to prevent parties from evading certain provisions in the Copyright Act. For example, the term of protection for a work of authorship varies depending upon whether it is a work made for hire.[20] In addition, the nationality of the author of a particular work may affect certain rights under the Act.[21] Thus, an agreement between an employer and an employee or an employer and an independent contractor (for works not fitting within one of the nine "work made for hire" categories of 17 U.S.C. §101) may transfer ownership of the copyright, but may not alter authorship of the work.

10.3 Departing Employees

(a) Noncompetition Agreements

Absent an agreement not to compete (also known as a restrictive covenant), an employer may not prevent a former employee from going to work for a competitor or going into business in competition with that employer. Whether or not an agreement exists, the former employee may not divulge his or her former employer's trade secrets or confidential business information to the new employer, nor may the employee use it in competition with the employer. The former employee is allowed, however, to compete against his or her former employer

[20]Under 17 U.S.C. §302(a), the copyright in a work authored by a person lasts for the life of the author plus 50 years. Under 17 U.S.C. §302(c), the copyright in a work made for hire lasts for 75 years from the year of first publication or 100 years from the year of creation, whichever is earlier.

[21]Under 17 U.S.C. §104(b), the author's nationality may determine whether the work is eligible for copyright protection.

by using the nonsecret knowledge, memory, skill, and experience he or she gained from the prior employment. The distinction between a former employee's general knowledge and experience and the employer's confidential business information is difficult to draw, particularly when the employee combined technical expertise with management duties or otherwise held an important position in the former employer's business. Courts have struggled to balance the interests of free competition and employees' rights to livelihood against employers' needs for protection against unfair trade practices.

Concerns for the protection of free competition and employees' rights to exploit their skills and experience lead many courts to disfavor noncompetition agreements. Courts will hold these agreements unenforceable if they are unreasonable. The reasonableness of a noncompetition agreement will be judged by the restrictions it places upon the employee's ability to practice his or her trade, by whether the agreement is necessary to protect a legitimate business interest of the employer, and from a standpoint of public policy.

Courts will not enforce a noncompetition agreement if it is more restrictive than is necessary to protect a legitimate interest of the former employer. Courts generally consider trade secrets and confidential business information to be protectable interests that properly may be the subject of a noncompetition agreement. Many courts also include customer information, good will, and other similar matters to be protectable.

Noncompetition agreements generally contain time and geographic restrictions on an employee's ability to engage in specified business activities upon the termination of his or her employment. For the agreement to be enforceable, the time restrictions must be relatively short. Although courts have enforced restrictions greater than three years in length, a court is much more likely to enforce a noncompetition agreement if it restricts the employee's activities for less than three years. Lengthier restrictions may be enforced against former employees who had access to confidential business and customer information than against former employees who did not have such access.

The reasonableness of a geographic restriction also is evaluated in light of the employer's interest that is being protected. Courts will not enforce noncompetition agreements that seek to restrict a former employee's right to do business or work in geographic areas not served by the former employer. Noncompetition agreements that limit geographic restrictions to the area in which the former employer does business or reasonably expects to do business in the near future are generally upheld. Of course, if the former employer's business is national, a nationwide restriction may be upheld.

The particular activities precluded by the noncompetition agreement must relate to the employee's responsibilities while employed by his or her former employer. For example, if the former employee worked as a research chemist assigned to develop a new pharmaceutical product for the employer, the noncompetition agreement probably cannot prevent the employee from working for a company that makes industrial solvents. In addition, if the agreement seeks to preclude an employee from competing in a geographic area in which the former employer does business, but the employee had no substantive responsibilities, the agreement may be unenforceable. For example, suppose an employer seeks to protect its interest in the good will it has developed with customers in a certain geographic area, and the former employee was a salesman for the company in a different geographic area. A noncompetition agreement may be unenforceably overbroad if it seeks to prohibit sales activities in the area not formerly served by the employee. The employee, having no sales contacts in that area, is not likely to harm the employer's good will interest by working in that area. Thus, there is no need to prohibit the employee from working there.

Whether a noncompetition agreement is reasonable, and thus enforceable, is a question of law to be determined by the court. As with other contractual provisions, noncompetition agreements are governed by state law. In some states, if the court finds any part of a noncompetition agreement to be unenforceable, the entire agreement is deemed unenforceable. In other states, courts will sever the unreasonable portions of a noncompetition agreement and enforce the remaining portions of the agreement. Occasionally, a court can rewrite unreasonable portions of an agreement to make them reasonable, and then enforce the entire rewritten agreement.

(b) Warning the New Employer

When an employee who has had access to an employer's trade secrets, or who has signed a noncompetition agreement, leaves to work for a new employer, it is often advisable for the former employer to contact the new employer. The former employer should advise the new employer that the employee had access to trade secrets and/or is subject to a noncompetition agreement. The new employer may be liable for trade secret misappropriation or tortious interference with contractual relationships if, with knowledge of what it is doing, it induces the employee to disclose trade secrets or to breach a valid and enforceable noncompetition agreement.

11

Protection of Computer Software

11.1 Introduction—The Economics of Protection

(a) Range of Protection

In the 1990s, the major growth area of the U.S. computer industry will likely be computer software. As hardware components become less expensive and faster, a key difference between one computer system and another is the type of software that runs on it. As this section will demonstrate, computer software is protectable by all forms of intellectual property. Nonetheless, because there is an array of legal protection choices, albeit awkward ones, the economic realities of software products and the industry that makes these products, as well as the position of the firm attempting to protect the software, become critical in making the right selection of legal protection. To determine that selection, it is first helpful to view intellectual property protection as a continuum which, at one end, is weak and at the other end, strong. The weak protection involves trade secrets and contractual protection (i.e., restrictions on licenses, assignments, joint ventures, etc.), the medium level of protection involves copyrights, and the strong protection involves patents.

The choices along this continuum depend upon certain factors such as: (1) the market for the software (e.g., commercial, government),

(2) the shelf life of the software, (3) the development costs of the software, (4) the cash position of the developer, (5) the technical complexity of the software, (6) the relationship among the software authors/inventors, (7) the potential for infringement, (8) the value and patentability of the programming ideas, and (9) the necessity for immediate protection of the software. Determinations of each of these factors help in defining which form of protection is best in a given situation. An additional consideration is that it may be possible to obtain more than one type of protection for a software product.

(b) Ramifications of Different Types of Protection

When employing the different forms of intellectual property protection, the software owner must consider the legal scope of what is actually protected, as well as the process for achieving the protection, the length or duration of the protection, and the manner in which the protection can be enforced.

A patent provides the broadest and strongest form of protection for the software product. The value of an issued patent is that it protects the underlying ideas of the program, which cannot be protected by copyright or trade secrets that have become public. Those ideas can be claimed and thus protected in the patent claims either very broadly or relatively narrowly. In fact, the exclusive rights of the patent need not be limited simply to cover the software, but can be described in "means plus function" language so that apparatus performing equivalent functions to the computer software would infringe the patent. Furthermore, a patent can be enforced against innocent parties who unknowingly infringe the claims of the patent. In other words, it is irrelevant whether or not an infringer knows that the patent exists. However, patents can be costly and take years to obtain.

Other than taking less time, efficiency can also be measured in terms of requiring less computer hardware to perform the task, requiring fewer lines of software, or software that is more readily recognizable to the end user (improved user interface). A final factor in considering whether to obtain patent protection is determining if the software simply yields faster results or if, instead, it yields better or different results. In many areas of technology, software is not merely automation of existing processes but may ultimately yield better or new results. For example, medically related computer software is now being used increasingly to perform analyses, such as determining nuclear magnetic resonance on three-dimensional arrays of data, which heretofore would have been impossible for a doctor to calculate. The result can also be expressed graphically so that the displayed information is clear to the user and is grasped visually. A further example of software that may yield entirely new results is in the computerization of the human genome; by placing this enormous quantity of data into the computer, new conclusions relating to the genetic structure of humanity can thus be drawn. These new results are patentable.

Copyright, by contrast, does not protect ideas—only the expression of those ideas. For computer software, copyright protects the code, the screens, and the flow charts and documentation associated with the program. Substantially similar versions of these works are also protected. In the early 1980s, courts were largely concerned with copyright infringements that involved exact copying. They did not deal with factual patterns involving software that was derived from or only close to protected works. In the early to mid–1980s, however, factual problems began to crop up in cases that did not involve exact copying. In a number of decisions, courts fashioned tests for substantial similarity that expanded copyright well beyond protecting the source code expression to protecting the program's structure, sequence, and organization. For a screen display, protection of the literal expression of the copyrighted screen displays was effectively broadened to cover its "look and feel." By the late 1980s and early 1990s, courts were generally taking more restrictive attitudes. One recent case[1] by the Court of Appeals for the Second Circuit has refused to recognize the structure, sequence, and organization standard and has instead developed a much more restrictive test, known as "successive filtering," that stringently separates out what is considered noncopyrightable matter from that material that is appropriately considered copyrightable. Accordingly, the legal ramifications of copyright can be characterized by the ease with which it is obtained and by the uncertainty as to its scope.

Finally, trade secret protection relies principally on licenses and confidentiality agreements for protection. As discussed in Chapter 9, the difficulty with trade secret protection, however, is the ability to maintain the computer program as a "secret." Secrecy is indeed difficult since it involves the issue of how to provide the program to users without any risk that the users can decompile and, hence, reconstruct the program. Licenses and agreements can reasonably guarantee secrecy for the software product with a relatively small number of end users, since

[1]Computer Assocs. Int'l v. Altai, Inc., 982 F.2d 693 (2d Cir. 1992).

such users can each sign agreements. However, for mass-distributed computer software, the problem is nearly impossible to overcome. Moreover, recent court decisions have effectively allowed copiers to reach the "trade secret" without infringing the copy protections available under copyright law. In *Sega Enterprises v. Accolade, Inc.*,[2] the Court of Appeals for the Ninth Circuit provided a limited "fair use" exception from copyright infringement for making a single copy in order to reverse engineer secret computer code. Thus, for those not obligated by a trade secret agreement, the freedom to reverse engineer secret code is effectively sanctioned by some courts.

Another fact to consider is whether the software is an improved product that enhances performance. An improved product may simplify and/or modify existing software so that it fits new applications. For example, if the client has determined that its accounting software, which was previously used for general books and ledgers, can now be applied to tax returns, then the application of the same method or process steps can now be applied to a new environment. Therefore, anyone using those same steps for tax returns would infringe. Alternatively, the improved product can involve the more efficient performance of tasks than previously accomplished by other software. Improved throughput is an important consideration that alone merits patent protection.

11.2 Patent Law: Nature and Limitations

(a) Introduction

Since the advent of computers, intellectual property rights in computer software and computer-based inventions have been difficult to define, obtain, and protect. Opposition to patent protection is based upon the statutory requirements of the Patent Act, specifically, 35 U.S.C. §§101 and 112.

Section 101 defines and limits the areas of technology that have patentable subject matter. Both the courts and the U.S. Patent and Trademark Office (PTO) have determined that specific categories, in-

---

[2] 977 F.2d 1510, 24 USPQ2d 1561 (9th Cir. 1992).

cluding mathematical algorithms, are excluded from protection. Section 112, first paragraph, requires that a patent application include sufficient disclosure for others to make or use the invention. This is a particular area of concern with respect to computer software because it is often difficult to determine when a disclosure is complete and sufficient to obtain a patent.

Some in the software industry are concerned that granting broad protection for software inventions will only stifle the fast-paced developments that have occurred in the past years in personal computer software. The increased protection that courts have been giving under copyright law has also fueled the argument that broad software protection under patent law is unnecessary.

(b) Patent Protection Fully Available for Software

Until 1981, patent protection for software inventions was relatively unobtainable. A case decided by the U.S. Supreme Court in 1981[3] resolved some uncertainty and forced the PTO to abandon its sweeping opposition to patent coverage for software inventions. Today, because of a combination of changes in the law and a strengthened patent system, more and more companies are recognizing that patent law has shifted. They can obtain broad and significant patent claims for their software. While the lack of prior art may ultimately result in overly broad claims being issued, there is a growing realization that opposing the notion of a software patent is simply cutting off one's nose to spite one's face. Nonetheless, the business attitude favoring software patents is still evolving. The legal acceptability of software as patentable subject matter still raises problems that require resolution and, for the practitioner, understanding.

(c) Mental Steps Doctrine

The main difficulty in patenting inventions arises from 35 U.S.C. §101, which prohibits the PTO from granting patents on inventions that do not fall within specified classes of statutory inventions that comprise "any new and useful process, machine, manufacture, or composition of matter, or any new and useful improvement thereof." The

[3]Diamond v. Diehr, 450 U.S. 175, 209 USPQ 1 (1981).

areas of exclusion are not explicitly stated in §101. The definition of subject matter that is not patentable has become a captive of the courts that, for software, has produced a confusing and conflicting definition of nonstatutory software. The area of court-made exclusion is known as the "mental steps doctrine."

At one time, the mental steps doctrine had been used to exclude any software or computer invention that contained algorithms. Recently, courts have held that this doctrine excludes only mathematical formulas. The close association between computer software algorithms and mathematical algorithms has led to the exclusion of many programs that clearly do not involve mathematics and to widespread confusion in the courts and the PTO.

Case law developments would seem to indicate, with some lack of complete clarity, that nonmathematical software is patentable. However, a recent shift in attitude by the PTO seems to indicate the acceptance of a much narrower standard to define a patentable algorithm. To understand the present uncertainty about §101, and to understand how a client's computer program may ultimately fare with this issue, it is important to have some background on the history and development of the mental steps doctrine.

One of the first articulations of the mental steps doctrine was that no patent can be obtained for a method that ordinarily consists of mental activity.[4] The mental steps doctrine was first applied to a software-related invention in the case of *In re Prater*.[5]

The *Prater* invention involved a method for analyzing the composition of gas mixtures by employing particular test equations performed either by the analyst or, more practically, by a digital computer. The court allowed the patent, finding that if a claim can cover a sequence of steps that could be accomplished either by hand or in a machine, then it is *not* precluded from protection under the mental steps doctrine merely because it could be carried out by hand.

The *Prater* decision was significantly changed (although not explicitly overruled) by the Supreme Court in *Gottschalk v. Benson*,[6] where the Court held that a method for converting numerals expressed as binary-coded decimals into pure binary numbers could not be pat-

---

[4]*See, e.g.*, Halliburton Oil Well Cementing Co. v. Walker, 146 F.2d 817, 64 USPQ 278 (9th Cir. 1944), *modified*, 329 U.S. 1, 71 USPQ 175 (1946).

[5]415 F.2d 1378, 159 USPQ 583, 160 USPQ 230 (C.C.P.A. 1968), *superseded*, 415 F.2d 1393, 162 USPQ 541 (C.C.P.A. 1969).

[6]409 U.S. 63, 175 USPQ 673 (1972).

ented as a process. (A binary-coded decimal is an intermediate step between binary numbers and decimals where individual binary numbers are substituted for numerals. Thus, 21 is 10 01 in binary-coded decimal, while in binary it would be 10101). The Court, in an opinion by Justice William O. Douglas, found that (1) a method that is equivalent to mental work is not patentable, (2) a method that does not physically alter an article is not patentable, and (3) a computer program is not protectable because of the difficulty that the PTO would encounter in trying to assemble a collection of prior art relating to this or any other computer software invention.

The sweeping rejection of software patents in the *Gottschalk* decision was subsequently criticized by the Court of Customs and Patent Appeals (CCPA), primarily for failing to adequately define or distinguish between nonmathematical algorithms (which are protected as "processes" under §101) and mathematical algorithms. Critics of *Gottschalk* focus on the Court's definition of algorithm, which they claim was imprecise and presupposed that all algorithms involve mathematical problems, when in fact, only some algorithms are purely mathematical.

However, the CCPA was still constrained to follow the Supreme Court's conclusion, although it attempted in several decisions to minimize *Gottschalk*'s sweeping rejection of software patents by allowing software claims that were drawn to machines, while upholding rejections of claims that described the program as a method.

Gottschalk was followed by the Supreme Court's decision in *Parker v. Flook.*[7] In *Parker,* the Supreme Court affirmed and extended the *Gottschalk* holding that a mathematical formula was unpatentable and could not become patentable merely by the addition of "conventional, post-solution application" language (i.e., language that would describe the application of the program's solution) to what would otherwise be a mathematical algorithm step. The Court concluded that placing conventional postsolution activity after a claim exalts form over substance. The dissenting opinion by Justice Potter Stewart argued that a claimed process, as a whole, could not be held unpatentable because one step was directed to a mathematical algorithm.

Following *Parker,* the CCPA still demonstrated a degree of resistance to the Supreme Court decision by developing a two-step analysis and thus a refinement of the rather broad-brush language of *Gottschalk* and *Parker,* which defined situations where software claims could still

[7]437 U.S. 584, 198 USPQ 193 (1978).

receive protection. As enunciated in *In re Freeman,*[8] the court first determined if the claims were purely mathematical and, if so, then tested if the claims preempted the algorithm. In this case, the second step was determined by considering whether the postsolution recitation effectively converted the claims into an application that was itself patentable.

The two-step *Freeman* test for §101 subject matter has remained the predominant test today. This is because it was accepted and was followed by the Supreme Court in its 1981 decision, *Diamond v. Diehr.*[9] In *Diehr,* the Supreme Court affirmed a CCPA decision that the software claims were statutory subject matter and thus subject to patent protection under 35 U.S.C. §101.

The claims at issue in *Diehr* were drawn to a method for operating a molding press in order to more accurately cure rubber tires. The method claim involved the steps of repeatedly measuring the actual temperature in the mold, repeatedly calculating the tire's cure time, and automatically opening the mold when the cure time was equal to the actual time. The Supreme Court noted that a claim drawn to subject matter that is otherwise statutory does not become nonstatutory simply because it uses a mathematical formula. Unlike *Parker,* the Court reasoned that in determining the eligibility of claims under §101, the claims must be considered as a whole. If then, under the *Freeman* test, this analysis determines that a claim, as a whole, is drawn to a mathematical formula, the exclusion of the claim under 35 U.S.C. §101 cannot be circumvented by merely limiting the claim to a particular environment. The Court attempted to reconcile *Parker* by stating that insignificant postsolution activity, such as computing an alarm limit, will not transform the claim into a patentable process. But the Court also noted that significant postsolution activity, such as the application at issue in *Diehr,* was indeed patentable.

Since *Diehr,* the Court of Appeals for the Federal Circuit has become relatively permissive on the issue of software algorithm patents. Two Federal Circuit decisions are of note. In *In re Grams,*[10] the Federal Circuit rejected the patentability of software claims based upon the *Freeman/Diehr* test. The claims in *Grams* were directed to a method for diagnosing an abnormal condition of an individual. The method included performing tests to measure parameters, computing and comparing actual values to reference values, and successively eliminating

[8]573 F.2d 1237, 197 USPQ 464 (C.C.P.A. 1978).
[9]*Supra* note 3.
[10]888 F.2d 835, 12 USPQ2d 1824 (Fed. Cir. 1989).

parameters and repeating the comparisons. The court determined that the computing and comparing steps solely constituted a procedure for solving a mathematical problem.

Although the first step of performing tests might have provided additional activity besides the "mathematical algorithm," the court in *Grams* reasoned that the tests were directed solely to providing the numbers for use in the equations. However, the court specifically did not determine that a physical step of obtaining data could not make a claim statutory. In this case, the disclosure provided no additional information on the nature of the tests. Furthermore, the specification indicated that the algorithm could be applied to any complex system, whether electrical, mechanical, chemical, biological, or combinations thereof. Therefore, the claim language simply attempted to limit the field of use claimed for the algorithm. As such, the court concluded that the claim, as a whole, attempted to claim the mathematical algorithm and was thereby nonstatutory subject matter under §101.

A few days later, the Federal Circuit held another software invention patentable in *In re Iwahashi*.[11] The *Iwahashi* invention related to an improved circuit for use in pattern recognition to obtain coefficients in an autocorrelation unit. Previous devices required the use of costly multipliers. The *Iwahashi* invention, by contrast, was able to accomplish the same result by obtaining the square of the sum of two factors and calculating the autocorrelation coefficient using a stated formula. The claim recited circuit steps for performing its calculations in "means-plus-function" language and the use of a read-only memory (ROM) containing a table of squares.

In considering the claim as a whole, the Federal Circuit concluded that the claims did not solely recite the formula. The court reasoned that the means-plus-function language in the claim was limited by 35 U.S.C. §112 to the structure disclosed in the specification and equivalents thereof. In this case, the specification had structural descriptions for the claimed elements. The claim was not solely directed to a mathematical formula, but set forth the application of the formula to specific structures. The Federal Circuit held that the claims in *Iwahashi* were patentable.

(d) PTO Practice

Until recently, the rationale of the *Diehr* decision was closely adhered to by the PTO. In determining whether a claim was statutory

[11]888 F.2d 1370, 12 USPQ2d 1980 (Fed. Cir. 1989).

under 35 U.S.C. §101, the PTO applied the two-part procedure set forth in *Freeman,* as modified by *Diehr*.

Over the past two years, the PTO has retreated from past practices and taken a very conservative view of what constitutes statutory subject matter for software-related inventions. The PTO practice guidelines, known as the *Manual of Patent Examining Procedure* (MPEP), were changed to recommend that patent examiners apply a more restrictive view of 35 U.S.C. §101. Specifically, the MPEP first explains, incorrectly, that the above-discussed Supreme Court decisions apply a broad interpretation to statutory subject matter, but that certain categories are not included. These categories are: laws of nature, physical phenomena, abstract ideas, scientific truths or the mathematical expression of them, algorithms, and mathematical formulas. This statement is misleading, however, since it lumps together all algorithms rather than excepting only mathematical algorithms from §101.

Next, the MPEP notes that any limitations that are defined in the patent specification using mathematical algorithms are construed as indirectly reciting a mathematical algorithm. To properly analyze the claims, the MPEP instructs patent examiners to remove all such limitations from the claim. The remaining limitations are then to be examined to determine whether they define statutory subject matter. If the remaining limitations could be broadly classified by the examiner as "field of use" limitations or "antecedent data gathering" limitations, and/or "inconsequential post-solution activity" limitations, the MPEP indicates that the claim will be regarded as nonstatutory under §101. However, this claim deconstruction technique runs up against *Diehr*'s requirement that the claim be "considered as a whole."

In sum, in the current environment patent practitioners and attorneys must closely follow past practices and avoid mathematical claims or applications unless there is ample support to apply that result to machines or processes.

(e) Adequate Disclosure of Computer Inventions

A patent application must provide sufficient disclosure to enable someone to make or use the invention.[12] Computer inventions generally contain three broad categories of elements: (1) hardware, (2) operational

[12]35 U.S.C. §112.

principles or applications, and (3) specifically coded software. The standards for sufficient disclosure for each of these elements are still developing. While PTO practice in this area has evidenced significantly less attention than the mental steps doctrine under 35 U.S.C. §101, exceeding the §112 standard with applications will ultimately aid in avoiding serious pitfalls.

As required by 35 U.S.C. §112, first paragraph, the invention must include sufficiency for *both* the disclosed hardware and software due to the interrelationship and interdependence of these elements. Also, since computer cases will generally involve two areas of the prior art—computer hardware and computer software—the knowledge of persons skilled in both technologies is an appropriate criterion for determining sufficiency of disclosure under §112.

When the disclosure is based upon block diagrams, the examiner is to focus on the diverse functions attributed to each block element and how it should be implemented. Furthermore, even if the components are known, how they are to be interconnected to function in the disclosed manner should not be considered inherent. Instead, these features should be explicitly set forth.

The PTO guidelines indicate that an examiner must establish a reasonable basis for questioning the adequacy of the disclosure to enable a person of ordinary skill in the art to make and use the claimed invention. However, the MPEP also states that the "guideline to generally follow is to challenge the sufficiency of such disclosures which fail to include either the computer program itself or a reasonably detailed flowchart which delineates the sequence of operations the program must perform."[13]

(f) Practical Advice Regarding Software Patenting

In view of the complicated history of §101 and the largely negative attitude toward software protection by the PTO, increasing attention must be paid to the preparation and prosecution of the patent application to avoid §101 and §112 pitfalls. In fact, a detailed and careful description of a computer invention and drafting of the application can completely avoid such problems.

---

[13]MPEP §2106.02, at 2100-7 (revision 6, Oct. 1987).

The first and most critical step toward this goal is to carefully define the software invention. Second, if from an initial review the patentable invention appears to partially or fully involve a mathematical algorithm, it is then critical to explore "significant" applications of the algorithm or hardware with the inventors.

Third, the explanation must not be drafted merely to satisfy a generic description of the program's application to an otherwise patentable environment or device. Instead, a minimum level of descriptive detail must be drafted. For example, if the application were directed to an artificial intelligence algorithm that could be applied to a control system environment, the mere mention of "control systems" would likely not avoid a §101 rejection for "insignificant post-solution activity" or as describing a mere "field of use." However, if that control environment were specified in the application, and in particular, described in hardware terms, then the specificity and particularity of the control system exemplified above would reach a level that would be considered satisfactory under §112 and support the recitation of structural elements in the claims as well as pass muster under the *Diehr*[14] test for statutory subject matter.

A trick to reaching the level of specificity is to "incorporate by reference" known hardware elements or arrangements. Many published patents contain basic teachings of typical hardware arrangements, the implementation of which may be easily adapted to new software control techniques. Thus, for example, if there is a statement in the specification that the present algorithm can be used in a P-I-D (Proportional, Integral, Derivative) controller, and a description of a P-I-D controller is incorporated by reference, along with a block diagram of that controller, a rejection of the allegedly insufficient disclosure can be readily overcome.

Even if the software does not appear to be truly mathematical, it is still helpful to include additional hardware description and drawings so that the patent examiner, who may normally examine hardware cases, is satisfied. An added advantage is that drawings and description can also support an apparatus claim relating to a computer for performing purely software steps. If adequate support is provided for the "computer," a §101 and/or §112, first paragraph, rejection would be altogether avoided.

The description of the software should also be modularized. It is not enough to describe the software as a series of "pseudo-code" equivalent steps (i.e., steps that are English equivalents to each line of com-

---

[14]Diamond v. Diehr, *supra* note 3.

puter source code). Although ultimately pseudo-code is helpful for a description of the algorithmic contents, it does not necessarily provide information about the program's data requirements, or a sufficient environment, or application, for the software.

To modularize the description, the application should take three views of the software: (1) a "system view" of the software, including its proposed application environments, (2) a "process view" of the algorithmic steps of the program, and (3) a "data view" of the necessary data structures and databases.

The "system view" would most likely be represented in the diagrams by "block"-type overviews, connecting functional pieces of the program to describe the program in broad modules that define, in a generic way, the functionality of the various pieces. In instances where the software is relatively discrete in nature (in terms of the functions that are performed), there may be some overlap with the "process view" of the software. One way to avoid, or circumvent, overlap is to include in the system view hardware element descriptions pertaining to the applications of the software. In a computer control application, for example, the output of the software can thus be connected to a controller, which in turn can have control lines to (and/or from) the controlled process or device. In this example, the drawings would include both viable pieces of hardware (controller, controlled device), and significant postsolution activity protected by patent law (controllers are protected in several categories by the PTO). The applicant can thus point to an environment for the software that is shown with "specificity."

In terms of the "process view" description of the software steps and functions, a pseudo-code level flow chart describing the important portions of the software should be diagrammed and explained. To the extent that portions of the software simply do not rise to the level of patentability or importance to the inventors, functional flow diagrams at a level somewhere higher than pseudo-code would suffice.

It is unnecessary to include source code as part of the application. The CCPA has ruled that an application need not contain source code in order for the description to be considered enabling under §112.[15] If it appears, however, imperative that source code be included, the expression of that source code should be minimized to show only the most critical contents of the program so that anyone reviewing it will not be able to immediately implement the software. Beyond *Sherwood,*

[15]In re Sherwood, 613 F.2d 809, 204 USPQ 537 (C.C.P.A. 1980), *cert. denied,* 450 U.S. 994, 210 USPQ 776 (1981).

most examiners do not appreciate source code in the specification. This is because they rarely have the time or the resources to review the code for accuracy or for meaning. The end result may ironically be that the examiner may shift the §112 burden back on the applicant to point out what parts of the claims are supported by the code.

The next level of description involves the database. A data flow diagram is often helpful for illustrating the relationship among data, data types, and the code manipulating that data. Another valuable aspect of describing a database is that it often inherently includes a description of the application of the software by virtue of describing the organizational framework for the data. Additionally, focus on the database organization and structure may yield patentable subject matter. It also may focus the inventor's thinking about the data aspects in the software invention (which are often ignored).

A final requirement is to describe, by way of example, applications of the program. One way to do so is to provide examples of the applications of the program in the specification. The use of examples also makes the disclosure more easily understood and again may provide sufficient support for overcoming §101 and §112 issues.

In providing the foregoing descriptions of inventions, it is imperative to deemphasize the mathematical aspects of any processes. Given the strict PTO policy on mathematical algorithms as discussed previously, the application should focus on physical aspects of the invention, the specific environment, and the real-world problems being solved.

Despite extensive opposition in the PTO, the patentability of software-based inventions is expanding. Both the courts and the PTO look to the structural elements in a claim or the application of an algorithm to a physical environment. By carefully describing the application of an algorithm and claiming a machine-based environment, many software-based inventions can be patented.

(i) Recognizing Patentable Inventions in Computer Software

Patent protection is largely available for computer software, but the practical problems arise when determining whether patents are the appropriate tool for maximizing the client's economic interest in this software. Several considerations can be used to recognize patentable inventions. First, a client must determine whether the software solves an important problem. If a problem in the relevant field is overcome by the software, then patent protection may be more effective than if the software were merely directed to automating a manual or mechanical process. By protecting the idea that solves this problem, an effective block to competitors may be achieved by obtaining a patent and, therefore, the client will have the opportunity to gain financial rewards.

(ii) Helping the Client Prepare for Patent Protection

Once a decision has been made to protect software, several steps must be taken to achieve that goal. Depending on the type of technology involved, different steps may be necessary.

One of the most difficult questions is defining what the client considers to be the invention. This is further complicated by the fact that patents protect not only existing inventions, but also those inventions that have not effectively been "reduced to practice." This is because a software patent can "constructively reduce to practice" in the patent application something that may not yet exist. For software, this becomes a particular challenge. Unlike computer hardware, computer software is malleable and is easily defined by functions. Thus, the potential patentee can look down the road relatively easily and craft a patent application that expresses present and future products. The need to define the full "life cycle" of an application therefore becomes critical if a patent is to be valuable in the long run. A second issue is the cost benefit of the patent. Often, a client approaches counsel with orders from management, the board of directors, or the sales division to "get a patent." However, economics need to be considered. The essential question is whether the software has long-term commercial prospects that will justify the time and cost of obtaining a patent. To answer this question, it is important to understand how the client intends to use the patent. If enforcement is entirely out of the question, then it needs to be understood whether the patent is at all effective as a defensive tool.

To pursue patent protection effectively, it is important for the client to interact with counsel in preparing the application. Two steps are critical. First, the inventor should not be the patent attorney. The more attention, feedback, and review that the inventor provides to his or her technical contribution, the better the patent application will be. However, it is important to note that the review should not be merely an editorial process. It should carefully look at whether the application, as drafted, would enable the reviewer to "make" or "use" the invention without resorting to significant additional work. An important caveat is that the client's involvement need not be overly time consuming.

Full disclosure of computer software inventions to the PTO does not require an explanation of every line of source code. Instead, the inclusion of a flow chart in the patent application, along with a written explanation that provides the functional description of the process flow and information flow is sufficient. Hence, it is important that the client closely interact with patent counsel in order to draft a flow chart that effectively describes the functional aspects of the invention.

A final issue is to determine whether international patents are desired. If so, certain issues first must be resolved. First, there cannot be any disclosure or offer for sale that, as described in Chapter 2, section 2.5(b), would prohibit patent protection as of the date of that public disclosure or offer for sale. This is an important issue and should be presented to patent counsel before proceeding with further protection.

(iii) Orienting Clients Toward Protecting Practices

In the software arena, it is critical that software designers follow practices that are followed in other technologies. Since the very nature of software creation is malleable, it is critical for software engineers to be concerned with statutory bar dates and having adequate factual backup to prove "priority of invention." To do so, clients must exercise care, organized recordkeeping, and diligence.

The essential rule for defining who has priority of invention is that the first to invent and effectively reduce the concept to practice is the first inventor. Usually, this means that the first person to conceive of the invention and to exercise reasonable diligence in reducing that concept to practice receives priority of invention. To prove priority, therefore, evidence of conception and reduction to practice must be presented.[16] It is also critical to note that activity in a foreign country cannot establish the date of invention under 35 U.S.C. §104. The types of records that are used to show priority include laboratory notebooks and data copies of successfully executed software. However, if there has not been a final software product created, but only the filing of a patent application (constructive reduction to practice), then diligence from the date of conception to the filing date of the patent application must be shown.

---

[16]35 U.S.C. §102(g).

Diligence, in turn, requires proof of continuous activity from the conception date to the date that the patent application is filed. "Continuous activity" can be proven by establishing through evidence (i.e., letters, notebook notes, and records of payments) that during the period in question work continued without any breaks. If gaps of time are evident, even short time gaps, then the ability to establish the "priority" date as the date of conception may be lost.

Keeping records is also critical for determining when a patent application must be filed. This is because 35 U.S.C. §102(b) bars the applicant from receiving a patent if his or her invention has been sold or published more than a year before the application is filed. The types of records applicable to this issue include copies of publications, advertisements, articles, and speeches about the product, and information concerning the date the software was first offered for sale or disclosed. To avoid the issue of a statutory patent bar and to improve the ability to establish priority, the client should be advised to regularly review protectable software. Often engineers, analysts, and programmers will assume their project is well known and will therefore never receive patent protection. Usually, these assumptions are incorrect. A process should be instituted for an internal review of ideas and the submission of ideas of economic value to patent counsel for follow-up.

In addition, defensive concerns regarding patents also should be carefully reviewed. It is important, particularly when a new software product is released, to obtain infringement opinions on the software. For example, a client may be marketing software that he or she knows infringes the patented software of a competitor. If a client is doing this knowingly, he or she could be liable as a willful infringer (with potential for treble damage liability). In addition, the client may also be liable for infringement even if he or she does not know about the patent. Therefore, an infringement opinion should be provided for products in the market. If it is determined that the client may be liable for infringement, several strategies may be pursued:

1. The client can change the product in order to circumvent the potentially infringed patent.
2. The client can conduct a validity investigation of the patent in question to determine if he or she has a right to use his or her product. Invalidity is the most common affirmative defense that is raised in response to an infringement lawsuit.
3. The client may want to contact the patent holder to investigate the possibility of a license.

If the date of the client's invention appears to predate that of the patent, the client can file a patent with identical claims in order to force an interference proceeding in the PTO which, if successful, would award patent protection to the client's invention and deny it to the later patent.

11.3 Copyright Law

In the United States, copyright law is the predominant method of protecting computer software. The Copyright Act of 1976 was amended in 1980 to include a definition for a computer program.[17] However, computer programs were never made into a separate category of copyrightable subject matter under 35 U.S.C. §102.

Instead, the 1980 revision classifies computer programs as literary works,[18] because the definition of "literary works" under §102 includes "words, numbers, or other verbal or numerical symbols or indicia" that would include the expressive elements of computer software. As a result, a computer program is protected by copyright regardless of the form in which it is expressed. This means that a program that can be understood only by a machine (i.e., object code) will be protected to the same extent as a program that is understandable to humans (i.e., source code). Furthermore, flow charts, pseudo-code, and diagrams of the program receive the same protection as that afforded to the program code itself.

(a) Originality

Even though "original works of authorship" for computer programs are eligible for copyright protection, this does not mean that any software or databases can be copyrighted. There must be something more than de minimis expression to qualify for protection under copyright law. Thus, words, phrases, slogans, names, titles, and lists of ingredients are not considered to have more than de minimis expres-

---

[17] 17 U.S.C. §101.

[18] Computer screens may be protected under several different categories—namely, literary works, pictorial or graphic works, or audiovisual works.

sions. Similarly, a short computer program with little more than several lines of code also likely will not qualify.

Moreover, the fact that a person has put forth a large amount of effort to create the work, that is, "sweat of the brow," has recently been discredited as a basis for establishing originality. In *Feist Publications v. Rural Telephone Service Co.*,[19] the Supreme Court held that an alphabetical listing of names and addresses in a telephone directory (a compilation work) does not contain sufficient original expression to warrant copyright protection. The Court stated that mere "sweat of the brow" was not enough to obtain protection; there had to be some element of originality. Because of this recent decision, one must be certain that other compilation works, such as computerized databases, contain sufficient originality to merit copyright protection. The information in a database may be analogous to the alphabetical entries in *Feist*'s telephone directory and, therefore, not deserving of copyright protection.

Because copyright protection is easier to obtain than patent protection, its scope is necessarily narrower. Therefore, an author who, by total coincidence, comes up with the same expression as one that is protected by copyright will not be guilty of infringing the original work.

(b) Particular Expression

Perhaps the most difficult area of copyright for computer programs is the issue of "what is protected." Copyright protects only original expressions embodied in the computer program or the selection of materials for the database. What it cannot protect, however, is any "idea, procedure, process, system, method of operation, concept, principle, or discovery."[20] The demarcation between protectable expression and unprotectable ideas will be examined below.

(c) Exclusive Rights

The owner of the copyright has the exclusive right to copy, sell, lease, distribute, perform, or display publicly and prepare derivative

---

[19]499 U.S. 340, 18 USPQ2d 1275, 18 Media L. Rep. 1889 (1991).
[20]17 U.S.C. §102(b).

works from the copyrighted work.[21] Special rules apply to computer programs with respect to these rights. Specifically, under 17 U.S.C. §109(a), the author's distribution right is limited by the owner's right to sell or otherwise dispose of the purchased copy as the purchaser sees fit. However, under §109(b)(1)(A), owners of copies of computer programs cannot rent, lend, or lease their copies. In addition, a special exception exists for video-game owners to repeatedly publicly display the game. Copyright law has also carved out a special "fair use" exception for owners of copies of computer programs to make another copy or adaptation of the program that is either essential (1) for its use in a machine or (2) is for archival purposes.

(d) Tangible Medium of Expression

Copyright protection attaches to the work when the work is fixed in any tangible medium of expression and proper copyright notification is given. Publication and registration are not required for a valid copyright.[22]

Fixation of a copyrighted work entails the requirement that the work be sufficiently permanent or stable to permit it to be perceived, reproduced, or otherwise communicated for a period of more than transitory duration. This does not mean that the work must be written or recorded exactly as it will be seen by the human eye. It is sufficient that the work is capable of being reproduced with the aid of a machine or device. Therefore, computer software that is stored in the memory of a computer and is capable of reproduction would clearly fall within the scope of the Copyright Act. The requirement of fixation would exclude only purely evanescent or transient reproductions, in other words, things that cannot be reproduced except by chance. Software can be copyrighted irrespective of the storage medium in which it is fixed. Software also can be copyrighted irrespective of the form it takes (e.g., source code, object code, screen displays, or microcode). Additionally, the copyright is available regardless of the functions performed by the computer software. It is irrelevant whether the software, for example, communicates directly with humans or only with

---

[21] 17 U.S.C. §106.

[22] 17 U.S.C. §102(a).

the machine itself (e.g., as an operating system).[23] Of course, if the writing of the code is a joint effort, all people who contributed would be considered authors of the work and would be entitled to joint ownership rights in that copyright.

(e) Works Made for Hire

If a work is made for hire, it is the employer rather than the employee who is considered the author for copyright purposes.[24] To qualify as a "work made for hire" under the Copyright Act, the work must either be "prepared by an employee within the scope of his or her employment" or "specially ordered or commissioned."[25] Unfortunately, no definitions for the key terms of "employee" or "scope of employment" can be found anywhere in the Act or the Congressional Committee Reports. Consequently, courts have differed on how to interpret those terms over the years.

Fortunately, the Supreme Court resolved this issue in the case of *Community for Creative Non-Violence v. Reid*.[26] In that case, CCNV, an organization that benefits the homeless, asked Reid, a sculptor, to create a work depicting homeless people in a nativity-like scene. He was paid $15,000 for that project. Some aspects of Reid's work were supervised by CCNV, but Reid acted independently in many other elements of the project. Reid claimed that he was not an employee of CCNV and, therefore, was the rightful owner of the copyright in the sculpture.

To decide this case, the Court interpreted the term "employee" under the general, common law rules of agency which state that a person is an employee if the hiring party has the right to control the manner and means by which the product on which the individual works is completed. The Court determined that Reid was in fact the copyright owner by looking at many factors, including the fact that Reid worked

---

[23]*See, e.g.*, Apple Computer v. Formula Int'l, 725 F.2d 521, 221 USPQ 762 (9th Cir. 1984); Apple Computer v. Franklin Computer Corp., 714 F.2d 1240, 219 USPQ 113 (3d Cir. 1983), *cert. dismissed*, 464 U.S. 1033 (1984).

[24]Because the nationality or domicile of the author is determinative of the rights that inhere in a copyright, the following rules pertain only to authors with U.S. citizenship or domicile. However, no copyright may be obtained if the U.S. government is the employer.

[25]17 U.S.C. §101.

[26]490 U.S. 730, 10 USPQ 1985, 16 Media L. Rep. 1769 (1989).

in his own studio in a different city, used his own tools, and was employed by CCNV for only two months.[27]

However, even if a person is considered an employee under the Copyright Act, his or her actions must be within the scope of employment for the employer to be deemed the author of the work. The fact that the employee used the employer's facilities or did work on company time is not dispositive of copyright ownership. Instead, courts will often look at the overall situation to determine if the person was acting within the scope of employment. Of course, two parties to a work may agree contractually to shift copyright ownership from one to the other, but it is important to note that this will merely be considered a transfer of ownership rights and cannot be converted into a work made for hire situation.

Certain commissioned works by independent contractors will also qualify as works made for hire if they fall within one of the following nine categories: (1) a contribution to a collective work; (2) a part of a motion picture or other audiovisual work; (3) a translation; (4) a supplementary work; (5) a compilation; (6) an instructional text; (7) a test; (8) answer material for a test; or (9) an atlas.[28]

However, falling within one of these categories is not, by itself, enough. Additionally, both parties to a specially ordered or commissioned work must specifically agree in a signed written instrument that the work will be made for hire.[29]

Computer software does not fall within any of the above categories of specially commissioned works unless the software performs a test, provides an answer for that test, or can operate as an atlas. By contrast, a database may qualify, since it is a compilation work. It thus becomes important that an employer obtain a written assignment of copyright rights from an independent contractor to protect its interests in the software or, if not possible, a written agreement stating that the works are made for hire if those works are databases.

(f) Notice

Section 401(a) of the 1976 Copyright Act, as amended by the Berne Convention Implementation Act,[30] eliminates the need to put

---

[27]The fact that a person does or does not receive compensation for a job is not, in and of itself, determinative of either employee status or copyright ownership.

[28]17 U.S.C. §101.

[29]These rules are a departure from the rules in existence prior to the 1976 Copyright Act and would not apply to any works prepared prior to January 1, 1978.

[30]Pub. L. No. 100-568, 102 Stat. 2853 (1988).

notice on a work to obtain copyright protection. However, while notice is no longer mandatory to obtain protection, there are several advantages to placing a copyright notice on a computer program. First, a defendant generally cannot claim innocent infringement to mitigate damages if adequate notice is present. Second, a U.S. citizen can avoid all formalities to copyright imposed by other countries if he or she complies with the formal requirements of notice. And lastly, notice is an inexpensive way to deter others from infringing a copyrighted work.

For notice to be adequate, it must include an indication of a claim to copyright by using any of the following: the copyright symbol (©); the word "Copyright"; or the abbreviation "Copr." Also, it must include the year of first publication and the name of the copyright owner. While the order of these elements is not important, it must be reasonably visible and legible to qualify as notice.

It is also important that the notice be placed in a position to give effective notice when the computer software is used in its intended manner. For a computer program, placement is advisable in any or all of the following positions:

1. At the beginning of the object code listing of the computer program or at the end of the work;
2. On the first screen displayed;
3. Continuously on each different screen; or
4. On a label securely affixed to the storage medium (i.e., diskette) or the box in which it comes.

It is advisable to place this notice in as many of these places as possible.

Prior to the 1976 Act, an error or omission in the copyright notice would usually result in a loss of copyright protection. However, the 1976 Copyright Act also added cure provisions for defective copyright notices in a limited number of situations.[31] Because notice has not been required for copyright protection since March 1, 1989, defective notice on a work first published after this date can always be amended.

(g) Registration

As with notice, registration is not a condition precedent to obtaining copyright protection. However, once again, there are many advantages to registering a work. A copyright claimant of a work

---

[31]*See* §§405 and 406 of the 1976 Copyright Act for a discussion of cure provisions.

originating in the United States cannot sue for infringement prior to registering that work with the Copyright Office. Furthermore, while a copyright claimant of a work not originating in the United States may institute an infringement suit without first registering, he or she may not ask for statutory damages or attorneys' fees if registration was not obtained. A registration is also required if the copyright holder seeks to have the U.S. Customs Service enforce the copyright against imports.

For works first published between January 1, 1978, and March 1, 1989, registrations can cure errors or omissions in copyright if made before or within five years of publication without notice. Additionally, instruments that transfer interests in copyrights will be viewed as affording constructive notice of those transfers to others only if that work is registered.

To register a copyright, one must submit a fee, fill out an application, and complete the deposit requirement of §408(b) or (c) (see Chapter 7). The application for copyright must contain the following information:

1. Name and address of the copyright claimant;
2. Name and nationality or domicile of the author(s). If any author has died, date of his or her death (not applicable for anonymous or pseudonymous works);
3. If the work is anonymous or pseudonymous, nationality or domicile of the author(s);
4. Statement indicating if the work is made for hire (as discussed in section 11.3(e));
5. Statement of how the copyright claimant became the owner of the copyright if he or she is not the author;
6. Title, including any previous or alternative titles under which the work can be identified;
7. Year creation was completed;
8. If the work was previously published, date and nation of first publication; and
9. If the work is a compilation or derivative work, identification of preexisting work(s) that it incorporates or is based upon and a brief, general statement of additional material covered by the copyright claim.[32]

For computer programs, this information must be filled out on Form TX, which is used for all nondramatic literary works, including

[32] 17 U.S.C. §409.

software. A single registration will cover both the codes (source and object), screen displays, documentation, and any associated flow charts.

(h) Deposit

Section 407 of the Copyright Act states that a deposit of a work is required within three months after publication of that work. However, this rule is enforced only when and if the Register of Copyrights makes a written demand. The penalty for noncompliance is a fine, not the forfeiture of a copyright. This is a departure from the rules of the 1909 Act, in which noncompliance may have resulted in copyright forfeiture. This deposit rule applies to both computer programs and databases but does not apply to databases that are available only on-line.[33] A deposit made under §407 that is accompanied by the necessary fees and applications will also satisfy the §408 deposit requirement described below.

Section 408 also imposes a deposit requirement on a copyright claimant of a published work that must be made in conjunction with registration. Generally, two copies of a work must be submitted to satisfy this requirement.[34] However, only one copy of identifying portions of computer programs and databases that are only stored in machine-readable form must be deposited.[35] These identifying portions must be visually perceptible without the aid of a machine or device. Any of the following will satisfy the deposit requirement:

1. First and last 25 pages of the program including the copyright notice;
2. If the program is 50 pages or less, the entire program;
3. If the program is a revision and the revisions are placed throughout the entire program, either (1) or (2) above;
4. If the program is a revision and the revisions are concentrated in a particular part of the code, 50 pages that are representative of those changes including the copyright page;

---

[33] 37 C.F.R. §202.19(c)(5).

[34] If the work was published prior to January 1, 1978, two copies of the work as it was first published must be submitted; otherwise, two copies of the best edition must be deposited.

[35] 37 C.F.R. §202.20(c)(2)(vii).

5. If the screen displays are being claimed, a visual representation of the copyrightable expression in the form of photographs, printouts, or drawings plus any of (1)–(4) above to register the literal code itself;
6. If it is a database, the first and last 25 or equivalent units of work submitted on paper or microform;
7. If the database has been revised, 50 representative pages or data records that have been added or modified;
8. If the database has multiple separate or distinct data files, 50 complete data records from each data file or if a data file is less than 50 records, the entire data file;
9. If an interest exists in the trade secrets of the program, the first and last 25 pages of source code can be deposited with trade secrets blocked out, as long as the blocked out portions are less than the remaining portions and an appreciable amount of the original program remains; and
10. Trade secrets can also be preserved by depositing the first and last 25 pages of object code for the program together with 10 consecutive pages of the source code (containing no blocked out portions) from anywhere in the program. However, this type of deposit will result only in a "rule of doubt" registration, which means that the owner has the burden to establish originality in court.

(i) Scope of the Copyright

Copyright law provides that expression is protected while ideas are not. Courts have long tried to differentiate between underlying ideas and the expression of those ideas to determine what falls within the scope of copyright protection. To accomplish this, many courts have used the idea expression test, which simply applies the general rules of copyrightability to a particular product (see Chapter 7, section 7.2(f)). The test states that the idea can be seen as the underlying purpose of the program, which is not copyrightable; and the expression can be seen as anything that is not necessary to that idea, which would therefore be deserving of copyright protection.

While this is the primary test used to determine copyrightable matter in a computer program, a problem arises because this test was developed before computer programs were copyrightable and, additionally, this test is not suited to the technical determinations necessary in the case of computer programs.

The National Commission on New Technological Uses of Copyrighted Works acknowledges that it is very difficult "to draw the line between the copyrightable element of style and expression in a computer program and the process which underlies it."[36] Courts have struggled with this analysis and often made contradictory determinations even though they were interpreting the same elements.

Other courts have used the "merger doctrine" to decide that a matter is uncopyrightable when there is no difference between the underlying idea and the expression. The merger doctrine states that even expression of ideas may be uncopyrightable if no practical difference can be found between an idea and its expression. In other words, if there is only one way to express this idea, copyright protection would not be available, because it would preclude others from using this idea. Therefore, protection cannot be granted regardless of the novelty of the expression. It is also important to note that when examining alternatives, the court should look not only at the technical feasibility, but also the economic feasibility to determine what constitutes a viable substitute.

Because Congress realizes that the computer industry is a quickly growing area, it has left the line-drawing problem of determining what is copyrightable to the courts to determine on a case-by-case basis.

If the idea/expression line is drawn too liberally in favor of protection, the first to create an application program would get an undeserved monopoly and thereby inhibit others from developing better products. If, however, the line is drawn too conservatively, there is a fear that authors will not continue to develop new programs and user interfaces.

This problem is especially evident when considering the protection of the nonliteral aspects of a computer program such as the screen display and the structure, sequence, and organization of the program, which is sometimes referred to as the "look and feel" of the program.

The first case to consider the issue of protecting the nonliteral aspects of a copyrighted work was *Baker v. Selden*.[37] In this case, the Supreme Court developed the method for determining what was copyrightable by distinguishing between the elements that were necessary to the concept (the ideas), and those that were unnecessary (the

---

[36]NEW TECHNOLOGICAL USES OF COPYRIGHTED WORKS 22 (Library of Congress) (1979).

[37]101 U.S. (11 Otto) 99 (1879).

expressions). The Court reasoned that this methodology encouraged creative expression by promoting arts and science through monopoly protection, while still allowing others to modify or enhance that idea.

In *Whelan Associates v. Jaslow Dental Laboratory,*[38] the Court of Appeals for the Third Circuit developed a test that was followed in other circuits, stating that the purpose of a given work is the uncopyrightable idea and everything not necessary to that purpose is protectable expression. In this case, Jaslow hired Whelan to write a program to automate the everyday operations of his dental laboratory. It was agreed that Whelan would own the copyright and that Jaslow would attempt to sell the work to other dental laboratories on Whelan's behalf. Several years later, Jaslow began selling his own program, which looked very similar to the one created by Whelan. Jaslow's computer program, however, was written in a different computer language and used different underlying logic structures.

The court, in using the above-stated test, found that the purpose of the program was to run a dental laboratory and that the structure and layout of the program were not necessary to that end. The court held that the structure, sequence, and organization of Whelan's program were copyrightable expressions and were therefore infringed by Jaslow's program, even though the programs, in a side-by-side examination, looked different.

Broderbund Software v. Unison World[39] expanded *Whelan* to cover screens as well as code when their "look and feel" are substantially similar. Broderbund claimed that Unison had infringed its program that created greeting cards and banners. The *Broderbund* court held that because there were other ways to design the display menus, the screens produced by the programs constituted protectable expression and had, therefore, been infringed. This decision, however, has been widely criticized because the court erroneously interpreted the *Whelan* decision.

The *Broderbund* court claimed that *Whelan* established that computer screens were covered by the copyright of the code. *Whelan* actually stated that it was the sequence and form of that computer code that were copyrightable. When addressing this issue, the *Whelan* court merely stated that the similarity of the screens may be used as evidence of infringement of the underlying program. The *Broderbund* decision

---

[38]797 F.2d 1222, 230 USPQ 481 (3d Cir. 1986), *cert. denied,* 479 U.S. 1037 (1987).

[39]648 F. Supp. 1127, 231 USPQ 700 (N.D. Cal. 1986).

greatly enlarged the protection of computer programs by stating that almost all of the nonliteral elements of the program, including the screen displays, were copyrightable, and that the analysis for determining substantial similarity merely needed to conclude an overall similarity in the look and feel.

Recently, in *Computer Associates International v. Altai Inc.*,[40] the Court of Appeals for the Second Circuit developed a substantial similarity test that limited the impact of *Whelan* and *Broderbund,* when it held that a copyright of the nonliteral elements of a computer program had not been infringed. This test examined (1) if the defendant had access to the plaintiff's copyrighted work, and (2) if the works were substantially similar.

The court performed the second test by going through three steps that it called abstraction, filtration, and comparison tests. In the first step, the court abstracted the work to a point in which the nonliteral expression broke down the program into its structural parts. Next, it analyzed those sections of the computer program to see what constituted unprotectable material, namely (i) ideas, (ii) expressions incidental to those ideas, and (iii) expressions that are already in the public domain. After pulling out all of these elements, only those elements that were protectable were left. This would therefore constitute the scope of the copyright. Lastly, the remaining parts of each program were then compared to see if they were substantially similar.

The court further stated that elements that are indispensable or at least standard to a particular type of program, known as scenes a faire, cannot be protected because this would virtually preclude others from developing programs to accomplish a particular application.

A review of the above cases shows that courts have routinely applied different standards to cases such as these and, as a result, have come to conflicting conclusions regarding both what constitutes the unprotectable idea and what constitutes the protected expression. Because of this, courts have also differed on what falls within the scope of the copyright. Until a definitive solution to this question exists, it is very important to examine all tests to see if a particular element of a computer program will fall within the scope of the copyright.

---

[40]982 F.2d 693, 23 USPQ2d 1241 (2d Cir. 1992).

11.4 Trade Secrets: Nature and Limitations

(a) Requirement of Secrecy

Like patent law, trade secret law provides protection for ideas incorporated into computer programs. Trade secret protection is thus broader than copyright, since it can protect more than just expressions. In addition, trade secret law does not require the careful description of the program as currently required by the PTO for patent protection. However, the ideas in the program must remain secret.

The principles of trade secret law grew out of and are rooted in the common law of torts. The offense of such law is in disclosing or using information that is discovered by improper means or that breaches a confidence of the one who communicated the information.[41] Unlike other forms of intellectual property, liability for trade secrecy violation does not come from the act of copying or using the protected information. Rather, liability derives from the use of an improper means to procure it.

Comment b to §757 of the Restatement (First) of Torts sets out, by exemplification, the definition of a trade secret, which has been adopted almost universally by the courts:

> A trade secret may consist of any formula, pattern, device or compilation of information which is used in one's business and which gives him an opportunity to obtain an advantage over competitors who do not know or use it. It may be a formula for a chemical compound, a process of manufacturing . . . , or a list of customers. . . . A trade secret is a process or device for continuous use in the operation of the business. Generally it relates to the production of goods, as, for example, a machine or formula for the production of an article. It may, however, relate to the sale of goods or to other operations in the business, such as a code for determining discounts, rebates or other concessions in a price list or catalogue, or a list of specialized customers, or a method of bookkeeping or other office management. . . . The subject matter of a trade secret must be secret. Matters of public knowledge or of general knowledge in an industry cannot be appropriated by one as his secret. Matters which are completely disclosed by the goods which one markets cannot be his secret.[42]

---

[41] RESTATEMENT (FIRST) OF TORTS §757, at 1–2 (1939).

[42] *See* Space Aero Prods. Co. v. R.E. Darling Co., 208 A.2d 74, 79 (Md.), *cert. denied*, 382 U.S. 843, 147 USPQ 541 (1965).

The value of a trade secret comes not from any inherent worth of the information, but derives from the fact that it is a *secret*. Therefore, the mechanisms for preserving the knowledge as a secret are important to the preservation of trade secret protection.

(b) Uniform Trade Secrets Act

Thirty-four states and the District of Columbia have adopted the Uniform Trade Secrets Act (UTSA)[43] since it was first promulgated in 1979. The UTSA was designed to codify and replace the common law of torts and provide consistent results in the adopting states. It did not displace contract or criminal law with respect to trade secrets.

The statutory definition of a trade secret under the UTSA is information, including a formula, pattern, compilation, program, device, method, technique, or process that: (1) derives *independent economic value,* actual or potential, from (2) *not* being *generally known to,* and (3) not being readily ascertainable by proper means by (4) other persons who can obtain *economic value* from its *disclosure or use,* and (5) is the subject of efforts that are *reasonable* under the circumstances to maintain its secrecy.[44] Based on the Restatement and common law, the UTSA has *eliminated* the requirement that the information be "continuously used in one's business" before qualifying as a trade secret.

The UTSA also provides broader protection for trade secrets and greater relief for improper disclosure than many state common laws. Courts may issue an injunction to last for as long as the information remains a trade secret, which could be indefinitely. In lieu of an injunction, a license or royalty may be awarded for use of the secret. Compensatory damages for disclosure can include a return for unjust enrichment as well as losses. Finally, the UTSA provides for treble damages. A more detailed discussion of the law of trade secrets can be found in Chapter 9.

(c) Secrecy and Reverse Engineering

Despite significant provisions for relief, protecting trade secrets is difficult, especially for computer software. As noted above, secrets

---

[43] 14 U.L.A. 433 (1985).

[44] UTSA §1(4), 14 U.L.A. at 438.

are protected only from being improperly obtained or disclosed. The ideas themselves are freely available for use, when known.

Disclosure, even if accidental or inadvertent, destroys the secrecy and, therefore, the protection.[45] Since some disclosure is necessary to use information in a business, absolute secrecy is not required. Reasonable measures must be taken to restrict the extent of disclosure.[46] Therefore, transmission of information should always be accompanied by express, or at least implicit, agreements of confidentiality. Otherwise, there is a substantial risk that a court will find that the trade secret protection has been lost.

It is not a trade secret violation to discover another's trade secret through one's own investigative efforts.[47] Such efforts, often called "reverse engineering," do not constitute a violation.[48] Despite the propriety of reverse engineering, the trade secret can remain as long as there is a substantial element of secrecy so that, except for the use of improper means, or difficult but allowable reverse engineering, there would be difficulty in acquiring the information.

Therefore, the distribution or sale of programs, especially mass distribution, inhibits the maintenance of secrecy. Once information is in the public domain, it can be freely analyzed, used, and copied.[49]

(d) Protective Procedures

With carefully established procedures, the underlying design concepts of the computer program can be protected as a trade secret. Restricted access to the program and agreements requiring nondisclosure of the program are essential to establish and maintain its trade secret status.

If there will be a mass distribution of the program, trade secret protection may not be available because the distribution of a large number of copies may negate a claim that the program is secret. Further, if the underlying design concepts must be disclosed in marketing the

---

[45]Defiance Button Mach. Co. v. C & C Metal Prods. Corp., 759 F.2d 1053, 225 USPQ 797 (2d Cir.), *cert. denied,* 474 U.S. 844 (1985).

[46]Restatement (First) of Torts §757 (1939).

[47]*Id.*

[48]*See* Kewanee Oil Co. v. Bicron Corp., 416 U.S. 470, 181 USPQ 673 (1974).

[49]Bonito Boats, Inc. v. Thunder Craft Boats, 489 U.S. 141, 9 USPQ2d 1847 (1989).

program, confidentiality and nondisclosure agreements with the customer will be necessary to maintain a claim of trade secret. While limited distributions of source code and other source documentation under restrictive agreements can preserve the secrecy of the program,[50] the greater the distribution, the less likely a claim to secrecy can be maintained.

Protective procedures for maintaining secrecy should include the following five steps:

1. Restrictive agreements with customers forbidding disclosure and limiting access to the source code and other source code documentation describing the underlying design concepts;
2. Nondisclosure and confidentiality agreements with employees;
3. Restricted access by employees and other individuals to the source code and other source code documentation;
4. Proprietary and confidentiality legends on all materials that embody the secrets; and
5. Filing deposits in the U.S. Copyright Office under the provisions to accommodate trade secrets.

These procedures must be regularly followed and closely monitored in order to preserve the secrecy of the program. To do otherwise could result in the loss of trade secret protection.

One approach to maintaining secrecy is to distribute only machine-readable materials (object code) to the customer, together with other program documentation (not source code documentation) to instruct the customer how to use the materials. This approach has been used to preserve the secrecy of the underlying design concepts of the program, particularly where the machine-readable materials are distributed under a license agreement. If licensees insist on source code backups, licensors should resort to an escrow arrangement that allows access only under certain extreme conditions.

(e) Agreements

Confidentiality agreements can protect trade secrets from losing protection upon disclosure. Express agreements should be executed

[50]Courts have held that restricted distribution of computer software does not negate trade secret protection. In Data Gen. Corp. v. Digital Computer Controls, 357 A.2d 105 (Del. Ch. 1975), the court found that disclosure to almost 6,000 users did

with all parties who may have contact with secrets, including employees, suppliers, and customers.

The common law often will impose an obligation on employees to maintain the secrecy of information based upon a duty of good faith. An implicit contract obligates the employee or former employee not to use or disclose the trade secrets to the owner-employer's detriment.[51] However, courts are less favorably disposed to imposing such relationships with outsiders. To find an implied contract, courts require evidence that a confidential relationship existed and that both parties realized the information was to be treated as confidential.

By licensing a trade secret, the licensor may avoid the problem of public disclosure through unrestricted sales, if the licensing agreement restricts the licensee and its employees from using or disclosing the information in a way that is inconsistent with the maintenance of the owner's trade secret, or, for example, from disassembling the product to determine its underlying processes.

The above approach has found some popularity in the area of computer software, where although the program is copyrightable, the underlying idea is not. Other terms to be considered when drafting the license agreement are those that require the licensee to observe the same protective measures discussed above with regard to maintaining the secrecy of a trade secret in-house, and restricting the hardware environment (stand-alone versus network) or location where the software is loaded.

Although written agreements provide the trade secret owner with a considerable measure of protection, they are not without attendant risks of their own. Contract law is not subordinate to the provisions of the UTSA. Contract principles thus will govern the rights and obligations of the parties. Failure to provide for the appropriate protection may result in a court concluding that the parties did not intend to include such protection. And where express conditions are set forth, a court may conclude that only those provisions and no others apply.

11.5 Software Contracts and Licenses

Computer software contracts can take numerous forms and they can treat the computer software as a good or service. Much software

---

not defeat trade secret status where adequate measures had been taken to protect confidentiality. In Management Science Am. v. Cyborg Sys., 6 Computer L. Serv. Rep. 921 (N.D. Ill. 1978), the court found that the computer software for payroll distribution could be a trade secret despite distribution to 600 licensees.

[51]In re Uniservices, 517 F.2d 492 (7th Cir. 1975).

is sold in retail stores as mass market products, considered goods. However, often software is specifically produced or modified for a single purchaser. Also, software can be included in conjunction with the provision of services, such as consulting or accounting. When the software is not independently marketed, it may be considered part of the service itself. Contracts can cover numerous situations, including software development, software servicing, and end uses.

Virtually all licensing rules apply to software. When software is considered a good, the Uniform Commercial Code (UCC) may apply to the sale or license.[52] This section is directed to the applicability of the UCC to software and particular types of software licenses. See Chapter 12 for a detailed discussion regarding intellectual licensing considerations.

(a) Computers and the UCC

If software is defined as a good under the agreement, then UCC article 2 would most likely apply. Article 2 would also appear to cover licenses that have all the attributes of a sale.[53]

The ultimate determination whether the software transferred is to be treated as a good or service for UCC purposes depends on how a court characterizes the predominant nature of the transaction.[54]

Whether or not a transaction falls within article 2 has an important impact on several aspects of a license agreement. Primarily, the UCC creates specific warranties with respect to the sale of goods. These warranties increase the burdens on software producers.

First, express warranties are automatically created under UCC §2-313(1) by virtue of any affirmation or promise, any description of the goods, or any sample or model. Under the common law, however, express warranties are usually created only in writing.

Second, if the UCC applies, the implied warranty of merchantability under UCC §2-314 becomes part of the agreement if the seller is a merchant. The merchantability warranty includes a warranty that the goods are fit for ordinary purposes for which they are used, and that they are adequately packaged. Disclaimer of this warranty must be

---

[52]UCC §2-102 (sales), §2A-102 (leases that include licenses).

[53]Hertz Commercial Leasing Corp. v. Transportation Credit Clearing House, 298 N.Y.S.2d 392 (N.Y. Civ. Ct. 1969), *rev'd on other grounds*, 316 N.Y.S.2d 585 (N.Y. App. Term 1970) (*per curiam*).

[54]RRX Indus. v. Lab-Con, Inc., 772 F.2d 543 (9th Cir. 1985).

conspicuous, specific, and in writing.[55] Under common law, however, implied warranties do not exist.

Third, the UCC also creates an implied warranty of fitness under §2-315 when the seller has particular knowledge about the purpose for which the goods are purchased and there is reliance on that knowledge by the buyer. Again, disclaimer of this warranty must be conspicuous and must be in writing under UCC §2-316(2).

Both implied warranties under the UCC can be critical. In *Jaskey Finance & Leasing v. Display Data Corp.*,[56] the defendant's attempts at disclaiming the implied warranty of merchantability were denied since the defendant failed to mention "merchantability" in writing. The implied fitness for a particular purpose warranty is particularly important in computer and software sales where purchasers rely on a computer salesman's recommendations on what computer system would meet the customer's needs. Under this scenario, the salesman's recommendations were held by courts to fulfill the conditions for creating the implied warranty of fitness for a particular purpose.[57]

Fourth, the warranty of title under UCC §2-312(1)(a) or the warranty of noninfringement under UCC §2-312(3) is automatically available as part of the general warranty of merchantability under the UCC. The warranty of title provides that title to the good is owned by the seller and that the transfer is rightful. More significantly, the warranty of noninfringement provides that a merchant of these kinds of goods warrants the goods to be delivered free of the rightful claim of any third person by way of infringement or the like. Given the confused nature of patent, copyright, and trade secret protections for software, a warranty of noninfringement places a high burden on the seller. In addition, all merchants, including wholesalers and retailers, are obligated by this warranty of the UCC. Moreover, these UCC warranties must be specifically disclaimed in the same manner described above.

Fifth, damages under UCC §2-714(3) include consequential damages and any incidental damages under the appropriate circumstances. The common law does not include such damages.

---

[55]UCC §2-316(2).

[56]564 F. Supp. 160 (E.D. Pa. 1983).

[57]*See, e.g.*, National Cash Register Co. v. Adell Indus., 225 N.W.2d 785 (Mich. Ct. App. 1975).

(b) Types of Computer Licenses

(i) Shrink Wrap Licenses

The most common form of software transfer is the sale of off-the-shelf software as mass-marketed products. Typically, this form of software is licensed under a "shrink wrap" license agreement. A shrink wrap license refers to the fact that the agreement is packaged with the product and is accepted when the purchaser opens the package.

Shrink wrap agreements, however, have serious drawbacks concerning whether or not there is an agreement by the end user. As yet, the issue has not been decided by a court. Without agreement, the terms of the license are not binding on the user.

Several practical techniques can be employed to increase the likelihood that a "valid" acceptance of the shrink wrap license by the end user occurs. The first approach is to provide a warranty card with the product, which provides the licensee with additional warranties *if* the user agrees to sign the card that he or she accepts the terms of the shrink wrap license and then sends the signed card to the warrantor. A second approach is to provide a capability in the software requiring the user to agree to the license to enable the further operation of the program and allow the user to move to the next screen. In other words, the software can tell the user, "If you accept the license terms, please indicate by typing 'Yes,' and you will be allowed to continue."

A second drawback to shrink wrap agreements is enforceability. Both Illinois and Louisiana have software enforcement statutes that indicate the appropriate format for shrink wrap agreements and the sanctions for their violation.[58] The Louisiana law, however, was judged to be preempted by federal copyright law and thus the shrink wrap agreements were found to be unenforceable under the statute in *Vault Corp. v. Quaid Software*.[59] The court ultimately failed to determine whether or not the license agreement was itself valid.

In 1986, ADAPSO, the Computer Software and Services Industry Association, adopted guidelines for shrink wrap agreements. These guidelines suggested that (1) software vendors provide express warranties that the program will perform substantially in accordance with the

---

[58] LA. REV. STAT. ANN. §§51:1962–51:1966 (West 1987).

[59] 655 F. Supp. 750, 2 USPQ2d (E.D. La. 1987), *aff'd*, 847 F.2d 255, 7 USPQ2d 1281 (5th Cir. 1988).

published specification, the documentation, and authorized advertising; (2) the warranties be of sufficient duration, such as 90 days, to enable customers to discover significant errors; and (3) if notified of significant errors, a company might either (a) convert the errors within a reasonable time period, (b) provide the customer with functionally equivalent software, or (c) provide the customer with a refund.

(ii) Other Licenses

Other forms of software license agreements are as varied as the types of situations those agreements cover. For example, contracts can be drafted to cover a "bundled" product consisting of both the computer hardware and the computer software combined. Software distributorship agreements are common, as well as joint development and programming services agreements, and third-party software licenses/assignments.

(iii) Escrow

An important concept employed in many of the above license agreements is the software escrow, whereby a third party holds a copy of the software source code. Under certain conditions, the purchaser may have access to the source code.

An escrow is particularly valuable when a vendor does not want the licensee or purchaser to see the source code. Generally, maintaining secrecy with respect to source code protects the code under trade secret law. However, the licensee/purchaser needs protection in the event he or she needs the source code to maintain the software and it is unavailable from the vendor. The source code may become unavailable for many reasons. The vendor could cease to exist, such as through bankruptcy, merger, or dissolution. The vendor may also fail to maintain prior versions of the source code when changes are made. This can be particularly important for significantly changed software. Also, the vendor may destroy or refuse to provide the source code in response to disagreements with the purchaser. A software escrow thus serves as a valuable tool that protects the vendor from having to disclose the source code, but also protects the licensee/purchaser, who may obtain a copy of the source code if the need arises.

12
Assignments and Licensing

12.1 Introduction

Intellectual property is intangible personal property. As personal property, the owner may sell or otherwise dispose of all or a portion of its interest in the property or may grant others permission to use the property. These transfers are treated under the law similarly to transfers of other kinds of personal property.

An assignment of intellectual property is a transfer of the title to the intellectual property from the assignor to the assignee. Title to property is the union of all the elements that constitute ownership of the property. In an assignment, the assignor generally must transfer *all* of its rights to the intellectual property to the assignee, although in some cases, the transferor can retain certain rights (see section 12.4). If the assignment is of less than the assignee's whole interest in the intellectual property, it may be considered a license rather than an assignment. On the other hand, an assignment of title may occur even if the parties label a transfer a license, if substantially all rights pass to the transferee. A partial interest can be assigned for most kinds of intellectual property. However, to constitute an assignment, all of the assignor's rights in that partial interest must be transferred. For example, the inventors named on a patent are joint owners of the patent. Each has an individual partial undivided ownership interest in the whole patent and all of the rights afforded by the patent.

A license is the grant of permission by the possessor of intellectual property rights to commit acts that the licensor has the right to exclude.

A license may also provide the licensee with the privilege to enforce the intellectual property rights against others. Generally, intellectual property rights may be divided in more ways for licensing purposes than assignment purposes.

An intellectual property owner is not required to grant licenses to others. The patent statutes expressly provide that there is no obligation on the part of the patent holder to license his or her patent or to practice his or her patented invention.[1] It is the prerogative of the patent holder to prevent others from using his or her patented invention and to not use it himself or herself.

12.2 Initial Ownership

As discussed below, initial ownership of intellectual property is governed by laws particular to the type of intellectual property at issue. Disputes as to initial ownership of intellectual property frequently occur in employment and independent contractor relationships. Thus, it is desirable to have employment agreements or contracts clearly spelling out who is to own the right to the intellectual property and placing obligations to assign title when necessary. This is especially important with independent contractors, where the hiring party may have a weaker claim to title in the absence of an agreement.

(a) Patents

An invention is originally owned by the inventors. The inventors are those individuals who conceived of the invention. No one but the actual inventors is entitled to apply in the United States for a patent on an invention. Accordingly, the ownership of the patent application and the resulting patent vests in the first instance in the inventors.

Patents and applications for patents usually contain several claims. The inventorship for all the claims does not have to be the same. For example, a patent may have 10 claims, Smith being the sole inventor of 3 claims, Jones being the sole inventor of 2 claims, and Smith,

[1] 35 U.S.C. §271(d)(4).

Jones, and Schmallman being the co-inventors of 5 claims. The entire patent is owned jointly by Smith, Jones, and Schmallman, each having an undivided one-third interest. Each can exploit the patent independently of the others, provided that each is entitled to a one-third share of the profits made by the others. Advantageously, joint owners will cooperate to exploit the property to avoid competition among themselves.

Another entity can obtain ownership of the invention from the inventors only by assignment or by operation of law, such as a court order in connection with bankruptcy or settlement of an estate. Thus, generally, an employer must obtain an agreement to assign inventions from its employee inventors. However, in some circumstances, such as when an employee is employed specifically to invent, an employer may be entitled to obtain ownership even if such an agreement was not obtained. Many employees have an implied or expressed contractual requirement to assign inventions made on the job to their employer. Such obligations to assign are not themselves assignments. Therefore, such an employee must execute an assignment for each patent application in which he or she is an inventor. When such assignments are made, an employer should be careful to ensure that the entire invention and all related rights are being transferred, not merely the particular patent application. The rules governing whether an employee or employer should be considered the original owner of an invention are discussed in Chapter 10, section 10.1.

(b) Trademarks

A trademark confers the right to eliminate customer confusion arising from a junior user's use of the same or similar mark. A trademark is initially owned by the first entity that uses the mark as a symbol of origin. The applicant for a federal registration must be the owner of the trademark. The registration rights are owned by the party that filed the application for registration. In a parent-subsidiary relationship, the parties may generally decide between themselves who owns a trademark and may be the applicant. But if the parent controls the use of the mark by the subsidiary, the parent is the owner of the mark and must be the applicant for registration. However, if the parent is using the mark, the subsidiary may not be the owner absent a license agreement giving the subsidiary control over quality of the goods and services provided by the parent.

A trademark symbolizes a single source of goods. Because use of a mark by two entities not commonly controlled can lead to customer confusion, joint ownership of a trademark, except in rare circumstances, is not permitted. Corporations, partnerships, and joint ventures are each considered a single entity for the purpose of trademark ownership.[2]

Because a trademark confers the right to prevent customer confusion of source, the owner of the trademark must exercise quality control to preserve trademark rights. Where there is no agreement between a manufacturer and a distributor of goods as to ownership of the mark, and the distributor is not exercising quality control over the production of the goods, it is likely that the manufacturer will be the owner of the trademark rights. This is because the manufacturer inherently maintains quality control of the goods through the manufacturing process. The manufacturer may own the mark even if the manufacturer's company name and either the distributor's company name or trade name appears on the goods as sold to the consuming public.

(c) Copyrights

The owner of a copyright in a work is initially the "author."[3] Unless the work is a "work made for hire" the author is the individual who creates the work. In two specific "work made for hire" circumstances, the author of the work, and therefore the owner of the copyright in the first instance, is an entity other than the creator.

First, when a work is prepared by an employee within the scope of his or her employment, the employer is the author of the work. An "employee" under the "work made for hire" provisions of copyright law includes not only regular employees, but also independent contractors if the employer exercises and directs sufficient control over the independent contractor in the creation of the work.[4] No transfer of title from the employee to the employer is required because title in the copyright initially vests in the employer upon creation of the work.

Second, if the author is not an employee, a work specially ordered or commissioned for any one of nine specified uses will be treated as

---

[2] 15 U.S.C. §1127.

[3] 17 U.S.C. §201(a).

[4] 17 U.S.C. §101; *see, e.g.*, Community for Creative Non-Violence v. Reid, 490 U.S. 730, 10 USPQ2d 1985, 16 Media L. Rep. 1769 (1989).

a "work made for hire" if the parties agree in a signed writing to treat the work as such. This applies only for works to be used as: (1) a contribution to a collective work, (2) part of a motion picture or other audiovisual work, (3) a translation, (4) a supplementary work, (5) a compilation, (6) an instructional text, (7) a test, (8) answer material for a test, or (9) an atlas.[5] If the above conditions are met, no transfer of title is required because title initially vests in the commissioning party. However, if the work is not one of the types specified, or if the parties do not sign a written agreement to treat the work as a work made for hire, title initially vests in the creator. Therefore, a subsequent transfer of title to the commissioning party is required.

Joint authorship of a copyright arises when a work is created by more than one author. Each joint owner has the independent right to use the work or license others to use the work,[6] provided that each joint owner has a right to share in the profits.[7] Recent cases hold that a joint owner must account to the other owners even for his or her own use, not just for licensed use.[8]

(d) Trade Secrets and Proprietary Information

The title to a trade secret or proprietary information initially vests in the creator. But when an employee is hired to design, title to trade secrets he or she develops in the course of employment vests initially in the employer, in the absence of an express agreement otherwise as to ownership of trade secrets.[9] The same rule has been applied to an employee who was not hired to design, but who nonetheless experimented and developed a trade secret and accepted pay for such work.[10] And when an independent contractor is hired for a specific task, the situation is treated as an employment relationship with the hiring party having initial title in any trade secrets developed by the independent

[5]17 U.S.C. §101.

[6]Werbungs und Commerz Union Austalt v. LeShufy, 6 USPQ2d 1153 (S.D.N.Y. 1987).

[7]Jerry Vogul Music Co. v. Miller Music, 74 N.Y.S.2d 425, 75 USPQ 205 (N.Y. App. Div. 1947), *aff'd*, 87 N.E.2d 681, 82 USPQ 458 (N.Y. 1949).

[8]Oddo v. Ries, 743 F.2d 630, 222 USPQ 799 (9th Cir. 1984).

[9]Standard Parts Co. v. Peck, 264 U.S. 52 (1924).

[10]Houghton v. United States, 23 F.2d 386 (4th Cir.), *cert. denied*, 277 U.S. 592 (1928).

contractor in the course of the job.[11] In both of these situations, no assignment of the trade secret to the employer is required.

12.3 Rights That Can Be Assigned or Licensed

(a) Patents

In the United States, an inventor does not have any exclusive patent rights in his or her invention until a patent issues. On the issue date, the patent confers the right to exclude others from making, using, or selling the claimed invention.

When an entire assignment is made, all three of these rights (make, use, and sell) are transferred to the assignee. If anything less than all three of these rights is transferred, for instance, only the right to make and use or the right to make and sell, then the transfer is merely a license, not an assignment. Courts will look to the substance of the transfer, not the label the parties place on it, to determine if a transfer is an assignment or a license. Therefore, if the parties intend to transfer title by an assignment, they should be certain to transfer the right to make, use, and sell the patented invention, without omitting any of these three rights.

A license allows the licensee to do what would be infringement in the absence of a license. Unlike an assignment, a patent license may be limited to any one or any combination of the make, use, and sell rights. It is also permissible to territorially divide licensed patent rights and to place other restrictions on the licensee. Such restrictions and limitations must be carefully applied to avoid possible violations of antitrust laws.

(b) Trademarks

The overriding purpose of a trademark is the right to prevent customer confusion caused by a junior user's use of the same or a

[11] *E.g.*, Mitchell Metal Prods. v. Berkeley Equip. Co., 36 F. Supp. 1010, 48 USPQ 254 (W.D. Pa. 1941); Jones v. Ulrich, 95 N.E.2d 113, 87 USPQ 331 (Ill. App. Ct. 1950).

similar mark. This right is assignable. However, the trademark by itself is valueless, and it must be assigned along with its accompanying good will to remain effective.

One of the changes under federal law from state common law is that it is possible to register an intent-to-use a trademark. The applicant may file an application based on a bona fide intention to use the trademark in commerce, although there need not be use of the trademark in commerce yet. This intent-to-use application is not assignable prior to filing a statement of use, except it may be assigned as part of the sale of an ongoing business.

Trademark rights may be assigned or licensed to different parties for different goods and services. However, to prevent the likelihood of customer confusion, the goods and services of one assignee must be unrelated to the goods and services of the other assignee.

(c) Copyrights

The Copyright Act of 1976[12] grants a copyright holder five specific rights in his or her copyrighted work as applicable to the particular work. These are the exclusive right to: (1) reproduce the work, (2) create derivative works, (3) distribute the copyrighted work, (4) perform the work, and (5) display the work. Any of these five rights may be freely separated and independently assigned or licensed to different parties. The so-called moral rights that have recently been added to the Copyright Act, the rights of attribution and integrity, are not transferable. These rights are inherent in the author of the work and for that reason may not be assigned.[13]

(d) Trade Secrets and Proprietary Information

A trade secret is information that has value from not being generally known and not being readily ascertainable by proper means, and that is subject to reasonable efforts to maintain secrecy. The right to

[12]17 U.S.C. §101.

[13]For a further discussion of the rights conferred by copyright, see Chapter 7, section 7.3.

use the information and prevent unauthorized use and disclosure may be licensed or assigned.

(e) Assignment of Rights to Enforce Against Past Infringement

The right to sue to enjoin infringement and collect money damages rests only with the title holder of the patent at the time the infringement occurs. Therefore, when a patent is assigned, the assignee takes only the right to collect damages for infringement that occurs after the assignment. However, the assignee may sue to enjoin infringement, no matter when the infringement began. If the parties intend to transfer the right to sue prior infringers to collect damages, this right must be expressly granted in the assignment document. There is no presumption that this right is transferred when a patent is assigned.[14]

Nor does an assignment of a trademark and its accompanying good will transfer the right to sue prior infringers.[15] If the parties intend to transfer this right, it should be expressly stated in the assignment that the right to enforce the trademark against prior infringement is being transferred. However, in the sale of an entire business, some courts have interpreted provisions that transfer all intangible assets as including existing causes of action.[16] Under such a construction, the sale of a business and all intangible assets includes the right to enforce a trademark against prior infringement even if this right is not expressly transferred.

Only the assignee or exclusive licensee of a copyright has standing to sue for infringement of his or her particular right, and only for infringement occurring after the transfer of ownership or license rights. Here, too, some courts have presumed the intent to transfer this right to enforce against prior infringement if an entire ongoing business is sold along with its copyrights.[17] However, if the parties intend to

---

[14]Crown Die & Tool Co. v. Nye Tool & Mach. Works, 261 U.S. 24 (1923); Arachnid, Inc. v. Merit Indus., 939 F.2d 1574, 19 USPQ2d 1513 (Fed. Cir. 1991) (and cases cited therein).

[15]H&J Foods v. Reeder, 477 F.2d 1053, 177 USPQ 612 (9th Cir.), *cert. denied,* 414 U.S. 859, 179 USPQ 322 (1973).

[16]George W. Luft Co. v. Zande Cosmetic Co., 142 F.2d 536, 61 USPQ 424 (2d Cir.), *cert. denied,* 323 U.S. 756, 63 USPQ 358 (1944).

[17]SAPC, Inc. v. Lotus Dev. Corp., 699 F. Supp. 1009, 9 USPQ2d 1467 (D. Mass. 1988), *aff'd,* 921 F.2d 360, 17 USPQ2d 1146 (1st Cir. 1990).

transfer this right, it should be expressly stated in the assignment document.

(f) Assignment of Royalty Rights

The right to collect royalties is treated in much the same way as the right to collect damages for infringement. When a patent, trademark, or copyright is assigned, the assignee has the right to collect royalties for licensed activity that occurs after transfer of the patent. However, the assignor retains the right to collect past due royalties for licensed use of the intellectual property occurring up until the time of transfer. The assignor may collect these past due royalties even after the transfer has occurred. As with the right to sue past infringers, the right to collect royalties for prior licensed activity may also be transferred when intellectual property is assigned.[18] This right must be expressly transferred in the assignment document.

(g) Assignment of Related Rights

An assignment should convey all rights to all patent applications that may be filed on the invention and not merely the current application, if that is the parties' intent. This is particularly true with employees who have an obligation to assign inventions to their employer. The employer should be sure that the assignment includes all divisions, continuations, continuations-in-part, reissues, and extension rights of U.S. patents and applications. The employer should also be sure to obtain all rights under international patent application conventions and treaties, and all rights to pursue applications in foreign countries.

In the United States, even if the invention and application are assigned to an employer, it is the inventor who remains the applicant. The employer is listed on the application and patent as the assignee. The employer may not in most circumstances pursue the application on its own, without the signatures of the inventors, until an assignment of the application has been recorded in the U.S. Patent and Trademark Office (PTO). If the inventors are unavailable or uncooperative, the

---

[18] *See, e.g.*, Chemical Found. v. E.I. DuPont DeNemours & Co., 29 F.2d 597 (D. Del. 1928), *aff'd*, 39 F.2d 366 (3d Cir. 1930), *aff'd*, 283 U.S. 152 (1931).

company may proceed by petitioning the Commissioner of Patents and Trademarks for permission to proceed without the inventors' signatures. In contrast, some foreign countries allow the employer/assignee to pursue patent rights without requiring the signature of the inventor.

Trademark and copyright assignments should be made for the full term of the trademark or copyright and any renewals thereof. All foreign rights should also be assigned if that is the parties' intent, or assigned on a country-by-country basis, as the case may be. Trade secrets should be assigned for the life of the trade secret, because there are no comparable renewal rights. Trade secret rights are recognized in virtually all industrialized nations, so an assignment should cover either all foreign rights or specified countries.

12.4 Assignment Versus License

Courts will look to the substance of a trademark transfer rather than the label the parties place on it to determine whether the agreement is an assignment or license. Courts will look at factors such as length of term, exclusivity, and method of payment in deciding whether a transfer of trademark rights is a license or assignment.[19]

A purported patent license agreement may be construed to be effectively an assignment if substantially all rights are transferred by the patent holder. This is so even if the patent owner retains some rights under the patent. If the transferee has been given the irrevocable exclusive right to make, use, and sell the patented invention and enforce the patent against infringers, this may be construed as an assignment despite the parties' labeling it as an exclusive license. One court has interpreted a transfer as being an assignment rather than a license despite the transferor's keeping the following rights: (1) the right to prohibit sublicenses, (2) the right to file foreign patent applications, (3) a reversionary right to the patent in the event of bankruptcy or termination of production by the grantee, and (4) the right to receive a share of infringement damages.[20]

---

[19] *E.g.*, Jones v. Pepsi-Cola Co., 223 F. Supp. 650, 142 USPQ 212 (D. Neb. 1963); Ste. Pierre Smirnoff, Fls. v. Hirsch, 109 F. Supp. 10, 96 USPQ 168 (S.D. Cal. 1952); Ex parte Teca Corp., 117 USPQ 367 (Comm'r Patents 1958).

[20] Vaupel Textilmaschinen KG v. Meccanica Euro Italia, S.P.A., 944 F.2d 870, 875, 20 USPQ2d 1045, 1049 (Fed. Cir. 1991).

In contrast, an agreement in which the patent transferor retained the following rights was deemed a license rather than an assignment: the right to receive royalties from sublicenses, the right to share in infringement damages awards, and the right to terminate the transfer. The transferee had a limited right to assign its rights only to its successor in interest.[21]

12.5 Elements of an Assignment

(a) Written Versus Oral

(i) Intellectual Property Subject to Federal Statutes

Ownership of patents, trademark registrations, and copyright registrations is subject to federal statutes. The patent statutes state that applications for patent, patents, or any interests therein are assignable in law by an instrument in writing.[22] The Lanham Act states that a registered trademark or a mark for which application to register has been filed is assignable by instruments in writing duly executed.[23] The Copyright Act provides that for a transfer of copyright ownership to be effective, an instrument of conveyance, or a notice or memorandum of the transfer, must be in writing and signed by the owner of the rights.[24]

(ii) Intellectual Property Governed by State Law

State common law trademark rights, trade names, and trade secret and other proprietary information are not governed by the federal statutes discussed above. Therefore, writing requirements for transfer of ownership are governed by state law. State laws such as the Statute

---

[21]Refac Int'l v. Visa USA, 16 USPQ2d 2024 (N.D. Cal. 1990).
[22]35 U.S.C. §261.
[23]15 U.S.C. §1060.
[24]17 U.S.C. §204.

of Frauds[25] and the Uniform Trade Secrets Act (UTSA)[26] will control as applicable. For instance, a contract that cannot be completed within a year is not enforceable under the Statute of Frauds.

(b) Wording of Assignment Grant

While federal statutes require written transfer of patents, federal trademark registrations, and registered copyrights, there is no required form for the writing. The only requirement is that the rights being transferred can be clearly understood from the writing. However, certain issues specific to the type of intellectual property being transferred should be addressed by the wording of the assignment.

(i) Right to Sue for Past Infringement

An assignee has standing to sue only for infringement occurring after the date of the transfer. Thus, if the right to sue prior infringers is intended to be transferred, it should be expressly stated in the assignment document.

(ii) Good Will Must Be Assigned With a Trademark

A trademark by itself has no value; it is the identification by consumers of the source of the goods with the quality of the goods that gives value to the trademark right. Therefore, transfer of a trademark or trade name alone conveys no legal rights. The transfer must include both the trademark and its associated good will. It is not necessary to transfer tangible assets in order to effectively transfer good will. Good will itself is an intangible asset that must be transferred in order to validate the transfer of the trademark.[27] A trademark assignment without

---

[25]Restatement (Second) of Contracts §110 (1979).

[26]Many states have enacted a version of the Uniform Trade Secrets Act, 14 U.L.A. 433 (1985).

[27]Money Store v. Harriscorp Fin., 689 F.2d 666, 676, 216 USPQ 11, 20 (7th Cir. 1982); White Tower Sys. v. White Castle Sys. of Eating Houses Corp., 90 F.2d 67, 69, 33 USPQ 573, 574 (6th Cir.), *cert. denied,* 302 U.S. 720 (1937); Sands, Taylor & Wood v. Quaker Oats Co., 18 USPQ2d 1457, 1465 (N.D. Ill. 1990), *aff'd in part and rev'd in part,* 24 USPQ2d 1001 (7th Cir. 1992).

the good will is null and void and can operate as an abandonment of trademark rights.

(iii) Trade Secrets/Proprietary Information

Title to unpatented technology may also be assigned. The requirements of a writing and of recordation of the assignment are governed by state law. This may include recordation with the secretary of state or other local official as part of a Form UCC-1 filing under the appropriate state's adoption of the Uniform Commercial Code (UCC). An effective assignment must transfer the right to prevent unauthorized use and disclosure of the technology and should require the transferor to maintain confidentiality.[28]

(c) Other Requirements

(i) Adequacy of Consideration

A patent assignment must be supported by valuable consideration. Reciting a nominal sum and other good and valuable consideration is sufficient to validate an assignment from an employee to an employer.[29] One court rejected an attack on an assignment by an employee who asserted failure to pay the recited nominal consideration.[30] So long as there is consideration to support a patent assignment, courts generally do not inquire as to its adequacy or type.[31]

Payment of a nominal sum for a trademark (e.g., $1.00) does not necessarily render a transfer ineffective, but may be a factor to consider in deciding whether good will has been transferred with the mark. Nominal payment and recitation that an assignment was for "good and

---

[28]E.I. DuPont DeNemours & Co. v. United States, 288 F.2d 904, 910, 129 USPQ 473, 477–78 (Ct. Cl. 1961).

[29]Diamond Scientific Co. v. Ambico, Inc., 848 F.2d 1220, 1225, 6 USPQ2d 2028, 2031 (Fed. Cir.), *cert. dismissed,* 487 U.S. 1265 (1988).

[30]Buckingham Prods. Co. v. McAleer Mfg. Co., 108 F.2d 192, 44 USPQ 91 (6th Cir. 1939).

[31]Transparent-Wrap Mach. Corp. v. Stokes & Smith Co., 329 U.S. 637, 72 USPQ 148 (1947); Bowen v. B.F. Goodrich Co., 36 F.2d 306 (6th Cir. 1929).

valuable consideration" are customary and do not themselves make an assignment ineffective.[32]

An exclusive license or assignment of copyright may be by gift or sale. Therefore, no consideration is required if the assignment does not recite that consideration is required.[33] Nonexclusive licenses are revocable if there is no consideration.[34]

(ii) Duress or Fraud

An assignment of intellectual property is subject to attack for duress or fraud as is any other form of contract. One situation involving duress might involve an employee who was forced to execute an assignment under threat of being fired. Fraud could entail misrepresenting the value of intellectual property to induce a buyer. For example, the owner of a patent might misrepresent the volume of sales of products under his or her patent to induce the assignee to purchase the patent.

(iii) Execution Formalities

Federal law only requires that an assignment be signed by the assignor of patents, trademarks, and copyrights. If the assignor is a corporation, the assignment must be executed by an officer authorized to bind the corporation. The assignee is not required to sign. Although there is no requirement that an assignment be notarized or witnessed to be effective, there are advantages to doing so. Notarization is prima facie evidence of the execution of the assignment. This means that the assignee will not be required to prove the authenticity of the assignor's signature in any litigation in which the assignment is enforced. Absent notarization, the assignee may have to obtain testimony from the assignor or others familiar with his or her signature, or other evidence that the assignor executed the assignment. Having the document witnessed by third parties provides identifiable persons who should be able to testify to the authenticity of the signatures. Many foreign countries require notarization as well as additional authentication referred to as legalization. Legalization includes additional verification of the notary's signature and the other parties' signatures on the documents.

---

[32] Money Store v. Harriscorp Fin., *supra* note 27, at 670, 216 USPQ at 15.

[33] 4 A. CORBIN, CORBIN ON CONTRACTS §909 (1951).

[34] McCarthy & Fischer v. White, 259 F. 364 (S.D.N.Y. 1919).

This verification is done by government officials such as clerks of court, state or federal secretaries of state, and the foreign country's consul having jurisdiction over the place of execution of the document.

Although assignments in the United States need not be signed by the assignee, it may be advantageous to have the assignee also sign when foreign rights are being transferred. Many foreign countries require that both the assignee and assignor sign an assignment for it to be effective. It is possible to file in some foreign countries a certified copy of an assignment of U.S. and foreign rights recorded in the PTO, instead of obtaining a separate document. Therefore, it is also advantageous to have the assignee sign any overall assignments covering U.S. and foreign rights. This may eliminate the need for the assignee to come back at a subsequent time to have a foreign document executed by both parties, when the assignor may have become uncooperative or unavailable for a variety of reasons.

12.6 Effect of an Assignment

(a) Transfer of Title

An assignment of intellectual property passes title to the assignee. The assignee may then assert the rights arising from holding title to the intellectual property. In contrast, a license merely grants the licensee permission to use the intellectual property in some defined way, with title remaining with the licensor.

(b) Assignment of Security Interests in Intellectual Property as Collateral

Transfers of security interests in property are governed by article 9 of the UCC. In most cases, there are provisions for recording the security interest locally, such as with the secretary of state. Article 9, however, provides that such filing is not necessary or effective to perfect a security interest in property subject to a statute or treaty of the United States that provides for a national or international registration or that specifies a place of filing different from that specified in article 9 for filing of the security interest. When there is such a federal priority, the UCC treats compliance with that system as equivalent to filing a financial statement under article 9.

Early court decisions held that no federal recordation is required to perfect security interests in patents and trademarks.[35] These analyses rested in part on interpretation of the statutes governing federal registration of ownership as being limited to full transfers and not including security interests. A more recent decision required federal registration to perfect a security interest in a copyright and criticized the earlier cases that held differently for patents.[36] Unless this issue is definitively resolved in the courts, the holder of a security interest in a copyright, patent, or registered trademark should record such an interest under both the local systems provided for under state law and in the PTO for patents and registered trademarks or in the Copyright Office for copyrights.

Trade secret ownership is not subject to federal law. Accordingly, recordation of a security interest will be pursuant to the appropriate state's version of the UCC. As a practical matter, the owner of a trade secret should ensure that any documents of transfer that are publicly recorded do not disclose the trade secret itself, thereby possibly eliminating the value or existence of the trade secret.

There is an additional consideration when using trademarks as collateral for a loan. Often, the lending party will seek an outright assignment of the collateral from the borrower subject to assignment back upon repayment of the loan. The lender will grant a license to the borrower during the time of the loan. However, it is unlikely the lender will actually exercise quality control while it holds title to the trademark collateral. This leaves the validity of the mark open to an attack based on abandonment. Accordingly, the borrower should insist on granting a security interest that does not require a license back from the lender. And the lender should recognize that insisting on an outright assignment jeopardizes the value of the property on which it seeks to secure repayment of the loan.

---

[35] City Bank & Trust Co. v. Otto Fabric, 83 B.R. 780, 7 USPQ2d 1719 (D. Kan. 1988); In re Transportation Design & Technology, 48 B.R. 635, 226 USPQ 424 (Bankr. S.D. Cal. 1985).

[36] In re Peregrine Entertainment, 16 USPQ2d 1017 (C.D. Cal. 1990).

(c) Recording Requirements

(i) Patents

The patent statutes provide that transfers of ownership in patents may be recorded in the PTO. If the assignment is recorded within three months of the date of the transfer, this provides constructive notice to future transferees and protects the initial assignee.[37] It is therefore important to record such transfers promptly to protect the transferee's rights.

(ii) Trademarks

The assignment of trademark registrations may be recorded in the PTO. An assignment shall be effective against subsequent purchasers for valuable consideration without notice if it is recorded within three months of execution, or prior to the subsequent purchase.[38] Assignments should therefore be properly recorded to protect the assignee's interest.

(iii) Copyrights

The Copyright Act provides that any transfer of copyright ownership may be recorded in the Copyright Office. Recordation provides constructive notice of the earlier transfer, provided the assignment is recorded within one month if executed in the United States, two months if executed outside the United States, or any time before the recordation of the subsequent transfer.[39]

(iv) Trade Secrets

There is no federal system of recording ownership and transfers of trade secrets. Therefore, recordation will be governed by the relevant state law, such as the UCC. However, the assignee should consider the risk of disclosing a trade secret through recordation. Any documents that are recorded should not disclose the trade secret itself.

---

[37] 35 U.S.C. §261.
[38] 15 U.S.C. §1060.
[39] 17 U.S.C. §205.

(d) Assignor/Assignee Estoppel

Both the assignor and assignee of a patent are estopped from attacking the validity of the transferred patent. The assignor is estopped from holding out to the assignee that he or she is selling something of value and then challenging the validity of the transferred property.[40] Therefore, if an assignee sues an assignor for infringement of the patent after the patent has been transferred, the assignor may not defend that the patent is invalid. Similarly, the assignee is estopped from challenging the validity of the patent.[41]

The doctrine of assignor estoppel may be an important consideration in deciding how to structure payments for a patent. A licensee is free to challenge the validity of the licensed patent and can thereby suspend or, if the challenge is successful, terminate his or her obligation to pay royalties.[42] In contrast, an assignee may not challenge the validity of the transferred patent. It may be beneficial for an assignor who wishes to spread payments for a patent over time (either as periodic payments or as payments based on sales or use) to structure the transaction as an assignment rather than a license. This will fix the assignee's obligation to make the payments and will prevent him or her from challenging the validity of the patent in an attempt to terminate his or her payment obligation.

The doctrine of assignor estoppel also applies to the employer/employee relationship. When an employee assigns his or her patent rights and invention rights to the employer, the employee is now estopped from challenging the validity of this patent. This doctrine is important in situations where the employee leaves the employer and begins practicing the patented invention in competition with the employer. If the former employer brings suit against the former employee for infringement, the employee is estopped from challenging the validity of the patent as a defense to the infringement suit.

The existence and scope of an assignor estoppel doctrine as applied to trademarks is not well-settled. One case has held that an applicant for a federally registered service mark who assigned the mark could not attack its validity as a defense in an infringement suit.[43] An assignor

---

[40]Diamond Scientific Co. v. Ambico, Inc., *supra* note 29.

[41]Sybron Transition Corp. v. Nixon, Hargrave, Devans & Doyle, 770 F. Supp. 803, 21 USPQ2d 1515 (W.D.N.Y. 1991).

[42]Lear, Inc. v. Adkins, 395 U.S. 653, 162 USPQ 1 (1969).

[43]Marshak v. Green, 505 F. Supp. 1054, 212 USPQ 493 (S.D.N.Y. 1981).

should not be estopped, however, from attacking the validity of a trademark for reasons arising after assignment of the mark, such as genericness or abandonment.

(e) Prior Licenses and Other Encumbrances

When a patent or trademark is assigned, the assignee takes the patent or trademark subject to all prior existing licenses. This is so even if these prior licenses are unrecorded and the assignee has no notice of them. An assignee, however, may have a cause of action against the assignor for breach of warranty provisions in the assignment if the assignor warranted that there were no prior existing licenses.

Assignment of copyright is taken subject to prior nonexclusive licenses, even if unrecorded. This is because the statute allows for oral nonexclusive licenses, the only exception to the writing and recordation requirements. For an exclusive license to survive a subsequent transfer, the exclusive license must have been recorded pursuant to statute.

Assignment of intellectual property is taken subject to liens and security interests that are properly recorded. The case law is not well-settled on whether security interests are perfected by recording pursuant to state law under the UCC or pursuant to federal recordation provisions (see section 12.6(b)). Accordingly, holders of security interests should record by both methods, and transferees of intellectual property should search both state and federal records when checking the title of intellectual property.

12.7 Assigning a Partial Interest

(a) Patents

(i) Territory

The assignment of the patent may cover the entire United States, or may be limited to any defined geographic territory within the United

States.[44] Transferring a patent and limiting the transfer to a specified territory will not in and of itself reduce an assignment to a mere license. The assignee in a particular territory is given the exclusive right to enforce the patent in that territory in much the same way the complete transferee would have the right to enforce a patent throughout the United States. Because of the antitrust issues inherent in any market division, territorial division of patent rights should be carefully exercised, especially with regard to the right to sell.

(ii) Claims

A U.S. patent contains one or more numbered claims that particularly define the patented invention, and define what the patentee has the right to exclude others from practicing. An assignment of a patent must transfer the right to all of the claims in a patent. If parties transfer less than all of the claims, the transfer will be construed as a license, not an assignment of title.[45]

(iii) Partial Term and Reversionary Rights

An assignment is normally for the duration of the patent. A transferor may seek to protect his or her rights by stating that the assignment may be "defeated by non-performance of a condition subsequent."[46] This is a condition that occurs after the time of the assignment that will negate the assignment. Upon occurrence of the condition, title reverts to the initial transferor. For example, the transferor may retain the right to cancel the assignment in the event the transferee stops making required payments or stops production under the patent, thereby depriving the transferor of payments that may be tied to production of sales.[47] One court held that an assignment of a patent "for so long as [transferee] shall continue in business" terminated when the transferee corporation ceased to exist. At that time, title to the patent revested in the original transferor without a subsequent assignment being re-

---

[44]35 U.S.C. §261.

[45]Pope Mfg. Co. v. Gormully & Jeffery Mfg. Co., 144 U.S. 238 (1892).

[46]Waterman v. Mackenzie, 138 U.S. 252, 256 (1891).

[47]*E.g.*, Vaupel Textilmaschinen KG v. Meccanica Euro Italia, S.P.A., *supra* note 20, at 874–75, 20 USPQ2d at 1048–49.

quired.[48] An assignment may obligate the transferee to assign the title back to the transferor in the event of some condition such as default. In such a case, the original assignment should obligate the transferee to preserve the patent rights. The transferee should have the duty to pay maintenance fees and to not act in such a way as to render the patent unenforceable, and the transferor should keep the right to maintain the patent if the transferee fails to.[49]

(iv) Limit Subsequent Transfers

An assignor may wish to limit subsequent transfers by the assignee. However, reserving such a right will probably prevent transfer of "substantially all rights" to the patent. It is likely such an arrangement will be held to be a license, not an assignment.[50] A transferor who wants to limit subsequent transfers should consider granting a personal, nontransferable license.

(b) Trademarks

(i) Territory

An assignment of a federally registered trademark must cover the entire United States. This is because federal registration of the trademark is effective throughout the United States. In contrast, common law or state-enforced trademark rights may be partially assigned on a state-by-state basis, provided that customer confusion does not result.

(ii) Different Goods

There may be partial assignment of a trademark as to specific goods. However, a trademark is only divisible for unrelated goods. Rights to use a trademark may not be assigned to more than one party

---

[48]Owens Generator Co. v. H.J. Heinz Co., 214 F. Supp. 864, 866, 136 USPQ 406, 408 (N.D. Cal. 1961), *aff'd*, 314 F.2d 66, 136 USPQ 404 (9th Cir.), *cert. denied*, 375 U.S. 815, 139 USPQ 566 (1963).

[49]*E.g.*, Sybron Transition Corp. v. Nixon, Hargrave, Devans & Doyle, *supra* note 41, at 808, 21 USPQ2d at 1519.

[50]*Cf.* Refac Int'l v. Visa USA, *supra* note 21.

if they are to be using them for similar goods, because of the customer confusion that will likely arise.

(iii) Partial Term and Reversionary Rights

An assignment of a trademark must be perpetual; if it is limited in time, it is merely a license. An assignment may be made subject to cancellation upon a condition subsequent, such as liquidation of the transferee.[51]

(c) Copyrights

(i) Term

A transfer of ownership of a copyright is presumed to be for the duration of the copyright if the agreement is silent on this and there is no evidence of contrary intent.[52] The right to renew the copyright or to terminate an outright assignment is peculiar to copyright law and is explained below. There are two statutory schemes currently covering renewal and termination copyrights. Works created before 1978 are covered by a modification of the 1909 Copyright Act[53], and works created on or after January 1, 1978, are covered by the 1976 Copyright Act.[54]

Under the 1909 Act, works had an initial copyright term of 28 years, with the right to a single renewal term of 28 years. If a copyright was not assigned during the initial term, only the *author* had the right to the renewal term. However, the author could convey the right to the renewal term prior to its occurrence. The renewal had to be expressly conveyed, because if the assignment of the initial term was silent, the author retained the renewal right. The transfer of the renewal right could be implied with the sale of a business. When the renewal was transferred, it was actually the transfer of an expectancy interest. The

---

[51]American Dirigold Corp. v. Dirigold Metals Corp., 125 F.2d 446, 52 USPQ 510 (6th Cir. 1942).

[52]Viacom Int'l v. Tandem Prods., 368 F. Supp. 1264, 181 USPQ 749 (S.D.N.Y. 1974), *aff'd*, 526 F.2d 593 (2d Cir. 1975).

[53]17 U.S.C. §304.

[54]17 U.S.C. §302.

author had to be alive when the right to renew could be exercised. Under the 1909 Act, the right to renew passed to the author's heirs. If the author died prior to renewal, it was the heirs who had the right to renew, not a previous assignee.

Under the 1976 Act, there is a single term of copyright: life of the author plus 50 years; or for anonymous, pseudonymous, and works made for hire, 75 years from first publication, or 100 years from creation, whichever expires first. In any case, there is no renewal term. Instead, there is a right to terminate a transfer of ownership. A transfer other than by will may be terminated during the 5-year period beginning at the end of 35 years from the date of execution of the transfer. Notice of the termination must be served between 2 and 10 years before the expiration of the transfer. A transfer may be terminated despite an agreement not to. And the right to terminate passes to the author's heirs.

(ii) Territory

Just as the five rights of a copyright holder are freely divisible, so too a copyright may be freely divided by territory. A transfer of copyright will be considered an assignment and not merely a license even if limited to only one of the rights of a copyright holder and limited to a small territorial area. The assignee would have the right to enforce a copyright against infringers of that particular right in his or her particular territory.

(d) Trade Secrets and Proprietary Information

In theory, it is permissible to assign a partial interest in a trade secret, for instance, limiting the assignment to a particular territory or to a particular field of use. However, for practical reasons, trade secrets should not be partially assigned. A trade secret derives value from not being publicly known. One of the rights of the owner of a trade secret is the right to disclose the trade secret. Therefore, parties generally do not want to be at risk of losing the trade secret through its disclosure by the owner of a partial interest. Limited transfers are better accomplished by licenses that include an obligation to maintain secrecy.

12.8 Other Considerations in Intellectual Property Assignments

(a) Checking Ownership

The assignee should check the appropriate title records for the intellectual property to discover any title defects or encumbrances on the records. Documents effecting title of patents and federal trademark registration may be recorded in the records of the PTO. Documents effecting title of copyrights may be recorded in the Copyright Office. The records of the PTO and the Copyright Office are open for inspection. In addition, documents effecting title to personal property may be recorded in the courthouse of the residence or domicile of the property owner. This may include the principal place of business of a corporation as well as its state of incorporation. These records should be inspected to make sure the assignor can convey unencumbered title to the intellectual property and that there are no gaps in the chain of title.

(b) Warranties

The assignee will want the following warranties to be made by the assignor in the assignment document: that the assignor has title to the intellectual property and has the right to make the assignment; that the property is unencumbered; that to the best of the assignor's knowledge, the intellectual property is valid; and that the assignor has not done anything to render the intellectual property unenforceable. The assignee will also want the assignor to indemnify the assignee against any breaches of these warranties.

(c) Further Acts

The assignee will also want the assignor to agree to take whatever subsequent steps may become necessary to perfect the transfer of title. This may include whatever formalities are required to ensure the assignments are validly recorded.

(d) Forms of Consideration

Often the transferee will make a single lump-sum payment at the time the intellectual property is assigned. This, of course, is valid consideration for the assignment. There are other methods of providing consideration for an assignment that may make the arrangement look like a license rather than an assignment. However, the following methods of payment are not inconsistent with an assignment and will not of themselves turn an assignment into a license.

One such method is an agreement to make periodic payments. Under this method, fixed dollar amounts are paid at fixed intervals for some defined time. As with installment payment methods for transfers of any type of property, the tax laws treat this as a loan, and the parties must impute a portion of the payment as being interest for the loan. This arrangement is considered a loan because the assignee is given a period of time to pay the full consideration for the property being transferred.

Another method to provide consideration for assignment of intellectual property is to base the payments in some way on the sales or use of the transferred intellectual property. This royalty-type payment is common to licenses. However, it too will not in and of itself turn an assignment into a license.

Lastly, an assignor may retain the right to share in any future damage awards that the assignee may recover. As part of the consideration for the assignment, the assignee may agree that in any suits for future infringement a certain percent of any damages award will be given to the assignor. This too does not change an assignment into a license.

(e) Tax Considerations

Whatever form it takes, consideration for assignment of a patent is subject to capital gains treatment. The Omnibus Budget Reconciliation Act[55] contains a provision for amortizing intellectual property including patents, trademarks, good will, computer software, and copyrights. This law was enacted to clarify confusing provisions in the Tax Code

[55]Pub. L. No. 103-66.

and to reduce disputes with the Internal Revenue Service over interpretation of the previous provisions.[56]

12.9 Elements of a License

(a) Written Versus Oral

There are no statutory requirements that a patent or trademark license be in writing. However, to prevent dispute over the terms of an exclusive or nonexclusive license, all such agreements should be in writing. The copyright statutes require that a transfer of ownership, which includes an exclusive license, be in writing and signed by the transferor to be effective against subsequent transferees.[57] An exception exists for oral or implied contracts for nonexclusive rights because these are excluded from the definition of transfer of ownership.[58] Trade secrets are governed by state law, and the issue of whether a written license is required is governed by provisions such as state enactments of the Statute of Frauds or UTSA. Under the Statute of Frauds enacted by most states, agreements that cannot be completed within one year must be in writing to be enforced. The model UTSA does not contain any provisions related to written licenses, but individual states modify the Act to varying degrees when enacting it.

(b) Exclusive Versus Nonexclusive

A license under intellectual property rights may be granted either on an exclusive or a nonexclusive basis. Generally, a nonexclusive license may be thought of as a mere covenant not to sue. The licensor permits the nonexclusive licensee to carry out whatever acts the licensor otherwise had the right to prevent under his or her intellectual property rights. However, the licensor may grant other licenses under the same

[56]For the text of the relevant portions and a discussion, see 46 Pat., Trademark & Copyright J. (BNA), No. 1142, pp. 311, 325–33 (1993).

[57]17 U.S.C. §205.

[58]17 U.S.C. §101.

intellectual property to others. All of the licensees will thus be in competition with one another.

However, in the case of an exclusive license grant, the licensee is the sole party authorized to operate under the intellectual property rights during the term of the license. Indeed, unless the licensor reserves rights to himself or herself, he or she will also be excluded from operating under the intellectual property rights. If desired, the licensor and licensee can modify the exclusivity in the license agreement and expressly provide for the allowance of additional licensees. Because of the lack of competition from other licensees, an exclusive license is much more valuable to the licensee than a nonexclusive license. Therefore, an exclusive licensee should expect to pay higher royalties in order to preserve his or her license.

(c) Transfer and Sublicensing of a License by a Licensee

A license of intellectual property is personal to the licensee and may not be assigned or transferred from the licensee to another party unless expressly permitted by the license grant.[59] If the owner of the intellectual property rights does not desire for the licensee to be able to sell or sublicense the licensed rights, this must be specifically provided for in the license. Licensors of trade secrets and trademarks are particularly likely to desire to limit the transferability of the license. In the case of trade secrets, maintaining the confidentiality of the licensed trade secret is crucial to preserving the value of the trade secret. Thus the licensor has a strong interest in maintaining control over the availability of the trade secret to third parties. The trademark licensor has an obligation to maintain control over the quality of the goods or services with which the mark is used. Therefore, trademark licensors are particularly interested in prohibiting the transfer to unapproved third parties of licensed rights to use the licensed marks. For all kinds of intellectual property, providing for nontransferability gives the licensor a degree of protection against the unintended use of the licensed property by his or her competitors.

---

[59]Hapgood v. Hewitt, 119 U.S. 226 (1886); Unarco Indus. v. Kelley Co., 465 F.2d 1303, 175 USPQ 199 (7th Cir. 1972), *cert. denied,* 410 U.S. 929, 176 USPQ 513 (1973).

Generally, the transferability issue will be addressed in the grant language of the license itself, for example, "licensor grants to licensee a personal nontransferable exclusive license." Using the term "personal" clearly indicates that the license may not be transferred to any other party and may be used only by the licensee himself or herself. This is true even in the case of the merger of a licensee company into another company. In such a merger the licensee company effectively ceases to exist and its assets are transferred to the surviving company. In this circumstance, a "personal" license will not be transferred to the surviving company.[60] Licensees who accept the grant of a personal license should require exceptions for those circumstances that are important to their business situation. Generally, transferability should be provided in the event of a merger or the sale of substantially all the licensee's assets, or if the licensee needs to use contractors or other third parties on a routine basis, or in specific circumstances, such as when workload is high, so that the intellectual property can be used for carrying out the licensee's business.

Sublicensing is the transfer by the licensee to a third party of a right to operate under the licensee's rights. The right to grant sublicenses is not inherently included with the license grant.[61] Therefore, if the licensee desires to in turn permit others to operate under his or her license, a sublicensing right should be specifically stated. This is true even in the case of an exclusive license.

For example, if an exclusive license without the right to sublicense is granted, no sublicenses can be granted and the licensee will be in the position of having to carry out by himself or herself all acts under the licensed intellectual property rights. The licensee cannot grant sublicenses and neither can the licensor. By virtue of granting the exclusive license the licensor has prohibited himself or herself from granting any further licenses.[62]

---

[60]PPG Indus. v. Guardian Indus. Corp., 597 F.2d 1090, 1093, 202 USPQ 95, 97 (6th Cir.), *cert. denied,* 444 U.S. 930, 204 USPQ 608 (1979).

[61]Rubber Co. v. Goodyear, 76 U.S. 788, 799 (1869); Ozyagcilar v. Davis, 221 USPQ 1064 (D.S.C. 1983); E.I. DuPont DeNemours & Co. v. Shell Oil Co., 498 A.2d 1108, 227 USPQ 233 (Del. 1985); Raufast S.A. v. Kicker's Pizzazz, 208 USPQ 699 (E.D.N.Y. 1980).

[62]Old Dominion Box Co. v. Continental Can Co., 273 F. Supp. 550, 155 USPQ 70 (S.D.N.Y. 1967), *aff'd,* 393 F.2d 321, 157 USPQ 353 (2d Cir. 1968).

(d) Trademark Considerations

(i) Quality Control

It is imperative that a licensor of trademark rights retain the right to maintain quality of the goods produced by the licensee to be sold under the licensed trademark. Not only must the licensor reserve the right to control quality in the license agreement, the licensor must actually exercise this control. Failure to do so may result in forfeiture of rights under that trademark.[63]

The exercise of quality control may be carried out in a variety of ways. For example, the licensor may inspect the manufacturing facilities of the licensee to ensure that the goods are being manufactured in accordance with the quality standards. Often the trademark licensees are required to submit product samples and samples of promotional material, product literature, and other materials bearing the mark to the licensor for approval. The licensee must recognize that the quality control is necessary. However, the licensee should ensure that the quality standards are clearly stated in writing, are reasonable, and do not form the basis for a subjective termination of the license agreement by the licensor.

(ii) Benefit of Use

The trademark licensor should be considered the entity that is effectively using the mark. However, if a question should arise regarding the degree of control or if the licensee is using the mark in other forms or somehow deviating from the original scope of the license grant, the licensee may be creating through such use his or her own independent trademark rights. Accordingly, it is prudent for the licensor to provide in the trademark license agreement that all use of the trademark and any confusingly similar marks by the licensee will inure to the sole benefit of the licensor.

(e) Royalties

Royalties are money payments made by the licensee to the licensor in consideration of the license. A license agreement may specify a

---

[63]*E.g.*, Sterling Drug v. Lincoln Labs., 322 F.2d 968, 139 USPQ 31 (7th Cir. 1963).

single up-front lump-sum royalty payment for a paid-up license. This would permit the licensee to act under the license for the time period specified in the agreement without making further payments. Another way of paying for the license rights is a running royalty based on sales or use of the licensed property. A third way is to specify periodic payments that are not based on sale or use of the patent. One or all of these types of royalties may be used in a single licensing arrangement.

(i) Running Royalty Base

The running royalty base is the event or revenue from which the amount of royalty is calculated. The royalty base may be determined in two parts. The first part is a definition of the activity that will result in the obligation to pay royalties. That activity should include something that falls under the license grant. In other words, some act that if not for the license grant would constitute infringement of the licensed intellectual property rights.

For example, in a license for a patented bicycle pedal, the making, using, or selling of the bicycle pedal would be an act that would give rise to the obligation to pay a royalty. The base could also be figured on the event of making, using, or selling of a bicycle that included the patented bicycle pedal, because this would also include an act that would otherwise infringe the patent.

In the case of a licensed copyright, the event could be the reproduction, distribution, or performance of the copyrighted work or some other activity that was licensed under the copyright. For a trade secret or other proprietary information, the relevant activity may be the use of the licensed proprietary information for the manufacture or sale of a product or the providing of a service. The timing of the event giving rise to the obligation to pay royalties may be further specified to coincide with the shipping of the product, the invoicing for the product or services, the receipt of payments by the licensee from its customers, or other events that occur in the course of the business using the intellectual property under the license.

The second part of the determination of the running royalty base is the definition of that portion of the revenues to which the royalty rate is applied. That portion may be the total revenue received, the "net sales value," or the net or gross profit. It is generally advantageous for the licensee to fix the royalty rate on the gross revenue or the net sales value rather than the profit. This is because the licensee may have considerable flexibility in calculating profit and may use this flexibility to decrease the amount of royalties owed. When used, net sales value should be defined in the license agreement; it usually includes the gross revenue minus shipping costs and taxes paid by the licensee. Other costs may be deducted or exempted as negotiated between the licensor and licensee such as those attributed to commissions, return of product units from customers, and promotional units shipped.

(ii) Running Royalty Rate

The royalty rate is the factor that is applied against the running royalty base to determine the amount of the royalties. The rate may be on a dollars per unit basis or may be a fraction of revenue or profit. As a rule of thumb, a starting point in negotiations of royalties begins with a rate that will give the licensor approximately one-quarter to one-third of the licensee's profit attributable to the licensed property. Royalty rates vary widely and are largely dependent on factors such as the market value of the licensed products and the relative bargaining power of the licensor and licensee. In some markets, however, royalty rates tend to be relatively uniform. Royalty rates typically will be higher where the intellectual property provides the licensee with an exclusive or unique product having a strong competitive advantage. Minor improvements and products that are in a very competitive marketplace will yield a lower royalty. Although the licensor and licensee will consider in determining the royalties the likely profit made by the licensee, the royalty rate, as discussed above, may advantageously be applied to a percentage of gross revenue or net sales value or calculated as a fixed amount per product unit. This provides more certainty for the licensor with respect to his or her likely monetary return from the license. This also eliminates the incentive for the licensee to minimize the profits made on the licensed activity. The simplest of all of the activities on which to base royalties is the manufacture or sale of product units. Commonly, royalty rates are applied against the net sales value of the activity falling under the licensed intellectual property rights.

A periodic royalty is an amount scheduled for payment at prescribed times, such as at the beginning of each calendar quarter. A periodic royalty may be fixed to provide the entire royalty payable by the licensee. Or, it may be a relatively minimal license fee calculated to be sufficient to ensure that the licensee does not maintain its license without engaging in significant business activity under the licensed rights. For example, a nonexclusive software license may provide for a lump-sum, up-front license fee of $100,000 and in addition a periodic royalty of $1,000 per year. The small royalty payable every year is relatively insignificant while the software is still in use. However, if the licensee ceases using the software, the periodic fee may be significant enough to the licensee that he or she will desire to stop paying. The license agreement can provide for termination if the periodic royalty is not paid. Thus, the license relationship can be ended effectively when the license loses its value to the licensee.

The royalty rate may be fixed or may vary over time, with the volume of units sold, or the amount of aggregate royalties paid. For example, a low royalty rate may be desirable in the initial year of a license if the licensee must undergo significant startup costs associated with manufacturing a product. In later years, the royalty can rise as the startup costs are no longer being incurred. Or, the royalty rate may decrease as the number of units sold increases, to provide some incentive for the licensee to increase the sale of units.

In the case of exclusive licenses, it is common to charge a minimum royalty to ensure that the exclusive licensee is adequately exploiting the licensed rights. Consequently, if the scheduled minimum royalty is not paid, the licensor has the option to terminate the license or may convert the license to a nonexclusive basis. The licensor will then be free to license others who may be better able to exploit the intellectual property.

(iii) Reports and Accounting

License agreements that include running royalties should include a provision setting forth the timing of the payments of the royalties. These are often on a quarterly basis but may be more or less frequent. Typically, reports are also required showing how the royalties are calculated and should be provided by the licensee regardless of whether a royalty is paid.

The licensee should be required to keep records of the relevant information needed to calculate the royalties. These records should be made available to the licensor for inspection at reasonable times to ensure accuracy of the royalty payments. Commonly, the record examination provisions of a license agreement provide that the inspection be carried out by an independent certified public accountant who is obligated to confidentiality with respect to the information obtained during the examination. The licensee should provide in the agreement for a copy of the report to be provided to him or her. The licensee will learn from the report what information is being passed to the licensor and will be alerted if he or she has overpaid his or her royalties. Licensors usually bear the expense of the record examinations unless significant underpayments of royalties are discovered.

(f) Term

The term, or period of time, during which the license will exist should be specified in the license agreement. Absent specification of a term, the license rights will continue for the life of the property or until the license is terminated pursuant to the agreement of the parties or operation of law. However, a trademark licensor has an obligation to maintain quality control over the goods or services with which the licensed mark is used. There is an inherent right of a trademark licensor to terminate an agreement, and even to sue the licensee to enjoin use of the mark, if the licensee fails to comply with quality standards, even if the agreement is silent on the licensor's right to terminate.[64]

It is desirable for a licensor to set a relatively short license term. If a licensee is not performing satisfactorily, another licensee can be chosen at the end of the licensed term. Often, renewal periods or automatic extension periods are provided in license agreements so that if the licensing arrangement is proving mutually beneficial to both parties, then additional execution of documents will not be required to extend the license term. However, each party may be given the opportunity to terminate the license prior to the beginning of the renewal license period upon notice to the other party. Performance goals may also be specified as a condition of entitlement to a renewal period. For example, if a certain amount of aggregate royalties is paid or if certain units of sales of product are achieved, then the licensee may have the right to renew for an additional renewal term without the opportunity for termination by the licensor.

A patent license may be granted for any length of time up to the duration of the patent itself. It is forbidden to license patent rights and collect payments for a term beyond the length of the patent.

---

[64]*Cf.* Baskin-Robbins Ice Cream Co. v. D&L Ice Cream Co., 576 F. Supp. 1055, 222 USPQ 225 (E.D.N.Y. 1983); Joseph Bancroft & Sons Co. v. Shelley Knitting Mills, 212 F. Supp. 715, 136 USPQ 120 (E.D. Pa. 1962).

(g) Territory

A license agreement may transfer the right to practice a patent worldwide or throughout the United States, or it may be limited to regions within the United States. One court has applied state law to interpret a license silent on the scope of the territory granted as providing for rights both throughout the United States and abroad.[65] It is therefore important for the parties to specify in a license agreement their intention as to the territory covered. When limiting the territorial scope of a license, antitrust aspects of the arrangement must be considered (see section 12.11(c)).

(h) Confidentiality of Trade Secrets

Strict safeguards should be imposed on a licensee of trade secret rights in order to ensure that the licensed information will not be disclosed, thus destroying the value of the information. Because trade secrets may have value for as long as the information is not common knowledge, royalty payments may be collected indefinitely. On the other hand, the licensee will want to ensure he or she is relieved from paying for use of the information if it becomes public knowledge by legitimate means.

(i) Field of Use

An owner of intellectual property rights often finds it desirable to grant a license limited to a particular "field of use." For example, the owner of a patent on a switch for use in a data entry key pad may grant a license to a first licensee limited to making, using, and selling key pads under the licensed patent in the field of personal computer keyboards. The licensor may also grant to a second licensee exclusive license rights under the same patent limited to the field of use, or market segment, of business telephone systems. Third and fourth licenses may be granted on a nonexclusive basis, each for the field of use of home

---

[65] Kabushiki Kaisha Hattori Seiko v. Refac Technology Dev. Corp., 690 F. Supp. 1339, 9 USPQ2d 1046 (S.D.N.Y. 1988).

security systems. In this way, the licensor can exploit his or her patent rights separately in each market segment.

12.10 Effect of a License

(a) Permission to Act

A license grants the licensee the right to do something that the licensor could otherwise have prohibited. Title to the intellectual property remains with the licensor, and the exclusive rights associated with the intellectual property return to the licensor upon termination of the license. A licensee accepts the license subject to all prior transfers.

(b) Recording Requirements

Any transfer of copyright ownership, including exclusive licenses, should be recorded in the Copyright Office within one month of the transfer if executed in the United States, two months if executed outside the United States, or any time before a subsequent transfer. This will provide constructive notice against future transferees and will preserve the exclusive license against subsequent transfers. Nonexclusive licenses need not be recorded and will survive subsequent transfers.

Recordation of a patent or trademark license agreement is not constructive notice, nor is it required by statute. Therefore, an assignee takes a patent or trademark subject to prior licenses whether the licenses have been recorded or not.

(c) Licensee Estoppel

There is no longer a doctrine of licensee estoppel under patent law of the United States. A licensee is free at all times to attack the validity of the patent he or she has licensed, and if successful is relieved from obligations to pay royalties for practicing the patented invention. A licensee is free to attack the validity of the patent despite contrary provisions in the licensing agreement.[66] The *Lear* court reasoned there is a strong public interest in permitting full and free competition in the use of ideas that should be in the public domain. A licensee may be the only party with an economic incentive to challenge a patent's validity and should not be estopped by a contractual relationship from doing so.

There is a doctrine of licensee estoppel as applied to trademarks, preventing a licensee from attacking the validity of the licensed mark.[67] Courts have declined to extend *Lear* to trademark cases.

Courts have extended *Lear* to copyright cases, however, holding that licensees are not estopped from attacking the validity of the licensed copyright.[68]

(d) Exclusive Licensee Has Right to Sue

In the case of exclusive licensees, the right to enforce the intellectual property rights against third parties is inherent in the grant of an exclusive license.[69] The exclusive licensee can enforce the property rights in his or her own name independently of the licensor. The licensor may not desire his or her exclusive licensee to enforce the property rights independently because of the risks to the licensed property that may be posed by litigation. For example, as a result of litigation a court may declare a property invalid. Litigation should be threatened or commenced only after a thorough examination of the merits and after the risks of the plaintiff's position have been thoroughly considered. Thus, the licensor will desire to provide in the license agreement for control over the litigation and any settlement of the litigation. Generally, if the licensee agrees to undertake the expense of litigation,

---

[66]Lear, Inc. v. Adkins, *supra* note 42.

[67]*E.g.*, Seven-Up Bottling Co. v. Seven-Up Co., 420 F. Supp. 1246, 192 USPQ 121 (E.D. Mo. 1976), *aff'd,* 561 F.2d 1275, 195 USPQ 106 (8th Cir. 1977).

[68]Hal Roach Studios v. Richard Feiner & Co., 896 F.2d 1542 (9th Cir. 1990); Golden W. Melodies v. Capitol Records, 274 Cal. App. 2d 713, 163 USPQ 429 (1969).

[69]Patents: Independent Wireless Tel. Co. v. Radio Corp. of Am., 269 U.S. 459 (1926). Trademarks: 15 U.S.C. §1125(a); *see* Frisch's Restaurants v. Elby's Big Boy, 670 F.2d 642, 214 USPQ 15 (6th Cir. 1982). Copyrights: 17 U.S.C. §§101, 501(b); *see* Eden Toys v. Florelee Undergarment Co., 697 F.2d 27, 217 USPQ 201 (2d Cir. 1982).

he or she will desire to have a greater degree of control over the conduct and settlement of the controversy.

In general, absent a provision to the contrary, a nonexclusive licensee has no right to enforce the licensed property rights against third parties. A nonexclusive licensee may not file a suit in his or her own name to enforce the licensed property rights. A nonexclusive licensee is permitted merely to use the licensed property and has no expectation that his or her competitors will not also have access to the licensed property. The nonexclusive licensee, however, does not desire to find himself or herself in the position of paying royalties for the use of intellectual property when his or her competitors are not. This results in a higher price or a lower profit margin to the paying licensee with respect to his or her product or services. A nonexclusive licensee may therefore desire to require the licensor to enforce the licensed property rights against infringers if the failure to enforce would put the licensee at a competitive disadvantage. The nonexclusive licensee may also desire to provide a consequence for the failure of the licensor to enforce the licensed rights against third parties. This consequence may include an abatement of the licensee's obligations to pay royalties.

12.11 Other Licensing Considerations

(a) No Contest Clauses

A licensor of intellectual property will want to prohibit a licensee from attacking the validity of the subject of the license. A "no contest" provision in a license seeks to prohibit the licensee from contesting the validity of the licensed property. The effectiveness of such a clause depends on the type of the intellectual property licensed.

As discussed in section 12.10(c), in patent law there is no longer a doctrine of licensee estoppel. Licensees of patent rights are free to challenge the validity of the patent, and contract provisions that limit this right are not enforceable.

One court has held that although there is no doctrine of licensee estoppel in the copyright field, a no contest provision in a copyright license is enforceable so long as there is no antitrust violation.[70] The

[70]Saturday Evening Post Co. v. Rumbleseat Press, 816 F.2d 1191, 2 USPQ2d 1499 (7th Cir. 1987).

court, however, would not extend the prohibition against enforcing no contest provisions of *Lear* from patent to copyright law.

Courts have also declined to extend *Lear* to trademark cases. Licensors may include a provision in the license prohibiting the licensee from attacking the validity of the licensed mark.[71] In fact, even without such a provision, trademark licensees are estopped from attacking the validity of the licensor's mark (see section 12.7(c)).

(b) Misuse

"Patent misuse" is the doctrine that the owner of a U.S. patent should not be entitled to enforce it while the exclusive rights of the patent are being used in certain impermissible ways. It is based on the belief that one who uses his or her patent in an attempt to exclude competition beyond what is allowed by statute should be prohibited from exercising even his or her legitimate patent rights. Patent misuse may be raised as a defense by a defendant in an infringement suit who claims that the plaintiff's misconduct regarding his or her patent should bar the plaintiff from enforcing his or her patent. Successful application of the defense bars recovery by the plaintiff until the misuse is purged. If the defendant is a licensee of the patentee, successful application of this defense will bar the patentee from recovering royalties under the license. Patent misuse is not a cause of action that may be asserted against the patent owner for remedies such as injunctions and damages. However, the same acts that are patent misuse may also constitute antitrust law violations, which can form the basis of an offensive action seeking relief. Misuse is a judicially created doctrine that is traditionally limited to patents, but has been recently expanded to copyrights.

(i) Common Misuse Activities

Prohibiting a licensee from producing or selling goods in competition with the patented goods covered by the license, often referred to as a "tie-out," is one classic type of patent misuse. Misuse also exists when the patentee promises not to compete with the licensee's activities

[71]Long John Silver's v. Washington Franchise, 209 USPQ 146 (E.D. Va. 1980).

under the license.[72] Other classic patent misuse activities are tying the purchase of unpatented goods to the license to use a patent, "tie-in" or "tying," and requiring a licensee to accept licenses on other patents beyond the patent he or she desires.[73] If a patentee's license provisions constitute misuse, this provides a defense in an infringement suit against defendants who are not even parties to the offending license agreement.[74] A 1988 amendment codified what had become well-settled case law by immunizing refusal to license from attack as patent misuse.[75]

As developed by the judiciary, the patent misuse defense was available whenever the patentee sought to extend his or her patent rights beyond the rights granted by statute. Unlike antitrust law, no analysis was required of the patentee's market power in the relevant market. The presence of an impermissible clause in a license was per se patent misuse.[76]

A 1988 amendment eliminated the existence of per se patent misuse for tying arrangements. Now, conditioning the license of any rights to the patent or the sale of the patented product on the acquisition of a license to rights in another patent or purchase of a separate product is not misuse, unless, in view of the circumstances, the patent owner has market power in the relevant market for the patent or patented product on which the license or sale is conditioned.

(ii) Misuse Doctrine Applied to Copyright Licenses

Application of the misuse doctrine has been expanding recently into U.S. copyright infringement cases dealing with tie-out schemes.[77]

---

[72]McCullough v. Kammerer Corp., 166 F.2d 759, 76 USPQ 503 (9th Cir.), *cert. denied,* 335 U.S. 813, 79 USPQ 454 (1948).

[73]For a discussion on the various activities constituting patent misuse, see generally 5 D.S. CHISUM, PATENTS §19.04[3] (Mathew Bender & Co., Inc. 1991); 1 S.Z. SZCZEPANSKI, ECKSTROM'S LICENSING IN FOREIGN AND DOMESTIC OPERATIONS §8.03 (Clark Boardman Callaghan 1992).

[74]Compton v. Metal Prods., 453 F.2d 38, 172 USPQ 263 (4th Cir. 1971), *cert. denied,* 406 U.S. 968, 174 USPQ 4 (1972).

[75]35 U.S.C. §271(d).

[76]*See, e.g.,* Senza-gel Corp. v. Seiffhart, 803 F.2d 661, 231 USPQ 363 (Fed. Cir. 1986). There, the Federal Circuit approved the district court's determination that the tie-in arrangement at issue was patent misuse barring recovery by the patentee, despite the arrangement not rising to the level of an antitrust violation. The Federal Circuit approved the district court's test for tie-in patent misuse that did not consider the patentee's market power.

[77]*See* Webb & Locke, *Intellectual Property Misuse: Developments in the Misuse Doctrine,* 4 HARV. J.L. & TECH. 257 (1991).

In *Lasercomb America v. Reynolds,*[78] the misuse defense was applied against a provision that is probably common in software licensing agreements. The plaintiff had licensed copies of its CAD/CAM software to the defendant. The plaintiff's standard license agreements included clauses that prevented licensees from writing, developing, producing, or selling computer software in competition with the licensed software. The defendant in the copyright infringement suit claimed that the plaintiff misused its copyrighted software by including in its standard license agreement the noncompetition, or tie-out, restrictions. The court first concluded that the misuse defense is inherent in copyright law just as it is in patent law. The court further concluded that because the copyright was being used in a way contrary to public policy, the misuse need not rise to the level of an antitrust violation to bar recovery by the plaintiff.[79]

(iii) Purging Misuse

Once misuse has been found, a patentee may not enforce his or her patent until the misuse has been purged, "the improper practice has been abandoned and . . . the consequences of the misuse of the patent have been dissipated."[80] Because there is no bright-line test for determining when the misuse has been purged, the determination is highly dependent on the facts of the case. It is the patentee's burden to demonstrate the misuse has been purged after a finding of misuse. When the misuse is caused by a provision in a license, mere nonenforcement is not enough to purge the misuse; the patentee must remove the clause from the license.[81] It has been considered sufficient to contact the licensees and authorize discontinuance of the restrictive provision.[82]

---

[78]911 F.2d 970, 15 USPQ2d 1846 (4th Cir. 1990); *see also* Atari Games Corp. v. Nintendo of Am., 975 F.2d 832, 846–47, 24 USPQ2d 1015, 1025–26 (Fed. Cir. 1992) (and cases cited therein).

[79]The misuse doctrine has also been applied to a copyright case in which the plaintiff acted in egregious bad faith in obtaining a preliminary injunction against the defendant. qad. Inc. v. ALN Assocs., 770 F. Supp. 1261, 19 USPQ2d 1907 (N.D. Ill. 1991), *aff'd in part and dismissed in part,* 974 F.2d 834, 24 USPQ2d 1145 (7th Cir. 1992).

[80]Morton Salt Co. v. G.S. Suppiger Co., 314 U.S. 488, 493, 52 USPQ 30, 33 (1942).

[81]Berlenbach v. Anderson & Thompson Ski Co., 329 F.2d 782, 784, 141 USPQ 84, 85–86 (9th Cir.), *cert. denied,* 379 U.S. 830, 143 USPQ 464 (1964).

[82]Automatic Radio Mfg. Co. v. Hazeltine Research, 339 U.S. 827, 835, 85 USPQ 378, 381 (1950), *overruled on other grounds* by Lear, Inc. v. Adkins, 395 U.S. 653, 162 USPQ 1 (1969).

(iv) Misuse Defense Distinguished From Antitrust Law

Although closely related to one another, patent misuse and antitrust law are distinct bodies of law. Patent misuse merely provides a defense for an accused patent infringer; it does not give rise to a cause of action against the patentee. A claimed antitrust violation can be grounded in the same conduct as that claimed to be patent misuse. Proving that patent misuse exists without regard to whether there is in fact an anticompetitive effect is all that is required in most circumstances to apply patent misuse as a defense to infringement, except for tying arrangements that now require a showing of market power. In contrast, an antitrust claim based on the same conduct must also include all of the other elements required by antitrust law.

(c) Antitrust Considerations

(i) Suspect Licensing Practices

As discussed above, activity that is misuse of intellectual property may form the basis of an antitrust claim. These misuse activities include tie-in provisions, tie-out restrictions, and improper patent packaging. Additionally, territorial restrictions on licensed activity, restrictions on field of use, or limits on access to customers may also be scrutinized under antitrust law. A "grant back" requirement, obligating the licensee to grant ownership to the licensor of improvements made by the licensee that arise from the licensed activity, also comes under scrutiny of antitrust law. The law is not well-settled with regard to grant backs, and they must be handled with caution.

(ii) Other Elements of Antitrust Violation

Outside of the patent field, courts generally apply a three-part analysis in attempt-to-monopolize claims, requiring: (1) proof of the relevant market, (2) proof of specific intent to acquire monopoly power, and (3) proof of dangerous probability of acquiring a monopoly.[83] A large share of market power in the relevant market can be a key element

---

[83]*See generally* W. C. HOLMES, INTELLECTUAL PROPERTY AND ANTITRUST LAW 6-30 nn.86–89 (Clark Boardman Callaghan 1993) (and cases cited therein).

in establishing a dangerous probability of success.[84] In appropriate circumstances, other antitrust issues, such as whether there has been an unreasonable restraint of trade or unlawful monopolization, may need to be considered.

Even though brought as part of a patent infringement suit that is appealable to the Court of Appeals for the Federal Circuit, an antitrust claim would be resolved under the law of the appropriate regional circuit.[85] Therefore, the Federal Circuit would perform an analysis similar to this three-part analysis.

A *Walker Process*[86]–type claim is probably the most common "attempt-to-monopolize" antitrust violation raised as a counterclaim in patent infringement cases.[87] In such a case, enforcement of a fraudulently obtained patent can be an antitrust violation if all of the other elements of a Sherman Act §2[88] violation are present. As to establishing the other elements, the court in *American Hoist & Derrick Co. v. Sowa & Sons*[89] required a showing of the relevant market and a dangerous probability of monopolization in addition to the fraudulent conduct. An illustrative analysis of relevant market and market power was provided by the district court in *FMC Corp. v. Manitowoc Co.*[90] The court explained that the relevant market consists of products that are generally usable for the same purpose as the patented product considering price, characteristics, and adaptability of the products. For a patented product to be in and of itself the relevant market, it must dominate a real market and be able to drive all or most substitutes from the market. To determine if the plaintiff had monopoly power in the relevant market, the court looked for a dominant market share or an ability to control prices and exclude competition.

---

[84]*Id.* at 6-34 nn.99–100.

[85]Loctite Corp. v. Ultraseal Ltd., 781 F.2d 861, 875, 228 USPQ 90, 99–100 (Fed. Cir. 1985).

[86]Walker Process Equip. v. Food Mach. & Chem. Corp., 382 U.S. 172, 147 USPQ 404 (1965).

[87]For a review of other bases for antitrust counterclaims in patent infringement actions, see Calkins, *Patent Law: The Impact of the 1988 Patent Misuse Reform Act and Noerr–Pennington Doctrine on Misuse Defenses and Antitrust Counterclaims,* 38 Drake L. Rev. 175, 204–14 (1988–89), discussing five categories of antitrust violations: (1) *Walker Process* claims; (2) patent pools; (3) sham or bad-faith litigation; (4) repetitive litigation; and (5) tying, package licensing, and price fixing.

[88]15 U.S.C. §2.

[89]725 F.2d 1350, 220 USPQ 763 (Fed. Cir. 1984), *cert. denied,* 469 U.S. 821, 224 USPQ 520 (1985).

[90]654 F. Supp. 915, 936–37, 2 USPQ2d 1969, 1984 (N.D. Ill.), *aff'd,* 835 F.2d 1411, 5 USPQ2d 1112 (Fed. Cir. 1987).

The law of some circuits is that a patent or copyright creates a presumption of market power.[91] However, in *Abbott Laboratories v. Brennan,*[92] the Federal Circuit reiterated its determination that a patent does not presumptively confer market power in an antitrust sense. In spite of the court's recognition that it is bound to apply the law of the regional circuit in antitrust issues, it looked at its own precedent to support its conclusion that there is no presumption of market power. When the Federal Circuit's view on presumptions is considered in light of the virtual monopoly the court has over antitrust counterclaims in patent suits,[93] it appears the need to affirmatively establish market power in the relevant market will be the law whenever an antitrust claim is raised in a patent infringement suit.

(d) Licenses Combining Intellectual Property Types

It is common for a complex license to include a transfer of patent, trademark, and copyright, or any combination of these. A problem then may arise if any one of these individual rights is held invalid apart from the others. If the royalty payments are expressly allocated to the various rights being transferred, it may be possible for the licensor to continue to enforce the license despite the invalidity of any individual type of licensed intellectual property. However, if the hybrid license is found to have the intellectual property types intertwined in a license and therefore not severable, if a patent becomes invalid or unenforceable, then the whole license may become unenforceable.[94]

---

[91]*E.g.*, Digidyne Corp. v. Data Gen. Corp., 734 F.2d 1336 (9th Cir. 1984), *cert. denied,* 473 U.S. 908 (1985).

[92]952 F.2d 1346 (Fed. Cir. 1991).

[93]The Federal Circuit has jurisdiction over appeals of all cases in which the district court's jurisdiction was based in whole or in part on any Act of Congress relating to patents. 28 U.S.C. §§1295(a)(1), 1338(a). Thus, the Federal Circuit has determined it has jurisdiction over appeals of antitrust issues even if the patent issues had been finally determined in a previous phase of the trial and no patent issues remain for appeal. Technicon Instruments Corp. v. Alpkem Corp., 866 F.2d 417, 9 USPQ2d 1540 (Fed. Cir. 1989). Similarly, the Federal Circuit has jurisdiction over appeals of antitrust issues even if tried separately before the patent issues have been tried. U.S. Philips Corp. v. Windmere Corp., 861 F.2d 695, 8 USPQ2d 1885 (Fed. Cir. 1988), *cert. denied,* 490 U.S. 1068 (1989).

[94]*See, e.g.,* Oshkosh Truck Corp. v. Lockheed Missiles & Space Co., 678 F. Supp. 809, 4 USPQ2d 1404 (N.D. Cal. 1987).

(e) Tax Considerations

(i) Ordinary Income

Royalty payments under a license are taxed as ordinary income. This is one consideration for an intellectual property owner in deciding whether to grant a license or an assignment. In contrast, payments for assignment of intellectual property are eligible for capital gains treatment (see section 12.8(e)).

(ii) Withholding Federal Tax From Foreign Royalty Payments

A licensee making royalty payments under a license with a foreign licensor must withhold a portion of the payment to comply with U.S. tax laws. The amount to withhold varies depending on whether the country involved is a treaty member or not. There is a higher withholding for licensors in countries that are not members of the relevant treaty. The licensee may be liable for failing to comply with this measure.

(f) Software Escrow Agreements

A licensee of computer software will usually receive technical support from the licensor in the form of upgrades to the software as they become available and help in fixing problems with the current version of the software. The licensee is at some risk of losing this assistance should the licensor cease to exist for some reason. Usually, the licensee will not have access to the source code of the licensed software, and will find it difficult to fix or upgrade the software himself or herself in the absence of assistance from the licensor.

An arrangement that protects the licensee in such an event, and preserves the confidentiality of the source code required to protect the licensor, is a software escrow agreement. A third party will hold a copy of the source code in escrow, and will have authority to provide it to the licensee in the event of specified conditions, such as bankruptcy of the licensor.

(g) Implied Licenses

A license grant may be implied by the acts of the licensor. In general, whenever the owner of intellectual property rights authorizes an act to take place, it is implied that permission is thereby granted under any rights the licensor has to enable the licensee and his or her customers to carry out the intent of the authorization by the intellectual property owner.[95] For example, if the owner of a patent sells a product covered by the patent, he or she need not grant either a written or oral express license to the purchaser. The purchaser will have an implied nonexclusive license to use and sell the product. The patentee has exhausted his or her patent rights by making the sale with respect to that unit of product.[96] Similarly, if a licensor expressly grants a license under only a first patent, and if a license under a second patent is necessary for the contemplated licensed activity by the licensee under the first patent, there may be an implied license under the second patent.[97]

(h) Bankruptcy

Often, a licensee may wish to have the right to continue operating under a license in the event of bankruptcy of the licensor. The bankruptcy laws were amended in 1988 to deal with this situation.[98] The amended statute allows the trustee of a debtor who is a licensor to reject an executory contract to intellectual property (trade secret, invention, patent, patent application, and copyright). The licensee may then elect to treat the license as terminated or may elect to continue operating under the license for its duration.[99]

Conversely, a licensor often wants the right to terminate a license upon bankruptcy of the licensee. However, once a licensee files a

---

[95] *E.g.*, Lukens Steel Co. v. American Locomotive Co., 197 F.2d 939, 94 USPQ 14 (2d Cir. 1952).

[96] United States v. Univis Lens Co., 316 U.S. 241, 53 USPQ 404 (1942); Ansul Co. v. Uniroyal, Inc., 448 F.2d 872, 169 USPQ 759 (2d Cir. 1971), *cert. denied*, 404 U.S. 1018, 172 USPQ 257 (1972).

[97] Lever Bros. Co. v. Procter & Gamble Distrib. Co., 668 F. Supp. 924, 939–41, 5 USPQ2d 1239, 1252 (D.N.J. 1987).

[98] 11 U.S.C. §365 was amended by Pub. L. No. 100-506.

[99] 11 U.S.C. §365(n).

petition for bankruptcy, a licensor is barred from terminating the license solely on the ground of the financial condition of the debtor or the filing of a petition for bankruptcy. This is so despite contrary license provisions.[100] To avoid this restriction, a licensor may include an obligation for the licensee to notify the licensor of its intention to file a petition for bankruptcy and grant the licensor the right to terminate the license upon such notice, prior to filing the petition for bankruptcy. The provision obligating such notice should state that failure to provide notice is a material incurable breach causing termination of the license.

12.12 Transfer of Intellectual Property in the Sale and Merger of Businesses

Of course, a transfer of intellectual property as part of the sale or merger of business entities is subject to all of the same rules and requirements of transfers made in other contexts. This includes recordation of transfers of ownership of patents, trademarks, and copyrights. However, certain issues particular to sales and mergers of businesses should be addressed.

Besides ownership of patents, the right to practice under an existing license is also a consideration in the sale and merger of business entities. The successor company may wish to continue operating under licensed patent rights that may have been granted to one of the predecessor companies. This can present a problem when the licensee was granted a nontransferable license to practice under the patent. One court has held that the merger of a corporation that was operating under a nontransferable license terminated the license.[101] The license agreement did not expressly list merger as an exception to the nontransferability prohibition. Problems such as this can be avoided when drafting the initial license agreement. Even if the intent is to grant a nontransferable license, the parties may wish to provide that the successors and assignees of the parties may operate under the otherwise nontransferable license.

---

[100] 11 U.S.C. §365(e).

[101] PPG Indus. v. Guardian Indus. Corp., *supra* note 60, at 1092, 202 USPQ at 100.

It is better practice to expressly provide for transfer of trademarks and their associated good will during the sale and merger of business entities. However, some courts have held that there is a presumed transfer of a trademark and its associated good will with the sale of an ongoing business if the agreement is silent in this respect.[102] This presumption can be rebutted, however, with evidence of contrary intent, such as the transferor's continuing to practice under the trademark after the sale or merger of the business. It is also better practice to expressly transfer copyrights in the written agreements, although some courts will presume that copyrights are transferred with the sale of an ongoing business.

Documents of sale or merger of business entities should expressly list all intellectual property being transferred, conveniently as a schedule to the agreement. However, the clause transferring intellectual property should not be limited to the schedule. And the provision identifying the intellectual property listed in the schedule must account for the vast number of potentially copyrighted works, regardless of the number of copyright registrations.

---

[102]Plitt Theatres v. American Nat'l Bank & Trust Co., 697 F. Supp. 1031, 9 USPQ2d 1226 (N.D. Ill. 1988).

Table of Cases

References are to chapter and footnote number. U.S. government parties are listed under the private-party litigant. Alphabetization is letter-by-letter.

D

H

I

P

Q

R

S

W

Index

D

E

R

S

T